THE INTERNET OF THINGS

WHAT EVERYONE NEEDS TO KNOW®

THE INTERNET
OF THINGS

WHAT EVERYONE NEEDS TO KNOW®

SCOTT J. SHACKELFORD

OXFORD
UNIVERSITY PRESS

Oxford University Press is a department of the University of Oxford. It furthers
the University's objective of excellence in research, scholarship, and education
by publishing worldwide. Oxford is a registered trade mark of Oxford University
Press in the UK and certain other countries.

"What Everyone Needs to Know" is a registered trademark
of Oxford University Press.

Published in the United States of America by Oxford University Press
198 Madison Avenue, New York, NY 10016, United States of America.

Published in the United States of America by Oxford University Press
198 Madison Avenue, New York, NY 10016, United States of America.

© Oxford University Press 2020

Library of Congress Cataloging-in-Publication Data
Names: Shackelford, Scott J., author.
Title: The Internet of things : what everyone needs to know /
Scott J. Shackelford.
Identifiers: LCCN 2019038627 (print) | LCCN 2019038628 (ebook) |
ISBN 9780190943813 (hardback) | ISBN 9780190943806 (paperback) |
ISBN 9780190943837 (epub) | ISBN 9780190943820
Subjects: LCSH: Internet of things. | Internet—Social aspects. |
Internet—Security measures. | Information society.
Classification: LCC TK5105.8857 .S53 2020 (print) | LCC TK5105.8857
(ebook) | DDC 004.67/8—dc23
LC record available at https://lccn.loc.gov/2019038627
LC ebook record available at https://lccn.loc.gov/2019038628

1 3 5 7 9 8 6 4 2

Paperback printed by LSC Communications, United States of America
Hardback printed by Bridgeport National Bindery, Inc., United States of America

To Cora

CONTENTS

TABLES AND FIGURES

PREFACE

Many of us go about our daily lives completely—some might say blissfully—unaware that we are surrounded by a cornucopia of devices that are running on various connected platforms and recording our physical presence, voices, heartbeats, and preferences.[1] Have a look around you. Beyond your computer, tablet, or smartphone, how many "things" that you see may be connected to the Internet, either directly or indirectly?[2] Are you wearing a Fitbit, Apple Watch, or using Airpods? Is Alexa in range? What about a connected fridge, oven, or smart laundry appliance? How far is the nearest Wi-Fi connected doorbell, light bulb, printer, or diaper?[3] What about your heating and air-conditioning and security systems? Now, do you know what data each of these devices is busily recording—or how that data is used or protected? What about the device itself—do you trust it to function consistently and safely? Does it matter?

There is a great deal of buzz surrounding the Internet of Things (IoT), which is the notion, simply put, that nearly everything in our physical world—from gym shorts to streetlights to baby monitors, elevators, and even our own bodies—will be interconnected.[4] The Internet of Everything (IoE) (a term that Cisco helped to pioneer) takes this notion a step further by referring to not only the physical infrastructure of smart devices and services but also their impacts on people, businesses, and society.[5] Thus, the IoE may be understood as "the intelligent connection of people, process, data and things[,]" whereas conceptions of IoT are often more limited to "the network of physical objects accessed through the Internet."[6] In other words, the IoT focuses on the smart devices pervading our homes and workplaces, while the IoE considers not only these products but also their impacts on business, culture, and society. It blurs the lines between the real world and cyberspace, creating a single, hyper-connected reality flush with both new opportunities and risks.

As the tech pioneer Kevin Ashton has said, "What the Internet of Things is really about is information technology that can gather its own information. Often what it does with that information is not tell a human being something, it [just] does something."[7] This broader lens is vital for considering the myriad security, privacy, and governance implications of smart devices becoming replete throughout society—and our lives. It should be noted, though, that there are other conceptions of this same idea. It has also been called Internet+,[8] while others, such as former Alphabet CEO Eric Schmidt, have suggested that the Internet itself will practically disappear in the future given the growing ubiquity of smart devices.[9] But such an outcome is also not a foregone conclusion given concerns over widening digital divides fueled in party by debates over 5G rollout.

The rise of IoT devices and services and the embedding of increasing intelligence, such as in self-driving cars,[10] could transform how we spend time or how businesses and societies operate, especially when they are deployed at scale. There are already billions of connected devices being used today—their number exceeds the number of people on planet Earth—and, while estimates vary, billions more are expected in the coming years. In short, there will be a mind-boggling explosion in Internet-connected stuff. Applications are seemingly endless, implicating an array of consumer products and other industries.[11] The Industrial Internet of Things (IIoT), sometimes also called the "Factory of Things" or "Smart Factory Wave," is only one facet of this trend toward an "embedded infosphere," and it involves the use of IoT technologies in manufacturing applications.[12] The financial implications of IoT's proliferation will also be significant; for instance, McKinsey Consulting has estimated the economic impact of the IoT, or what more technical communities may describe as the "Network of Things,"[13] at $6.2 trillion by 2025.[14]

Part of the reason the IoE presents such a mind shift is the enormous amount of data being generated, stored, and processed. According to former Federal Trade Commission chairwoman Edith Ramirez, "We're now in a world where data is being collected all the time . . . We're bringing these devices into our homes, into what used to be private spheres, and the data that is being generated is increasingly much more sensitive. It's really in my mind fundamental that consumers continue to be in the driver's seat, that they have a say in their own information and how it's being used."[15]

We are swimming in a sea of Big Data, and it's rapidly getting both wider and deeper. One way to begin to wrap your head around its vastness is to think about our smartphones. While generally not considered IoT devices themselves, smartphones are often a critical part of the IoT ecosystem, allowing users to interact with and control IoT devices through apps. More than three quarters of Americans had smartphones as of 2018—the same year that half of US households had tablets, and 20% had smart speakers.[16] Smartphones, which are loaded with sensors, collect data about, for instance, your location (one study has suggested as often as every three minutes),[17] air pressure, temperature, which way you're holding or twisting your phone, how bright it is in your vicinity, whether and how loud you're talking, whether you're moving, and so on.[18] Pre-installed or third-party search, social media, health care, and other apps may also track and store a trove of data, including personal data shared through platforms such as Facebook.[19]

Likewise, IoT devices are often full of sensors that are constantly collecting and reacting to data, such as a request for Alexa to "say grace" before a meal.[20] Combined with intelligence, that data can even help a device be responsive to what you want out of it. For instance, what if you could lace up your Bluetooth-enabled Nike sneakers with an app—and then have their tightness automatically adjust as they collect and process data about whether and how much your feet are swelling during a basketball game?[21] While some of this data collection and usage is intuitive to a device's intended function, IoT devices and services may also be sweeping up more than what you'd expect. For instance, smart speakers may not only be collecting and storing data shared through voice interactions but also, to the extent they are connected with other smart home sensors, information about when lights are turned on or off, the channel that TVs are set to, or when front door locks are engaged.[22] Such information, it almost goes without saying, would be of interest not only to marketers but also to criminals, and even provide a new dimension to domestic disputes.

Such statistics and examples related to the rise of smart consumer devices tell only a part of the story.[23] Beyond saving you the step of retying your shoes, what can devices, integrated software functionality, and data *do* when they are combined in interesting new ways? Consider Virginia Tech's Goodwin Hall, which is equipped with hundreds of sensors that together collect more than 12GB daily—they are even able "to identify occupants based on gait[.]"[24] In other words, such smart floors and walls can now identify you based on the way you walk. Even underground, our world is quietly evolving—South Bend, Indiana, for example, now boasts one of the smartest sewer systems in the world.[25] From the deepest depths of the oceans, to the final frontier of space, these systems of intelligent devices and services, saturated with data, are set to transform our lives and our world.[26]

Beyond the new capabilities and opportunities that an ever-expanding "Internet of Everything" presents, we should also ask what challenges are in store for us. In other words, as Socrates famously quipped during his trial, "The unexamined life is not worth living."[27] Consider October 2016, when a distributed denial of service (DDoS) attack emanating from a vast network of small, cheap, Internet-connected devices, which collectively came to be known as the Mirai botnet,[28] paralyzed Internet servers run by a tech firm called Dyn. That, in and of itself, might not have been a big deal, but the consequences certainly were. Because Dyn managed (and continues to operate) a significant part of Internet infrastructure, access to a number of important Internet services was slowed, or even stopped entirely, for much of the eastern United States during the attack. The Mirai botnet was so successful, and noteworthy, because it took advantage of security weaknesses in Internet-connected devices such as security cameras and home routers. Initially, some thought that the attack was politically motivated, but investigators determined that, in fact, it was not a shadowy criminal group or nation state behind the botnet; instead, it was three college students, trying to get an edge in the Minecraft computer game.[29] "They didn't realize the power they were unleashing," said FBI agent Bill Walton. "This was the Manhattan Project."[30]

In the context of IoT and more broadly, cyber attacks are continuing to increase in cost and complexity,[31] and some have both economic and national security implications. IoT might be used to send spam, eavesdrop on kids, and power DDoS attacks. A 2017 study found that nearly half of IoT security buyers have experienced a breach in the last two years; moreover, the financial impact of those breaches was reportedly significant—"13.4% of the total revenues for smaller companies and hundreds of millions of dollars for the biggest firms."[32] Compromised IoT technologies also escalate the risk of kinetic attacks with greater potential consequences. As Bruce Schneier has argued, "With smart homes, attacks can mean property damage . . . [but] [w]ith cars, planes, and medical devices, they can mean death."[33] Some scenarios with smart ovens might also be catastrophic.

Consider that, in 2014, for only the second time in history to that point, a cyber attack was confirmed to have caused physical damage.[34] This time, the target was not Iran's nuclear program, but a steel mill in Germany. Specifically, a blast furnace was compromised, causing " 'massive'—though unspecified—damage."[35] Attackers had gained access to the plant through the firm's business network, highlighting the insecurity that can stem from interconnected systems even when a firewall is in place. IoT devices might be targeted directly or serve as an entryway to a network. For instance, there have been unconfirmed reports of similar incidents to that of the German steel mill, such as one involving a petrochemical factory that was compromised by a coffee maker,[36] and a Las Vegas casino that was hacked through a smart aquarium.[37] Widely varying estimates for the cost of these attacks range from $275 billion to $22.5 trillion,[38] with US government entities regularly warning that the danger from cyber attacks now "exceed the danger of physical attacks."[39]

Whether cybersecurity and data protection will scale along with IoT devices—or whether low-cost imperatives, increasing complexity, or other challenges will derail progress and exacerbate insecurity—remains an open question.[40] What we do know is that "cybersecurity," a term that, like "cyberspace" and the "Internet of Things," did not even exist a generation ago outside of science fiction, has fast become a central tenet of twenty-first-century life.[41] From the US intelligence-attributed Russian government's hack of the Democratic National Committee's email servers to Yahoo!'s disclosure that more than one billion of its customers' records were compromised, mitigating cyber risk has become a topic of conversation in boardrooms and at the White House, on Wall Street and on main streets in many cities around the world. While increasing attention is being paid to how we should go about protecting smart devices,[42] there's still uncertainty regarding how cybersecurity more broadly should be enhanced or how we can better safeguard privacy across networks and borders. Moreover, managing the growth of the IoE impacts a diverse set of interests: US national and international security, the competitiveness of firms, global sustainable development, trust in democratic processes, and safeguarding civil rights and liberties in the Information Age, to name a few.[43]

Yet, for all the press that the IoT and broader but intersecting cybersecurity and privacy topics have received, it remains a topic little understood or appreciated by the public. One 2014 survey, for example, found that fully 87% of respondents had never even heard of the "Internet of Things."[44] More recently, those numbers have almost certainly changed, but not necessarily for the better. In 2017, a Unisys survey indicated that most American consumers support the sharing of personal data via smart devices in some circumstances.[45] In its global survey in 2018, Unisys documented slightly higher levels of support for its proposed use cases, such as "sensors in luggage that communicate with an airport baggage management system."[46] In surveying reasons for not wanting organizations to have access to data, there is some variance depending on the circumstance, but lack of a compelling reason for an organization to have data, concerns about data security, and a discomfort with an organization having data were all cited.[47] Still, one 2019 survey of 2,045 US households found that 69% of households reported owning IoT technology while 56% reported feeling "comfortable" with it.[48] Another global survey published in 2019 found that 63% of people find connected devices "creepy," and even more distrust how data is shared.[49] During the 2018 Black Hat cybersecurity conference, 93% of respondents "saw the future of IoT not necessarily as something smarter, but more dangerous, [in particular] as they predict nation states will target or exploit connected devices."[50]

The goal of this book is not necessarily to let readers know everything about IoT that they wanted to know but were afraid to ask, but it aims at least to unpack some of the outstanding

security, privacy, ethical, and policy challenges and opportunities in play. In essence, *The Internet of Things: What Everyone
Needs to Know* is intended to be true to this series by providing
real-world examples and straightforward discussion about
how the IoT and IoE are impacting our lives, organizations,
and nations—and about how they are increasingly shaping the
international community in the twenty-first century. What are
some of the benefits of increasingly ubiquitous IoT sensors? Is
my smart speaker always listening, even when it appears to be
turned off? Are there any downsides to my phone's being able
to unlock my front door, start my car, and control my thermostat? Can someone really take over my connected car? How
are other countries working to protect user privacy? This book
answers these questions and more, along with offering practical ideas about how to build an IoE that is as secure, private,
innovative, sustainable, and yes, even as fun as possible.

There is certainly a lot of ground to cover, and this book
covers topics from the practicalities of navigating the IoT, such
as understanding the utility of the Consumer Reports Digital
Standard, to wrestling with the big questions, such as the
meaning and promise of cyber peace. This is done, beginning
in chapter 1, which is entitled "Cyber-What," by charting out
a hopefully helpful guide to the lay reader on the big questions of cybersecurity and Internet governance, such as: What
is cyberspace? How has it expanded, and what are some of the
major policy issues that are driving its evolution?

Chapter 2, "Welcome to the Internet of Things," picks up
by investigating the evolution of the IoT concept, before surveying its myriad applications. In particular, we discuss everything from how your phone communicates with your smart
refrigerator to defining the "Internet of Bodies." Chapter 3,
"Securing Everything: Deep Dives into Internet of Things
Security," then analyzes why your smart lightbulb does not
come with better security and what some of the risks are,
along with what lessons may be gleaned from the efforts and
experiences of various industries as they roll out and support

an array of smart devices. Chapter 4, "Protecting Privacy in an Internet of Everything," reviews the evolution and meaning of the right to privacy, and how new technologies from the camera to the Google Nest have forced us to reevaluate our preconceptions about the private and public spheres.

Chapter 5, "Governing the Internet of Things," takes a deep dive on managing the security and privacy of IoT technologies, including a summary of efforts by the US government at the state and federal levels. We also analyze various cybersecurity and privacy frameworks, including those from the National Institute for Standards and Technology (NIST), along with expanding the lens to see how other cyber powers—including the European Union—are grappling with these same challenges. Chapter 6, "Analogizing the Internet of Things," looks at lessons from other contexts and applies them to the IoE. We ask and answer, for example, how the tragedy of the commons applies to cyberspace. What if we took an ecosystem-based approach to cybersecurity—what might that look like? And, should cybersecurity be a human right? Finally, chapter 7, "How Can We Do Better? Finding Cyber Peace in the Internet of Things," explores a number of potential solutions to these issues, including new technologies like blockchain and artificial intelligence, and revamped policies ranging from establishing a Cyber Peace Corps or a National Cybersecurity Safety Board to new international agreements for protecting civilian critical infrastructure.

In the end, no book—dare we say, no stand-alone volume—can do justice to the myriad opportunities and risks replete in the IoT. But our hope is that, by the end, you will feel like we at least did justice to unpacking some of the most important issues and concepts in this new frontier of technology and governance. There are no panaceas or magic bullets, and necessary policy or technological changes will not happen overnight; even the "Blockchain of Things" has its limits, as we will see. Dealing with formidable challenges, such as the pace of technological change or the realization of social and political rights online and offline, takes sustained effort. But as the Rev. Dr. Martin Luther King Jr. said in reference to the US civil rights movement, "If you can't fly, then run. If you can't run, then walk. If you can't walk, then crawl, but by all means, keep moving."[51] In that spirit, let's get started!

ACKNOWLEDGMENTS

This book would not have been possible without the help and support of numerous scholars, practitioners, policymakers, and research assistants. First and foremost, I would like to thank Amanda Craig. Her numerous insights and invaluable contributions greatly improved this text, and she deserves credit for drafting, refining, and in some cases originating many of the best ideas presented herein, especially in chapters 1, 2, and 3. I am also indebted to Professors Lee Alston, Fred Cate, Dan Cole, Todd Haugh, Jeff Kosseff, Michael McGinnis, Elinor Ostrom, Joshua Perry, Angie Raymond, and Timothy Fort for their helpful comments and suggestions on portions of this manuscript.

An extremely talented team of graduate students worked hard to help bring this book to fruition, including Dakota Coates, Shreya Fadia, Dhruv Madappa, Kalea Miao, Jared Stancombe, Phillip Walter Smith II, and James Theesfeld. I am indebted to them for their invaluable research and citation-checking support. My thanks also go to the Kelley School of Business administration, staff, and colleagues in the Department of Business Law and Ethics for their much-appreciated support and enthusiasm for this project, along with the faculty affiliates and fantastic staff at the Ostrom Workshop, including Patty Lezotte.

In addition, I would like to thank Angela Chnapko and the staff at Oxford University Press for this opportunity, and for their incredible professionalism, patience, and dedication throughout every stage of the production process.

Above all, I am indebted in countless ways to my wonderful wife, Emily

ABBREVIATIONS

5G	5th Generation Cellular Network Technology
AI	Artificial Intelligence
APEC	Asia-Pacific Economic Cooperation
ARPA	Advanced Research Projects Agency
ARPANET	Advanced Research Projects Agency Network
ATM	Automated Teller Machine
AV	Autonomous Vehicles
AWS	Amazon Web Services
BCI	Brain-Computer Interface
BSA	Business Software Alliance/The Software Alliance
C2	Command-and-Control
CAGR	Compound Annual Growth Rate
CBPR	Cross-Border Privacy Rules
CCDCOE	(NATO) Cooperative Cyber Defense Centre of Excellence
CCPA	California Consumer Privacy Act
CCTV	Closed-Circuit Television
CDC	Centers for Disease Control and Prevention
CEO	Chief Executive Officer
CIA triad	Confidentiality, Integrity, and Availability
CIO	Chief Information Officer

Cong. Res. Serv.	Congressional Research Service
CONSENT Act	Customer Online Notification for Stopping Edge-Provider Network Transgressions Act
COP	Conference of the Parties
CPS	Cyber-Physical Systems
CSIS	Center for Strategic and International Studies
CSR	Corporate Social Responsibility
CTIA	Cellular Telecommunications and Internet Association
CVD	Coordinated Vulnerability Disclosure
DARPA	Defense Advanced Research Projects Agency
DDoS	Distributed Denial of Service
DICE	Device Identifier Composition Engine
DNC	Democratic National Committee
DNS	Domain Name System
DSM	Digital Single Market
DVR	Digital Video Recorder
EC	European Community
EEG	Electroencephalogram
ENISA	European Union Agency for Network and Information Security
EPA	Environmental Protection Agency
FBI	Federal Bureau of Investigation
FCC	Federal Communications Commission
FDA	Food and Drug Administration
FIDO Alliance	Fast Identity Online Alliance
FIPPs	Fair Information Practice Principles
FTC	Federal Trade Commission
FVEY	Five Eyes (Australia, Canada, New Zealand, United Kingdom, and United States)
G2	Group of Two (United States and China)
G7	Group of Seven
G20	Group of Twenty
GAO	US General Accountability Office

GB	Gigabyte (10^9 bytes)
GDP	Gross Domestic Product
GDPR	General Data Protection Regulation
GGE	(UN) Group of Government Experts
GRI	Global Reporting Initiative
HTTP	Hypertext Transfer Protocol
HTTPS	Hypertext Transfer Protocol Secure
HVAC	Heating, Ventilation, and Air Conditioning
IANA	Internet Assigned Numbers Authority
IBM	International Business Machines
ICANN	Internet Corporation for Assigned Names and Numbers
ICCPR	International Covenant on Civil and Political Rights
ICS	Industrial Control Systems
ICT	Information and Communication Technology
IDC	International Data Corporation
IEC	International Electrotechnical Commission
IEEE	Institute of Electrical and Electronics Engineers
IETF	Internet Engineering Task Force
IGF	Internet Governance Forum
IIoT	Industrial Internet of Things
IoBs	Internet of Bodies
IoE	Internet of Everything
IoT	Internet of Things
IoT Consumer TIPS Act of 2017	Internet of Things Consumer Tips to Improve Personal Security Act of 2017
IP	Internet Protocol
ISO	International Organization for Standardization
IT	Information Technology
ITU	International Telecommunications Union
JTC	Joint Technical Committee
K-12	Kindergarten through Twelfth Grade (US)

LEED Standards	Leadership in Energy and Environmental Design
MCU	Microcontroller
ML	Machine Learning
MRI	Magnetic Resonance Imaging
NASA	National Aeronautics and Space Administration
NATO	North Atlantic Treaty Organization
NATO CCDCOE	NATO Cooperative Cyber Defence Centre of Excellence
NCCoE	National Cybersecurity Center of Excellence
NICE	National Initiative for Cybersecurity Education
NIH	National Institutes of Health
NIS	Network and Information Security
NIST	National Institute of Standards and Technology
NIST CSF	NIST Cybersecurity Framework
NSA	National Security Agency
NSFNET	National Science Foundation Network
NSTAC	National Security Telecommunications Advisory Committee
OECD	Organisation of Economic Co-operation and Development
OFPA	Organic Foods Production Act
OHCHR	Office of the (United Nations) High Commissioner for Human Rights
OPM	Office of Personnel Management
OSCE	Organization for Security and Co-operation in Europe
P2P	Peer-to-Peer
PC	Personal Computer
PII	Personally Identifiable Information
RFC	Regulators, Facilitators, and Collaborators
RFID	Radio Frequency Identification
RoI	Return on Investment

SC	Subcommittee
SCADA	Supervisory Control and Data Acquisition
SEC	Securities and Exchange Commission
SOC	Security Operations Center
TCG	Trusted Computing Group
TCP/IP	Transmission Control Protocol (TCP) and the Internet Protocol (IP)
TPM	Trusted Platform Module
UNCTAD	United Nations Conference on Trade and Development
UNESCO	United Nations Educational, Scientific, and Cultural Organization
UNHRC	United Nations Human Rights Council
VPN	Virtual Private Network
WLAN	Wireless Local Area Networks
WNAN	Wireless Neighborhood Area Networks
WPAN	Wireless Personal Area Networks

1

CYBER-WHAT?

The Internet of Things (IoT) exists at the intersection of "cyberspace" and physical space, though the line between the two is increasingly blurry. As Nicholas Negroponte, founder of the MIT Media Lab, has said, "This is just the beginning, the beginning of understanding that cyberspace has no limits, no boundaries."[1] But what does "cyber" mean—and how did it become such a dominant twenty-first-century prefix? Is it here to stay in its current form, and is its meaning distinct from other terms like "information" and "digital"? As an important and evolving technical, conceptual, and even political backdrop, understanding this context—and, in particular, having a clear conception of cyberspace itself—is helpful for digging into the Internet of Everything (IoE).

The "cyber" prefix had humble beginnings and emerged in a very different context. Indeed, the first use of the term was in the 1940s, when "cybernetics" ("the study of communication and control systems in living beings and machines") was all the rage.[2] Today, while some readers may never have heard of cybernetics, "cyber," which is Greek for "steersman" or "to govern," has taken off, being tacked in front of a range of nouns and trends, from cyber bullies to cyber war.[3] Moreover, it has been used for foundational, sweeping terms, like "cyberspace," which, as Professor Stephen J. Lukasik explains, "couples the idea of communication and control with *space,* a domain previously unknown and unoccupied, where 'territory' can be claimed, controlled, and exploited."[4] Still, little agreement exists as to the meaning and relevance of this concept in an era in which seemingly everything is on the verge of being connected. As Professor Milton Mueller has observed, "The tension between global cyberspace and the territorial state is the primary factor that drives internet governance and cybersecurity debates."[5] This opening chapter outlines the basics of cyberspace and addresses some of the questions and issues that will be important in our increasingly hyper-connected world.

What is "cyberspace," and how is it different from the "Internet"?

At the outset, it is important to note that cyberspace is *not* synonymous with the Internet—or, even more so, the World Wide Web, or "web"—even though the terms are sometimes used interchangeably. The Internet may be thought of as a global network of wired and wireless networks (you will often see it referred to as a "network of networks"). Interconnection among these networks requires a massive physical infrastructure, including copper and fiber-optic cables, which permit packets of information to transit to homes and businesses around the world (though, as will be discussed later, there is significant global disparity in access to broadband infrastructure). It also requires the use of "Internet protocols,"[6] which are specifications or standards that allow systems to interoperate (including, principally, the Transmission Control Protocol and Internet Protocol, or TCP/IP). Think of them as a kind of universal translator as popularized by *Star Trek* (with major tech companies making strides toward its realization).[7] The web, though incredible in its reach and impact, is just an "information space"[8]—a bunch of public resources that are interconnected and accessible via the Internet owing to the consistent use of application-layer Internet protocols, that is, Hypertext

Transfer Protocol (HTTP) or Hypertext Transfer Protocol Secure (HTTPS).[9] Notably, a number of foundational Internet and web protocols were built "without security in mind."[10]

So, then—what is "cyberspace"? Relative to the Internet and the web, cyberspace is a more abstract and symbolic term. As was mentioned in the beginning of this chapter, the Greek prefix on which the term is based takes us only so far in understanding the word's meaning (and impressive staying power—describing the cutting edge of science for more than half a century, from cybernetics to cyber warfare). Science fiction writer William Gibson first defined the term "cyberspace" in 1984, describing it as: "A graphic representation of data abstracted from banks of every computer in the human system. Unthinkable complexity. Lines of light ranged in the nonspace of the mind, clusters and constellations of data. Like city lights, receding."[11] Such a fanciful understanding wound up being not far from a fair description, especially when conceptualizing cyberspace as, at a high level, being composed of routers and servers running in fiber-optic networks on which users collaborate via pulses of light to form communities.[12]

Since its early days, though, the term "cyberspace" has remained ambiguous in many ways. Even the use of the prefix "cyber" is debatable (see the next question for a quick review of sometimes-preferred alternatives)—or even comical.[13] It has evolved to describe an expansive world of technologies as well as human and machine interactions despite a lack of consensus on the part of computer scientists and policymakers as to the term's meaning and scope.

Elements of the US government, which played a foundational role in creating the Internet (including through the development of the Advanced Research Projects Agency Network, or ARPANET, a project of the US Defense Advanced Research Projects Agency described later in chapter 1) have evolved their definitions of cyberspace over time. The George W. Bush administration defined it as "hundreds of thousands of interconnected computers, servers, routers, switches, and fiber optic cables that allow our critical infrastructures to work."[14] In 2008, an internal US Department of Defense memo defined it is as "a global domain within the information environment consisting of the interdependent network of information technology infrastructures, including the Internet, telecommunications networks, computer systems, and embedded processors and controllers."[15] Meanwhile, while serving as chief of the Air Force Cyberspace Command, Major General William T. Lord defined it as being synonymous with "the entire electromagnetic spectrum."[16]

Expanding our purview beyond one government's perspectives does not necessarily bring satisfactory clarity, either. In 2012, Cisco summarized how nations around the world view "cyberspace," finding a remarkable lack of consistency, though there was some agreement that it included: (1) "tangible elements" such as a global network of hardware,[17] (2) information, (3) virtual spaces, and (4) some degree of interconnection.[18] Yet, there are also natural tensions within those elements and how governments treat them. For instance, even as there is a shared belief (especially on the part of many Western academics and policymakers) that cyberspace is a "global networked commons," as is explored further in chapter 7, many established and emerging cyber powers wish to protect or extend their "cyber sovereignty."[19] Yet as former Estonian president Toomas Hendrik Ilves has said, "In cyberspace, no country is an island."[20]

Despite laudable efforts from many corners of academia, government, industry, and the press, foundational work still needs to be done to further clarify the scope and meaning of cyberspace and ensure consistent use of terminology. Indeed, among the most consequential elements often ignored by efforts at defining cyberspace are us—users (or netizens or even digital citizens, if you prefer), including our rights (e.g., to privacy, the topic of chapter 4) and responsibilities (e.g., practicing cyber hygiene, which is further discussed in chapter 7). Without people, there would be much less content to translate into packets and send as pulses of light on fiber-optic cables. And, without people, the technology innovation that makes cyberspace so dynamic would dissipate. Despite often being defined by the broader integration of many more devices and machines, then, the IoE requires and will be impacted by our nebulous conception of cyberspace, which is in the process of expanding still further to encompass the physical world.

Is "cyber" the only applicable prefix?

In line with many scholars, practitioners, and policymakers, as well as popular references in US and international media, this book primarily (but not exclusively) uses "cyber" terminology. But numerous other terms have been used and continue to be relied upon to refer to similar concepts. Understanding the dimensions of debates about terminology—whether they be technical, political, or otherwise—provides important context as well as the ability to identify and thoughtfully engage with materials aimed at different communities.

Many engineers and practitioners, for example, prefer "information technology" and "information systems" to "cyber" when referring directly to networks, hardware, and software.[21] Many also prefer "information security" or security of information systems to "cybersecurity."[22] There may also be a need to use both terms simultaneously for sufficient clarity of scope. For example, recently a key group within the technology and security standards community formally (and at long last) included cybersecurity within its title (whereas its title had previously been limited to information security and privacy protection).[23]

There is also variability among governments. Russia and China prefer "information security" to "cybersecurity" to connote content regulation along with broader security measures.[24] Some governments use "cybersecurity" and security of "information systems" in different contexts—including the United States, which tends to frequently use the terms "cyberspace" and "cybersecurity."[25] Many governments also refer to "information and communications technology," or ICT, especially when referring to sectors of the economy. ICT is also used in multilateral fora, such as the G20, in reference to technology development as well as security measures (i.e., "security in the use of ICTs").

Recently, there has also been a resurgence of the term "digital" (e.g., digital information, digital ecosystem, digital revolution, digital security, and digital peace), especially among policymakers and multilateral organizations. "Digital" has long roots in the Information Age, as it refers to technologies that generate, store, and process data as fixed numbers—binary digits or "bits" in the form of zeroes and ones (unlike analog electronic and mechanical devices with voltage or signals that vary continuously rather than in steps or increments). The transition to digital technologies is also associated with the third industrial revolution in the late twentieth century. In 1995, for instance, Nicholas Negroponte wrote *Being Digital*, a book that hypothesized that we would someday stop reading books in paper form and instead read them on a screen—and that we would use digital technologies with touch screen interfaces.[26]

Today, "digital" may be resurging as a way to manage political challenges with terms like "cybersecurity" and "information security." It may also have less of an association with national security and military efforts in cyberspace given its strong tie to conceptions of the global "digital economy" (also referred to as the "Internet economy"). One key example is the 2018–2019 United Nations Secretary-General's High-Level Panel on Digital Cooperation, which considered issues related to digital technologies, including inclusion, trust, and "digital security."[27] Notably, though, in multilateral and multistakeholder fora, the "cyber" and "information" prefixes persist as well—as is evident in the Global Commission on the Stability of Cyberspace, the Paris Call on Trust and Stability in Cyberspace, and the United Nations groups working on developments in the field of information and telecommunications in the context of international security[28] (more on each of those in chapter 7).

How has cyberspace expanded and evolved?

In the predawn of the Information Age, and only a few months after Apollo 11's historic mission to the Moon, on October 29, 1969, ARPANET was activated by a UCLA graduate student named Charley Kline.[29] Kline was called upon to type "LOGIN," but the system crashed after "LO." This, the first message in the Internet's history, was sent to the Stanford Research Institute some 350 miles away.[30] Although Kline is not remembered today like Neil Armstrong and Buzz Aldrin, in many ways, his two keystrokes that day continue to reverberate into the twenty-first century, much like those first footsteps on the lunar surface.

Since 1969, cyberspace has experienced incredible growth across numerous dimensions, including the number of users, the physical and virtual resources of technology infrastructure, the number and variety of applications and services, and the amount of available data.[31] While growth in the number of individual users was relatively slow initially, from ARPANET to the National Science Foundation Network (NSFNET) to the Internet we know today,[32] it began to skyrocket in the early 1990s with the emergence of the web. While estimates vary, the World Bank reports that 0.8% of the world's population was using the Internet in 1995; that number was 6.7% in 2000, 15.7% in 2005, 28.7% in 2010, and approximately 43% in 2015.[33] As of January 2019, that estimate is 57%—or 4.4 billion people (an increase of 366 million users since January 2018—or about 1 million new Internet users per day).[34]

Many of these users are increasingly connecting thanks to surging broadband penetration and the growing penetration of mobile devices.[35] Across Organisation of Economic Cooperation and Development (OECD) countries, which include the United States and many European countries as well as Australia, Japan, and South Korea, broadband became accessible between 1997 and 2003, reaching penetration rates of 13–38% by 2008.[36] In the United States specifically, from 2000 to 2010, home connections to broadband jumped from 4% to 68%, and average broadband speeds doubled from 2009 to 2013.[37] Today, there's also new growth in edge devices that provide entry points into networks such as routers, due in part to the development and deployment of new types of IoT technologies—as is discussed in more detail in chapter 2. This prompts the question—when almost everything is a computer, in what other ways should we measure the growth and evolution of cyberspace?

One candidate is measuring the amount of data being generated, which is colossal; in 2000, Peter Lyman and Hal R. Varian published a study in which they calculated that "about 1.5 exabytes of unique information—about 250 megabytes" per person—was produced in 1999. They also hypothesized that, while, "even today most textual information is 'born digital' . . . within a few years this will be true for images as well."[38] By 2020, it is estimated that 1.7 megabytes per person will be created every *second*[39] (about 146,880 per person per day)—nearly what we were collectively creating in a year in 1999. In other words, by this measure, the data being generated by one person in 2020 is on par with the entire Internet some twenty years before. As Domo has highlighted, much of this data is user-generated; in 2018, users posted 49,380 Instagram photos, shared 2,083,333 Snapchat "snaps," conducted 3,877,140 Google searches, sent 12,986,111 texts, and submitted 18,055,555 Weather Channel forecast requests *every minute*.[40] Even in 2015, more data had been created "in the past two years than in the entire previous history of the human race."[41] Going forward, IoT devices will result in further exponential growth, in part because, beyond user-generated data, they will also create streams of data from sensors, including temperature, pressure, proximity, image, and other sensors.[42]

(To what extent all of this data, whether user-generated or otherwise, can be relied upon by the larger ecosystem or should be marked as "misinformation" remains to be seen.)

While there will likely also continue to be significant growth across the capabilities and services available in cyberspace—especially as software and applications are developed for new IoT devices and the data streams they will come to instantiate—it's also worth noting the consolidation of services built by Facebook, Apple, and Google and functioning as curated, semi-closed Internet platforms.[43] Compete, a web analytics company, found that "the top ten Web sites accounted for 31% of US pageviews in 2001, 40% in 2006, and about 75% in 2010."[44] This trend continued through 2018, with over 1 billion websites on offer worldwide but only a few generating the vast majority of hits. Google.com, for example, was the most visited website worldwide in 2018, owing to more than 42 billion visits per month (YouTube, which is also owned by Google, was number two with 23 billion hits, hinting at monopolistic concerns explored in chapter 5).[45] Consumers seem to favor semi-closed, proprietary networks, like those common in many smartphones, due to their ease of use, while companies favor these networks since they can make it simpler to make a profit, including through marketing.[46] According to *Wired Magazine*, single-purpose apps are preferred over the general-purpose browser; or, put differently, fast is beating flexible.[47]

What are some of the major policy issues affecting cyberspace today?

Access and inclusion,[48] governance, and trust have enormous impacts on cyberspace. While we have catalogued incredible growth across multiple dimensions of cyberspace, global access to broadband infrastructure remains a fundamental challenge and major policy issue. In rural areas, including in the United States as well as in developing regions around the world, technology adoption is limited, due in large part to the lack of a supporting infrastructure,[49] resulting in what's commonly referred to as a "digital divide." In 2017, nearly half of the world's population was using the Internet, but numbers vary dramatically across regions. For example, the Internet penetration rate in the United States then was 75%—tucked in between Belarus (74%) and Argentina, Moldova, and Russia (76%), but well behind the United Kingdom (95%).[50]

The numbers speak clearly to a divide in connectivity, but the impacts of that divide are both hidden and wide ranging. For one, studies have shown that there is a direct economic impact; countries experience growth in GDP per capita as broadband is introduced and subsequently diffused more broadly.[51] In addition, technological adoption can be compounding; certain technologies are foundational to the integration and use of others. For example, Internet access enables the use of cloud services, which power the storage and processing of more data, which in turn supports machine learning applications. Moreover, today, most people who use the Internet live in urban and densely populated areas; "the scale of infrastructure that must be built or upgraded to bridge the digital divide [in rural and remote areas] and deploy emerging technologies is considerable"—an estimated $450 billion will be required to bring the next 1.5 billion people online.[52] What's more, just increasing Internet access is not sufficient; inclusive approaches are critical across multiple policy areas, including security. For instance, more broadband connectivity in nations with low awareness of cyber hygiene practices[53] and weak governance increases the risk that they will become havens for cybercriminals.[54] Ultimately, then, both the near- and longer-term challenges posed by today's digital divide are significant, and, meanwhile, limited Internet access may have cascading effects on economic growth and innovation opportunities in struggling communities.

Numerous organizations are attempting to address major gaps in Internet access, both conceptually and through pragmatic action. In 2010, then–Secretary General of the International

Telecommunications Union (ITU) Dr. Hamadoun Touré argued that governments must "regard the [I]nternet as basic infrastructure—just like roads, waste, and water."[55] A 2011 UN report argued—as have the governments of Spain, France, and Finland—that Internet access is a basic human right, even though practitioners, including Vinton Cerf, the "Father of the Internet," have taken umbrage with this position, as is explored further in chapter 4.[56] In 2018, the Broadband Commission for Sustainable Development, which brought together senior leadership from the ITU and UNESCO, published a series of recommendations to boost broadband access, including the development of National Broadband Plans and the reduction of affordability threshold targets from less than 5% to less than 2% of monthly gross national income per capita.[57] Public[58] and private sector[59] organizations have also created loan and grant programs, driven research, and supported policy proposals to sustain and strengthen the build out of broadband infrastructure and other connectivity solutions in rural America[60] and around the world.

Another major policy issue affecting cyberspace today is governance, including issues related to sovereignty and control. These issues are not new; since the Internet emerged as an economic driver and national security priority—a major platform for commerce and conflict—governments have been concerned about and sought to influence its governance. However, there are numerous challenges. First, while some aspects of cyberspace are undeniably global, different regions have different values, norms, and laws that test (and increasingly undermine ideas about) whether it can or should be managed through consistent global rules. One early manifestation of this issue concerned the sale of Nazi memorabilia on Yahoo.com (Yahoo's English-language platform); in 2000, a French court ruled that (and in 2006, a US court upheld that[61]), consistent with French laws, Yahoo must ban French users from English-language sites where Nazi memorabilia were sold by auction.[62] More recently, this issue has resulted in broader efforts to control information and been associated with concerns of political leadership, including in Egypt during the Arab Spring[63] and with China's infamous Great Firewall.[64] As is evident in the passage of a new law in Russia in 2019, security and privacy concerns are also being used to justify such measures; cumulatively, these efforts are also buttressing and furthering consistent and growing concerns about fragmentation of the Internet—and cyberspace.[65]

Second—and, in some ways as an extension of the above issues about local sovereignty within a global system—there are challenges related to global governance institutions and control within multilateral or multi-stakeholder fora. Numerous organizations that have managed some governance issues—such as the development of technical protocols and standards, the disbursement of IP addresses (each device connected to the Internet needs one!), and the maintenance of the Domain Name System (which enables us to use a "domain name," like weather.com, to get to a numerical IP address, which would be much harder to remember)—have long been associated with the United States, even if there have recently been concerted efforts to ensure a stronger global role in them.[66] (For instance, in 2016, the US Department of Commerce formally transitioned coordination and management of functions of the Internet Assigned Numbers Authority (IANA)—an entity that has its roots in the work of US citizen Jon Postel, whom media organizations called an early "god" of the Internet—to the private sector; see Figure 1.1.[67]) But some governments have pushed for a broader role for multilateral organizations like the ITU, an agency of the United Nations, over multi-stakeholder fora like the Internet Corporation for Assigned Names and Numbers (ICANN) or Internet Governance Forum (IGF).[68]

As with access and inclusion issues, governance issues will likely continue to pose major policy challenges for some time, and IoT may increase tensions. For a "network of networks" that many different stakeholders are contributing to and leveraging for an array of commercial and national security

Figure 1.1 Jon Postel ("God" of the Internet)

purposes, governance is dispersed—and not just among the alphabet soup of institutions referenced above. Much of the private sector owns and operates Internet infrastructure and services, from broadband to devices to software. As IoT devices (and applications and services) proliferate, there will be a greater diversity of industry organizations at the table, seeking to contribute to multi-stakeholder discussions—not just telecommunications and IT companies, but also appliance manufacturers that need IP addresses, car firms that need reliable connectivity in remote areas, and industrial system operators that need global data flows to inform threat intelligence models. Whether, to what extent, and how multilateral and multi-stakeholder governance approaches are leveraged will likely impact a range of issues, including the use of and control over IoT. One way to conceptualize the challenge is through the literature on polycentric governance, discussed in chapter 5.

Governance decisions (along with increased Internet access) will also affect the third major policy issue that impacts cyberspace today: trust—and related issues of privacy, security, and stability. Each of these issues is covered in more detail later in the book, but in short, our collective ability to trust that our data is being protected and not misused, that we can rely on resilient connected systems and services, and that cyber conflicts will not escalate and threaten our digital activities, infrastructure, and livelihoods is foundational to our continued use of cyberspace as well as our growing use of the IoT. Embedded within these broad issues of privacy, security, and stability are not only topics related to laws, policies, and norms intended to advance industry practices, protect consumers, and constrain offensive cyber attacks, but also efforts to improve global law enforcement cooperation, enhance cyber hygiene, and prepare for new technologies, including the rollout of machine learning and artificial intelligence services discussed in chapters 6 and 7.

How is cybercrime different from cyber war, espionage, and terrorism?

Before we dive more deeply into IoT in particular, one final note on the "cyber" prefix—and on challenges with ensuring sufficient trust in cyberspace: cyber threats have often been categorized into four buckets—cybercrime, cyber war, cyber espionage, and cyber terrorism.[69] Because they are also used in contexts outside of cyberspace, these categories are helpful for understanding different types of threatening cyberspace actions and actors, even if the lines can sometimes be blurry. Cybercrime, which is becoming increasingly organized,[70] is typically understood as financially motivated; attackers might steal users' identities or credentials to direct or redirect money (and, today, often cryptocurrencies) to their accounts. Cyber war is typically understood as involving conflicts among governments, whether those conflicts are confined to cyberspace or also involve conventional (kinetic) attacks;[71] notably, there have also been significant challenges with defining the application of international law for cyber incidents that fall below the threshold of armed conflict (a subject of ongoing exploration through the *Tallinn Manual*[72]). Cyber espionage might involve state-on-state activities (e.g., targeting military plans or diplomatic information) as well as the stealing of private sector information (e.g., targeting intellectual property information to short-circuit research and development efforts or reduce the cost of bringing new products to market).[73] The US government has tried to establish a norm against the state-sponsored theft of intellectual property for commercial purposes, with some initial success as seen in the 2015 G2 Cybersecurity Code of Conduct, though that agreement was derailed in the wake of ongoing trade disputes.[74] Finally, the "general term, terrorist, is used to denote revolutionaries who seek to use terror systematically to further their views or to govern a particular area."[75] Cyber terrorists, on the other hand, use cyberspace to "disrupt computer or telecommunications service[s]" to elicit widespread panic and loss of public confidence in the ability of government to function effectively, such as by interrupting critical infrastructure.[76] The term tends to refer to non-state actors using the Internet to spread propaganda and engage in recruiting and financing activities, including through cyber attacks.[77]

The expanding IoT will increasingly undermine the utility of these categories, which already suffer from problems of overlap and attribution, among other issues.[78] Connectivity across a range of devices—along with the new data streams they create—will result in new opportunities and motivations for stealing information and conducting disruptive or destructive attacks. For instance, whereas cyber terrorists may not find stealing health records sufficiently compelling for their cause, they may consider targeting health monitors or devices that could cause more havoc. If they need greater expertise to do so, then they may try to work more closely with cyber criminals to conduct attacks that serve the interests of both groups.

Today, we already see partnerships across nation-state cyber operatives and cybercriminals—in particular in Russia.[79] As IoT devices proliferate, so will investments in cyber attacks—creating a need not only for continued investment in risk management but also flexibility in our understanding of the evolving cyber threat and how to mitigate it.

2

WELCOME TO THE INTERNET
OF THINGS

New inventions often open the door to unanticipated impacts that are difficult to foresee as they interact with and influence the evolution of systems around them. Take tractors, for instance.[1] Today, they are everywhere—in lots of different forms. Before the late nineteenth century, though, farms required many more people and animals to produce significantly less food. As tractors have enabled more efficient food production, they have also displaced horses—and farmers, especially in certain regions of the world. In the United States, where agriculture was long the backbone of the economy, tractors ultimately pushed many people out of and sometimes into new jobs, often in factories, powering a new period of industrialization and technological development—and helping (along with other technological innovations and trends) to catapult the 1890s US populist movement.[2]

Smartphones are another example. While adoption was relatively slow with early models (e.g., the Ericsson R380 in 2000, the Palm Treo in 2002, and the Blackberry Quark in 2003), and there were initial concerns about whether relatively expensive iPhones (which first hit the market in 2007) would sell, ultimately smartphones have ushered in a wave of connectivity, supporting new e-commerce models, creating a whole new world of apps, and changing the way in which we interact with and rely on technology. While not generally considered part of the IoT, they are at the leading edge of the emerging Internet of Everything (IoE) era—prompting potential transformations akin to the move from yesterday's landlines to today's iPhone and Android devices. As the utility and appeal of "computerizing devices" increases and their price point decreases, so too will the reasons against further expansion of the IoE, making possible a variety of scenarios—such as smart washing machines communicating with the smart clothes inside to optimize a spin cycle.[3]

What makes IoT unique, and potentially more problematic than other mobile computing technologies, though, is the sheer scale and variability of devices and platforms in play. Indeed, while IoT offers promising value propositions with greater connectivity and functionality through ubiquitous networking, there are major challenges that impact its implementation, some of which are summarized in Table 2.1.[4]

We discuss concerns with security and privacy in some detail in chapters 3 and 4 as they pose arguably the most significant near-term challenges to the continued development and

Table 2.1 Challenges Impacting the Adoption of IoT

Challenge	Description
Security	Increasing number of design weaknesses or vulnerabilities that could be potentially exploited to conduct identity theft, steal information, penetrate networks, and even cause physical damage[94]
Privacy	Direct collection of sensitive personally identifiable information and analysis of massive volume of granular data to make inferences about a person's behavior[95]
Data control and governance	Collection of a vast amount of real-time data overwhelming our capacity to understand how it's being used and to protect it[96]
Standardization	Lack of a standard, universally accepted architecture and potential domination of proprietary protocols, interfaces, and equipment designs[97]

deployment of IoT systems; the related issues of governance and standards are unpacked further in chapters 5 and 6.[5] As we will see, the dual issues of cybersecurity and privacy have been serious concerns throughout the rise of Internet commerce and other activities, though IoT raises the stakes further. If someone's identity is hacked, then that can hurt him or her financially.[6] If someone's autonomous car is hacked, the results may be even more damaging and immediate.[7] Similarly, customized advertisements that are routinely seen while browsing highlight the implicit trade-offs in the privacy bargain we have struck with tech firms.[8] As more dimensions of our behavior and aspects of our lives are tracked, aggregated, and analyzed, without safeguards in place, we may increasingly be at risk of being manipulated (whether maliciously or not) without even being aware of it,[9] especially in a world of ubiquitous sensors.

To get a sense of what's coming and what it all means for questions of security, privacy, and governance, we begin here by considering some of the questions about definitions, scope, and practical impacts of IoT technologies. (This grounding can also provide a foundation for larger questions introduced later in this book and explored further elsewhere, such as the broader social, economic, and political impacts of the IoE.[10]) Ultimately, whether our future is one in which the Internet is so pervasive and trustworthy that it practically disappears depends on a number of factors.[11] What it would mean for how future generations organize, work, or engage political leaders may be hard to anticipate, but we can expect ripple effects—like the tractor's contributing to a populist wave in the United States, or a quest to connect vending machines catalyzing advanced IoT research.

What is the "Internet of Things," and how did it emerge?

Today, the "Internet of Things" (IoT), as a term, enjoys widespread use in both technology and policy circles, as well as in popular culture (having mostly surpassed alternatives such as "cyber-physical systems"), but there are differing accounts as to its origin story.[12] The technology pioneer Kevin Ashton is often credited with first using the "Internet of Things" as the title of a presentation for Procter & Gamble in 1999.[13] He wanted to link the idea of the Radio Frequency Identification (RFID) technology, which he had a hand in creating, to the Internet, and thus attract the attention of senior executives.[14]

But the idea of "intelligent" devices communicating with one another dates back to long before the late 1990s, all the way to the emergence of ARPANET (an undertaking that would eventually evolve into the Internet[15], under the heading of "pervasive computing").[16] Moreover, connecting computers to machinery predates IoT; "factories and large industrial machines have long been controlled by computerized [industrial control systems], and supervisory control and data acquisition (SCADA) systems[,] that monitor and adjust those industrial machinery based on operating conditions."[17] Researchers at Carnegie Mellon University are credited with first deploying sensors and switches in a vending machine and connecting it to the Internet in the early 1980s. The connection enabled the researchers to count the number of bottles present and check their temperature.[18] Around the same time, students at the Massachusetts Institute of Technology (MIT) deployed a server that could tell you which bathrooms were available.

Limited infrastructure and prohibitive costs delayed the realization of what we think of today as IoT. In the 1990s, although more enterprises began to achieve more widespread Internet connectivity, slow speeds and poor network architectures continued to restrict the usage of connected machines.[19] The potential of IoT technology arguably has been realized only since 2010,[20] the result of the confluence of at least three factors. First, the increasingly widespread availability of broadband Internet provided high-speed network connectivity that enabled devices to communicate with each other over a wireless network across large parts of the developed world.[21] Second, enhanced computational capabilities enabled the real-time analysis of large amounts of unstructured data.[22] Third, the decreasing cost of sensors allowed manufacturers to add small wireless chips to any device for a minor incremental cost.[23] The combination of these factors created the perfect environment for the proliferation of smart, interconnected devices, giving rise to IoT (and, in time, the IoE). Further advances,[24] such as improved computational capabilities resulting from machine learning and AI or improved connectivity and communications, including through the rollout of 5G, will enable even greater growth as well as new functions. Indeed, as Schneier argues, trend lines from IoT, machine learning, AI, cloud computing, and robotics reinforce one another, leading to "an Internet that senses, thinks, and acts."[25]

There's no universal IoT definition, perhaps in part because the term describes "a new concept that defines how we interact with the physical world" rather than a type of technical architecture.[26] Still, organizations and individuals have proposed ways of describing it, highlighting some common elements and themes. In 2014, the US National Security Telecommunications Advisory Committee (NSTAC) described IoT as a decentralized network of devices, applications, and services that can "sense, log, interpret, communicate, process, and act on a variety of information or control devices in the physical environment . . . ."[27] In 2015, an Institute of Electrical and Electronics Engineers (IEEE) publication considered the architecture of IoT to have three tiers: sensing; networking and data communications; and applications.[28] In 2017, a director at Leverage, an IoT company, explained IoT as a system that "integrates four distinct components: sensors/devices, connectivity, data processing, and a user interface."[29] Sensors generate data, which is often sent (i.e., through a cellular, satellite, Bluetooth, Wi-Fi, etc. connection) via and/or to a cloud service for processing (anything from checking that a temperature reading is within an acceptable range to using computer vision to identify objects, such as intruders in your home); finally, a user can access that information and potentially act on it.[30] Cloud services can also help to maintain the software being used to power an IoT device, providing updates or security monitoring. Cumulatively, these capabilities add a level of "digital intelligence" to physical devices.[31]

IoT has now progressed a long way from a smart vending machine to include constellations of quite dissimilar networks.[32] Indeed, one further way to describe IoT is to distinguish between "small" scenarios with a low degree of relative complexity (e.g., a few things on one network) and "large" scenarios with greater complexity (e.g., many things and/or networks).[33] From smart thermostats that use predictive analytics to learn about user behavior patterns so as to create customized heating schedules to smart sidewalks, there is information to be gained, and value to be gleaned.[34] But as connectivity, analytics, and management capabilities improve, HVAC systems could be integrated with other networks, such as those for telephone service, security, and lighting, to create a remotely controllable, interactive smart home environment. As IoT matures, disparate smart residential and commercial networks will also be able to communicate with one another, creating smart (and potentially more resilient) cities.[35] At a macro level, this outcome resembles the early days of networking when Cisco used multi-protocol routing to join dissimilar networks. This eventually led to the creation of a common networking standard called the Internet Protocol (IP), which was foundational to the Internet and continues to be heavily relied upon today. IoT looks set to follow a similar route, albeit on a larger scale, spanning myriad sectors and industries.

What are projections for the growth of different types of "things" on the Internet, are they accurate, and why do they matter?

In 2018, Samsung committed to making *all* of its devices—including TVs and refrigerators as well as wearables—connected and intelligent by 2020.[36] Eric Schmidt, the former

Google chairman, has gone further, predicting that "the Internet will disappear. There will be so many IP addresses . . . so many devices, sensors, things that you are wearing, things that you are interacting with, that you won't even sense it. It will be part of your presence all the time."[37] Although unlikely in the near term, the possibility that many, perhaps most, devices will be connected to the Internet in the medium term is real. In launching Azure Sphere in 2018 (see chapter 3 for more on Azure Sphere, an IoT solution intended to increase security), Microsoft highlighted that, today, many everyday devices have a microcontroller (MCU)—a tiny chip often smaller than the size of your thumbnail. Indeed, over 9 billion MCU-powered devices are deployed every year, but few are connected to the Internet today.[38]

As IoT hype ebbs and flows,[39] there have been a number of reports about current IoT deployment and wide-ranging estimates for IoT device growth. While some of these projections have been proven overly optimistic and continue to vary,[40] it is undeniable that smart devices are proliferating across multiple categories. In early 2017, Gartner predicted that the number of IoT devices installed that year would increase to 8.3 billion (up from 6.3 billion in 2016), surpassing the number of people on the planet for the first time.[41] However, midway through 2018, IoT Analytics stated that "just" 7 billion IoT devices were in use; they forecasted that the number of connected and in-use devices would reach 8.3 billion in 2019 and increase to 11.6 billion in 2021 (equaling the anticipated number of connections of non-IoT devices, such as smartphones, tablets, PCs, laptops, and fixed line phones, that year).[42] Meanwhile, in late 2018, Gartner forecasted that 14.2 billion things would be connected in 2019 and that 25 billion things will be connected by 2021.[43] Representing a middle ground between two well-respected analyst firms, Ericsson has forecasted that 18 billion IoT devices will be in use by 2022.[44] All in all, recent estimates for 2020–2021 range from about 9 to 25 billion, though more dated estimates for 2020 have been as high as 75 billion.[45]

There are at least a few ways to think about such mind-boggling and variable estimates. One is deployment globally, both today and in the future. Reports from 2015 and 2019 highlight North America as the region with the most extensive IoT deployment and Asia Pacific as the most rapidly growing;[46] in 2017, Gartner expected that 67% of IoT devices would be used in China, North America, and Western Europe.[47] Relatedly, we could consider *how* devices are connecting—for instance, through wireless personal area networks (WPAN) such as Bluetooth or via wireless local area networks (WLAN) such as Wi-Fi—as well as where growth is projected.[48] While IoT analytics shows that, today, most devices connect via WPAN or WLAN, it also highlights the potential growth of low-power wide area networks and the introduction of wireless neighborhood area networks (WNAN), including mesh networks discussed in chapters 6 and 7,[49] and 5G in the coming years.[50] How devices are connecting will impact global adoption—given variations in infrastructure that's currently deployed or available in the near term (e.g., mesh networks might help to fill gaps in broadband access)—as well as security and privacy given that different types of networks might have varying risks or capabilities.

We can also consider what these numbers will mean for people and businesses. If, by 2025, there are 8 billion people and 25 billion IoT devices on the planet, that means an average of 3.13 devices per person. However, given variability in connectivity and income (as well as among different age groups), we can expect that many people will not have IoT devices by that time; on the other hand, for numerous others—and many Western households—that number will be much higher. International Data Corporation (IDC) has estimated that, by 2025, every "connected person" in the world will have a "digital data engagement," many of which will be related to IoT devices. They estimate this engagement will occur over 4,900 times per day, which means that we will be interacting with some device on average about once every 18 seconds.[51]

There will also be variability in adoption across market segments and within individual businesses. In firms, for instance, sales, marketing, and operations tend to be the most active early adopters of IoT as they recognize its potential for obtaining real-time customer feedback and operational goals.[52] Among industry verticals, consumer IoT—think "smart home" devices as well as wearables—has the broadest deployment as well as the greatest anticipated growth in spending (overall, though, businesses pay more).[53] Manufacturing, transportation, and logistics have had the broadest deployment and highest anticipated spending, but significant usage and growth is also being tracked and expected in the energy and utilities, financial services, healthcare, and retail sectors (among others).[54]

Across these business contexts, one key to broadening and deepening IoT adoption seems to be helping business make sense of the landscape of options and use cases. IoT solutions can also be helpful in optimizing resources, including through the use of IoT services,[55] the bundling of components from several vendors into "complete" IoT solutions,[56] and cost-efficient use of data for advanced analytics, visualization, and data mining.[57] In addition, addressing the security, privacy, and governance challenges described in the following chapters will be key to ensuring an enabling environment for both businesses and individuals.

Across individual users, businesses, and governments, what sorts of IoT functions, devices, and applications are being offered?

How many technologies can you say are intended to help protect your home, improve a manufacturing facility's energy efficiency, enable better health outcomes, drive your car more safely, manage stop lights and traffic flow, and prepare for floods or earthquakes? Not many, most likely. The incredible expanse of potential IoT functions, devices, and applications is part of the point of why IoT technologies are incredibly exciting and full of hype—and why they have the potential to transform so many aspects of our lives and societies, for better or worse.

In the meantime, what can you, your business, or your government do to take advantage of IoT opportunities today? In short, the list is already near endless. Here's a non-comprehensive roundup to give a flavor for the types of IoT functions, devices, and applications on offer as of this writing. First, consumer IoT. In the "smart home" context, existing devices and services relate to appliances (such as refrigerators and washers and dryers); entertainment (TVs); utilities (plugs or outlets, irrigation controllers, thermostats, home energy monitors, bulbs, and vents); and security (locks, garage doors, motion sensors, smoke detectors, home alarm systems, etc.). In the consumer gadget context, existing functions, devices, and applications include personal assistants (such as Amazon's Echo or Google Home); wearables (e.g., watches and fitness trackers); and daily personal and home management devices (everything from key or wallet trackers to toothbrushes to pet feeders).

Industry examples are broader still. In the context of manufacturing or industrial IoT, functions, devices, and applications include: monitoring and optimization of processes and resources (with the help of many sensors and analytics as well as digital twins[58]); predictive maintenance; error reduction (such as by integrating sensors to tools and machines and giving working wearables); and transparency and compliance (with parts traceability).[59] In the transportation and logistics sector, examples include: fleet and transit management, smart inventory systems, and connected or semi-autonomous cars.[60] In the financial services sector, increasing deployment of sensors and data analytics is already impacting credit underwriting, lending (e.g., sensors might monitor the condition of financed goods), trading and investing activities, and the providing of insurance to businesses and individuals.[61] In the energy sector, common sensor deployment examples include smart meters and smart grids, along with IoT to optimize their operations.[62] In the health sector, increasing healthcare data generated from IoT-enabled devices, such as EC, MRI, X-ray, and Sonography machines, is leading to a more rapid deployment of IoT analytics.[63] Retail use cases range from tracking inventory in stores to providing personalized marketing for shoppers to understating operational versus customer-oriented tasks of employees.[64] There are also potential functions, devices, and applications in agriculture, education, hospitality, and other sectors, some of which are discussed in Table 2.2.[65]

Governments are also using IoT devices and applications to enhance operations, provide better public infrastructure and services, and improve emergency response, policing, and national defense. Examples include using smart energy systems in government offices, building and maintaining smart roads, optimizing trash collection, tracking wildlife, monitoring the weather and the environment (e.g., river levels, forest fires, underwater volcanic activity), managing military supply chains, analyzing the flow of traffic especially in high-accident areas, and understanding water usage trends. It's even being deployed to help with parking headaches.[66]

In short, it is difficult to find a sector or industry that neither is already, nor will be, impacted by the widespread availability of IoT technologies. This includes something very personal to all of us—our very selves.

What is the "Internet of Bodies"?

We know from the previous question that IoT devices and applications could be used to reduce external stresses (like finding a parking spot more quickly), but IoT may also be able to address bodily woes from the inside. This phenomenon, known as the "Internet of Bodies," is based on the same concept as IoT itself—except that it is a network of smart devices that are attached to, or exist inside, the human body.[67] As such, it is inclusive of but goes beyond devices like fitness trackers,

Table 2.2 Current and Future Applications of IoT Devices across Industries

Industry	Current Application	Future Scope
Retail	Supply chain operations, personalized marketing, and customer service[98]	Real-time monitoring of in-store and fleet operations, consumer behavior prediction[99]
Healthcare	Diagnostic smartphones for patient vitals, pill bottle for prescription adherence[100]	Reducing device downtime using sensor data, tele-health services for elderly care, and a fully realized Internet of Bodies[101]
Insurance	Existing technologies by businesses are used to collect data for compliance[102]	Tailoring policies by using collected data to make business predictions[103]
Smart Home	Disparate networks like HVAC, lighting, and security use smart devices like intelligent thermostats, smart meters for electricity, and analytical security solutions[104]	Creation of a single smart home-based network that consists of all devices seamlessly connected to each other[105]
Automobile/Transport	Tracking traffic data, driver performance, environmental conditions, system alerts[106]	Connecting automated vehicles to other automated vehicles and other smart devices and infrastructure[107]

smart glasses, and smart watches to an uncertain future full of both promise and potential peril: as described by Meghan Neal of *Motherboard*,

Computers will become so tiny they can be embedded under the skin, implanted inside the body, or integrated into a contact lens and stuck on top of your eyeball.

Naturally, those machines will be WiFi-enabled, so it's feasible that anything you can do with your phone now you could do with your gaze or gestures [in the future].[68]

This concept, though, is already becoming a reality. In 2017, the US Food and Drug Administration approved the use of ingestible technology or "smart pills," which are being used by doctors at the University of Minnesota Health Clinics to monitor whether chemotherapy patients are taking their medications.[69] Medtronic, the world's largest medical device company, launched a mobile app in 2019 called MyCareLink Heart, which has the ability to communicate directly with patients' pacemakers through their smartphones and tablets.[70] Another company has introduced a "smart bimodal hearing solution" that can be connected to and managed directly from a smartphone.[71] There is also significant investment going toward the development of an "artificial pancreas," which would have the ability to automatically monitor blood sugar levels and provide insulin to people with Type 1 diabetes, replacing the need for constant monitoring and the delivery of insulin through shots.[72] Similarly, in 2014, Google announced an effort to develop a smart contact lens that could continuously measure glucose levels in tears using a tiny wireless chip and miniature glucose sensor, enabling those with diabetes to get a signal rather than having to prick their finger and test drops of blood.[73] That same year, the company also filed a patent for an intra-ocular device that could automatically adjust the eye's focus, take photos, and connect to wireless devices, replacing traditional glasses or contact lenses (especially for focusing at a close distance) and enabling data to be sent to an optometrist's office or a clinic, which could then provide a wireless update for the equivalent of corrective lens prescriptions.[74]

Of course, security and privacy concerns are manifest when connecting something as delicate as the human body to various IoT devices. The problem made national news, for example, when the FDA mandated a recall of more than 400,000 pacemakers that were found to be vulnerable to hackers, necessitating a firmware update.[75] It can be further imagined when considering the challenges of interacting with implanted devices or considering how criminals or nation states might use the personal health records of their targets.[76] We delve deeper into these security issues in chapter 3, after first assessing some further benefits of replete, embedded sensors.

What are some benefits of having sensors in connected personal devices? Or in industrial control systems?

According to ZDNet, the best smart home gadget of 2018 was Ring.[77] It's a device and app "doorbell" system that alerts you (through your smartphone, tablet, or PC) when motion is detected near your home entrance and then provides you the option of communicating directly with visitors through an in-built microphone—or to capture video footage (which wound up getting Ring in trouble in late 2019 in the form of a $5 million class action lawsuit over vulnerabilities in its camera software).[78] Second on the list: Kuri, a "cute mobile robot" that can wander around your house, acting as a personal assistant and documenting the chaos of daily life.[79] Just three months after ZDNet's recognition, though, Kuri production (at least temporarily) ended after Bosch made the decision not to integrate this initiative of the Bosch Startup Platform into its existing business units.[80]

Even though the functions (and success to date) of Ring and Kuri are rather different, at least some of their sensors are similar. For instance, both Ring and Kuri have proximity and motion sensors as well as image sensors, whether they are used to identify and record people at your door or family and friends within your home. Sensors have come up quite a lot already in this exploration of the benefits of the coming IoE—as foundational components of IoT (whether bundled or embedded). But what are these sensors that are used consistently across IoT devices and applications to record so much about us, and what are some of their benefits and drawbacks?

There are many different types of sensors used across devices for different functions. One way to categorize them is by physics domains: there are "light and electromagnetism sensors," "thermal sensors," "vibration and sound sensors," "matter and materials sensors," and "time and space sensors."[81] More specific categories include pressure, water quality, chemical, gas, smoke, humidity, or infrared sensors—and those are just some of the relatively intuitive ones.[82] Gyroscope sensors, which measure angular rate or velocity, are used in everything from car navigation systems to game controllers and drones,[83] and they are so sensitive that they have been used "to pick up acoustic vibrations . . . [to] eavesdrop on conversations."[84] These sensors are used in combination with accelerometer sensors, which measure the rate of change of velocity over time (and are used in smartphones to detect acts like tilting—as well as for anti-theft protection).[85] Level sensors, which are used to determine the amount of liquids that flow in an open or closed system, are deployed in everything from the recycling industry to beverage and pharmaceutical operations to fuel gauges and instruments for monitoring sea levels.[86]

In a home environment, these sensors can help provide safety, energy efficiency, convenience, novelty, expertise (i.e., to make you cook like a pro or to track your running form), or human connectivity.[87] In the safety context, beyond Ring, smart home security systems use image and motion sensors to monitor who comes and goes (or the well-being of children or the elderly), and smart ovens might use temperature or gas sensors to send a signal if they are malfunctioning. In the case of induction cooktop stoves, expertise might be enabled by pressure and chemical sensors that heat exclusively when a metal pan is placed on top—no more burners running uncovered, and no more pans being overheated.[88] To further energy efficiency, motion detection and optical or infrared sensors can provide localized heating, and level and humidity sensors can help enable smart water heaters and washing machines to alert you to leaks or HVAC systems to signal that they require predictive maintenance. Roombas, providing convenience and novelty (check out those cat videos on Instagram), require proximity and pressure sensors. To improve human connection, image and motion sensors might not only help transmit faces of loved ones but also create a sense of physical proximity or awareness by triggering when someone moves through a space with a connected device.

In industrial IoT, many of the same sensors are used for similar purposes, but there are also differences; for instance, even in especially harsh environments, industrial sensors should be able to signal that a particular condition is being preserved.[89] While sensors have been used in manufacturing for decades, before IoT technologies they were constrained by issues like signal noise, signal attenuation (i.e., a weakened signal), and response dynamics; IoT has transformed sensors, enabling them to be used in more machines (because they can be smaller and much more flexible), carry out more complex calculations, and have more features.[90] Broadly speaking, industrial IoT sensors can increase visibility into existing workflows and processes, help predict outcomes in different environments, or create new business models; for instance, Kaeser Compressor, a German company that traditionally made and sold compressed air machines, realized through the use of IoT sensors that they could also offer compressed air as a service.[91] More specifically, industrial IoT sensors tend to monitor and measure conditions like temperature, speed, weight, location, operational failures, changes in operations, object movement, and valve status—as well as machine performance, oxygen levels, and employee heart rates—in real time.[92] Ultimately, these sensors offer a few key benefits, including: maintenance of equipment and environmental conditions, meeting of regulatory requirements, improvement and automation of logistics and asset management, and controlling of energy costs.[93]

Sensors are at the heart of IoT devices, enabling the collection of data that can be used to enhance functionality. Then the data gets processed on a device, leveraging connectivity, and some function is performed, either automatically or in response to user input. This is the real value-add of IoT devices and services—and also where much of the risk is introduced, which brings us to the more challenging aspects of the IoE revolution.

3

SECURING EVERYTHING?

DEEP DIVES INTO INTERNET OF THINGS SECURITY

Success sometimes has unexpected or counterproductive consequences. For example, as the makers of Kleenex, Q-Tip, and Band-Aid know, widespread success can cause a trademark to become "genericized" in the United States and elsewhere, undermining a brand's investment in a unique identifier. In the case of the Internet, success undercut assumptions about how security would work. Early Internet developers focused on interoperability more than security as they were building a network for a relatively small, trusted community of technology experts, but exponential growth brought in many new Internet users, making built-in security more important.[1] Moreover, speed, efficiency, and a desire to be first to market has long won out over security, at least until the headline-making viruses of the early 2000s.[2]

Today, as the Internet of Everything (IoE) proliferates and impacts many aspects of our lives, this backdrop sets the stage for security concerns across an ever larger ecosystem, sprawling from consumer products to smart manufacturing and beyond; even NASA is now helping to bring the Internet of Things (IoT) to the final frontier.[3] Thus, IoT poses tremendous challenges for security, layering new threats, vulnerabilities, and consequences as well as techniques and technology architectures on top of cybersecurity issues that have been mounting for decades, even as those issues are increasingly taken seriously and efforts to address them proliferate. This chapter takes some deep dives into these implications, beginning with foundational security issues before moving on to the seemingly bright idea of smart lightbulbs.

What are some of the foundational security challenges, and benefits, of IoT?

IoT devices themselves and the services and networks they leverage all face security challenges. For starters, the networks and infrastructure on which an IoT device relies (including mobile networks) must be protected and made resilient. In addition, IoT devices and services are facing issues similar to those faced by other systems and programs composed of hardware and software and interacted with by users, such as vulnerabilities (i.e., weaknesses in code)[4] and poor user hygiene (e.g., weak passwords, delayed patching or installation of updates, and successful "phishing" or "spear phishing" scams).[5] Challenges with mobile technologies also highlight some potential issues that IoT devices could pose as they're deployed more broadly and interact with users across home and work environments in a more integrated way. While increased user functionality has driven mobile device growth among consumers, just as it has with IoT applications,[6] that growth has also expanded the "attack surface" that must be defended.[7]

Some organizations have struggled to successfully deploy Bring-Your-Own-Device (BYOD) programs, wherein users bring their personal devices to work, often reducing costs and improving user productivity while increasing concerns around remote network access and confidential data protection.[8] Mobile Device Management (MDM) solutions have been instrumental in helping to address some of these security gaps,[9] but IoT broadens the array of threats with which enterprises need to cope;[10] some even see IoT as "BYOD on steroids."[11]

More broadly, many consumers and organizations still lack awareness of cybersecurity issues as well as insight into how to evaluate the security of what they are buying, making it unlikely that they will pay more for better security. Cybercrime is still "cheap, profitable, and comparatively safe" for cybercriminals, while cybersecurity can be expensive, difficult, and have an unclear return on investment (RoI); in other words, the economics of cybersecurity remain challenging, as is explored in chapter 5.[12] The deployment of IoT devices and services will also complicate cybersecurity risk management efforts by broadening supply chains that must be tracked, creating automated functions and new interdependencies[13] that must be monitored, and multiplying the systems and data that must be updated and protected. As Stanford professor Robert Cannon remarked, "Everything that can be automated will be automated."[14]

In other ways, IoT security challenges represent not only an exaggeration of or new twist on old problems, but also an entirely new game. For one, unlike our laptops and smartphones, we will likely not be able to replace many IoT devices every few years, though the newest technology often incorporates the most advanced security techniques and capabilities—just think how often you replace your refrigerator or thermostat, let alone how often capital-intensive machines are exchanged in factories or healthcare facilities.[15] The UK's National Health Service, for example, was still running Windows XP in the majority of its hospitals as of 2016, despite the fact that XP was released in 2001 and Microsoft stopped supporting it in 2014 (and provided free upgrades to Windows 10 starting the following year).[16] It may be even more difficult to regularly upgrade IoT devices given the scale of their deployment and the cost of some individual devices; for instance, MRI machines may cost as much as $1–$3 million.

In addition, the consequences of IoT-enabled cyber attacks have the potential to be especially severe: after all, "When cars or infusion pumps are hacked, people can die."[17] Confidentiality, integrity, and availability—which are generally referred to as the "CIA triad"—have always been at the center of efforts to protect computer systems and the information they store, process, or communicate.[18] Together, they help defenders ensure that computer systems and data are not accessed or altered without authorization, and that users can access systems and data when they need them. All three principles continue to be important for the IoE, but the importance of integrity and availability may be the most pronounced.[19] IoT technology is distinct because it is integrated with the physical systems of our world—including our cars and homes as well as medical devices, electrical grids, and manufacturing facilities that manage complex equipment and a variety of materials. The manipulation or lack of availability of some of these physical systems may have catastrophic consequences, including fatalities or long outages. A Lloyd's of London study estimated that a worst-case scenario cyber attack on the grid could cost up to $1 trillion and last weeks.[20] According to Schneier, "On the Internet of Things, integrity and availability threats are much worse than confidentiality threats. It's one thing if your smart door lock can be eavesdropped upon to know who is home. It's another thing entirely if it can be hacked to allow a burglar to open the door—or prevent you from opening your door."[21]

It's not all bad news, though. IoT technologies do present some meaningful opportunities to potentially improve cybersecurity. First, the IoE is being created in an era that is much more security-conscious than in the early years of Internet communication and commerce. Whereas cybersecurity awareness and spending remained low throughout the 1990s and 2000s, by 2010, cybersecurity had emerged as a top security threat for many large organizations.[22] Today, enterprises and other organizations are still in the thick of trying to understand how to manage cyber risk effectively, but many are certainly paying attention.[23] According to former FBI director Robert Mueller, "I am convinced that there are only two types of companies: those that have been hacked and those that will be. And even they are converging into one category: companies that have been hacked and will be hacked again."[24]

While the ecosystem of vendors contributing and managing IoT technologies is broad and diverse, creating complexity, at least some IT companies, cybersecurity firms, and insurers are seeing security as a differentiator.[25] Likewise, governments are increasingly leading efforts to promote best practices or ensure the use of baseline measures, which also helps to cultivate awareness and, ideally, effective processes and investments (see more in chapter 5).

Second, IoT technology, the data it generates, and the automated functions it enables have the potential to drive improvements in AI-based security technology as well as help deploy security efficiently at scale. Specifically, "IoT can provide unprecedented detailed information to predict and counter attacks. For example, information from multiple types of sensors can provide data for advanced, automated threat diagnostics."[26] While progress will likely be "more muddled and incremental than marketers would want to admit," researchers at companies and in academia largely agree that there will be benefits (as well as challenges) in leveraging AI technology for cybersecurity.[27] Components may even be able to learn to detect new vulnerabilities and, if necessary, isolate themselves.[28] Due to the interconnectedness it will involve, IoT may also help shift thinking toward ecosystem-wide tactics wherein IoT devices "cooperate with one another to provide the appropriate security levels for an entire system."[29] Smart routers could collect and analyze their own data, sharing findings across a decentralized network, or collectively identify malicious patterns and deny traffic en masse, acting like an automatic, organic Security Operations Center (SOC), explored further in chapter 6.[30] In responding to various threats, such as distributed denial-of-service attacks (DDoS),[31] approaches that "leverage truly autonomous, self-improving security bots" can result in positive emergent behavior (i.e., the development of larger systems from smaller, autonomous units) that "counters negative emergent behavior."[32]

Overall, then, the impact of the IoE on cybersecurity will be both positive and negative. To see how the dynamics are playing out in the real world, we next focus on an increasingly popular consumer product—the smart lightbulb—before moving on to discuss broader trends in IoT security.

How secure is my smart lightbulb, and why should I care?

While smart lightbulbs can allow lighting to be remotely controlled as well as customized and scheduled, they can also provide an inroad for criminals, who might hack IoT devices for malicious purposes, and security researchers, who might compromise the same devices to test their skills or help to improve security. The latter is not, in fact, that uncommon. In 2014, researchers at a UK-based cybersecurity consultancy shared that they had successfully captured and decrypted Wi-Fi credentials by hacking an LIFX smart lightbulb—as well as informed LIFX of their findings and worked with the company to develop a fix.[33] In 2016, security researchers in Canada and Israel discovered that they could use a drone to remotely take control of a Philips Hue smart lightbulb—as well as install malicious firmware (i.e., deeply embedded software that allows hardware to be updated).[34] The malware enabled the researchers to block wireless updates, including any that could have shut off their remote access, from being processed by the lightbulb, thus making their infection irreversible.[35] The researchers reported the vulnerability that they exploited to Philips, which then developed and delivered a patch to fix the issue.[36] In 2018, another security researcher demonstrated that a different LIFX smart lightbulb was not encrypting Wi-Fi credentials, so passwords were "plainly readable" in the bulb's memory; LIFX again fixed the relevant vulnerabilities through firmware and app updates.[37] Yet, this should be tempered with the "industry rule of thumb" that "a quarter of us install patches on the day they're issued, a quarter within the month, a quarter with the year, and a quarter never do."[38]

While these sorts of issues—and cooperation across security researchers and responsive, proactive vendors—are not limited to smart lightbulbs, they are an interesting case as a relatively inexpensive and popular consumer device. One significant challenge facing smart lightbulbs and other inexpensive consumer IoT devices is that the vendors that produce them are often working on tight profit margins,[39] and even for buyers that are cognizant of security when making new PC and mobile device purchases, security is not often top of mind when purchasing lightbulbs—or cameras or DVRs (see more in the next question). Whereas an increasing number of consumers might have dealt with a crashing computer, identity fraud, or even ransomware, they likely have not experienced many negative impacts associated with unsecure lightbulbs (even if the broader ecosystem has). As security expert Bruce Schneier has written, our PCs and smartphones are

> as secure as they are because there are teams of security engineers working on the problem. Companies like Microsoft, Apple, and Google spend a lot of time testing their code before it's released, and quickly patch vulnerabilities once they're discovered. Those companies can support such teams because [they] make a huge amount of money . . . from their software—and, in part, compete on its security. This isn't true of embedded systems or home routers.[40]

It also isn't generally the case for smart lightbulbs, even though large and diversified companies like Philips are in the game. In 2019 consumer reviews, both Philips and LIFX fared well, getting top scores for individual products and the diversity of their offerings.[41] However, despite smart lightbulbs being described as not "quite a commodity" but also "getting close to maturity as far as the market goes," security still does not even get mentioned in product reviews or marketing pages,[42] though it is a growing focus at *Consumer Reports*, as is discussed in chapters 4 and 5. By way of comparison, security does not necessarily feature prominently in product reviews or marketing pages for PCs and smartphones, but it does get mentioned; for instance, security features related to chips, biometric sensors, payment platforms, and Trusted Platform Module support as well as security highlights from case studies at least sometimes make the cut.[43]

How does the scale of insecure IoT devices create new risks?

Producers of smart lightbulbs and other consumer devices may not be as focused on competing on security at this stage as producers of PCs and smartphones are, probably at least in part because of the extent to which consumers have dealt with risks and consequences with these different generations of devices. In 2017, for instance, about 16.7 million US consumers were victims of identity theft or fraud (which was 81% more likely online than at point of sale), and even if the direct financial impact of the nearly $17 billion in damages was limited for consumers, they still needed to be vigilant in monitoring their accounts, especially if they were otherwise active online.[44] Meanwhile, relatively few consumers have dealt with "nightmarish" smart home scenarios, such as strangers' voices helicoptering into their kids' orbits.[45] Indeed, as a December 2018 study shows, an understanding of security issues associated with smart home platforms and integrated third party products is still being demonstrated, even among academics.[46] (Notably, the researchers demonstrated that "an attacker can compromise a low-integrity device/app integrated into a smart home (e.g., a light bulb), and use routines to perform protected operations on a high-integrity product (e.g., a security camera)."[47]) Moreover, few consumers have yet experienced especially and immediately dangerous attacks resulting from integrating and using IoT devices that might provide an

entryway into their home networks—such as the manipulation of smart locks or security systems, the shutting down of
HVAC systems, or the blowing up of connected ovens.[48] Even
if those sorts of attacks have not hit mainstream—and even
if their doing so is not likely in the near term due to other
lower-risk and high-reward online financial crime, such as the
stealing of bank credentials and even trade secrets (and we
hope they never do!)—insecure consumer IoT devices escalate
ecosystem-wide risk.

Consider this story from the Washington, DC, Department
of Transportation. Back in 2013, it overhauled its traffic management system by deploying a network of more than 1,300
wireless sensors to provide accurate data and insight for
real-time congestion management, emergency response, and
urban planning.[49] Less than a year later, Cesar Cerrudo, CTO
at IOActive Labs, strolled the streets of the city and demonstrated how to hack into the deployed traffic control systems
from as far as two miles away, or even from a drone flying
at more than 650 feet.[50] He exposed the vulnerabilities in the
vendor's (Sensys Networks) sensors, confirmed that the communications were not encrypted, and also that the sensors and
repeaters could be controlled without any authentication.[51]
This meant that it was possible to compromise the sensors and
feed traffic control systems with fake data to manipulate traffic
at will.

To take another example, many IoT cameras have hardcoded
credentials,[52] but numerous mobile applications do not encrypt
traffic.[53] While this may seem less than significant, in fact the
absence of encryption leaves the video stream open for anyone
to view, meaning that somebody watching a video stream on
her mobile phone connected to a public network allows others
to sniff this information and watch the same video of the live
traffic stream. This happened when TRENDnet, a marketer of
IoT cameras and baby monitors, "failed to use reasonable security to design and test its software, including a setting for the
cameras' password requirement."[54] These devices also stored

and transmitted login credentials in clear text, making them easily acquired and utilized by attackers.[55] Indeed, in early 2012, a hacker exploited these flaws and posted links to the live feeds of nearly 700 cameras.[56] Unfortunately, this vendor is not unique, as has been shown; many firms do not build in cybersecurity from the inception of new product lines, choosing instead too often to bolt it on after the fact. This problem is not restricted to smaller companies. Even Nike Fuelband had a default pin on every device.[57] If someone knew the default pin (which was not difficult to retrieve), one could connect to anybody's Fuelband. D-Link and Asus routers also have had backdoors with default credentials that could not be changed.[58] The list goes on. In 2014, researchers at the French technology institute Eurecom discovered thirty-eight vulnerabilities in the firmware across 123 products of IoT device manufacturers, which included poor encryption and backdoors that could allow unauthorized access.[59] Symantec analyzed fifty smart home devices available in the market in 2015.[60] None of them enforced strong passwords or provide mutual authentication between the client and the server.[61] This is important since, according to one study, "80% of breaches are the result of abuse or misuse of credentials."[62]

A significant part of the reason why insecure IoT devices escalate risk, even in the immediate term, has to do with the scale at which they're being introduced into our home, work, and industrial environments. The proliferation of billions of IoT devices with default credentials and minimal security features of the type described means that many devices can be compromised by an outside attacker who controls aspects of their functionality without an owner's awareness, ultimately forming a "botnet," or collection of "bots" (i.e., compromised devices).[63] Botnets can then be used for nefarious purposes (as well as legitimate ones, including cryptomining), such as distributing spam, stealing credentials at scale, or bombarding a target server with traffic until it's knocked offline, the last of which is known as a "distributed denial-of-service attack," or DDoS.[64] Many devices cannot be released from the botnet because they cannot be patched, in some cases because tight budget constraints meant that insufficient space was allowed for the (often Linux-based) operating system kernel to be updated; in other challenging situations, manufacturers might be out of business or no longer supporting outdated systems (e.g., Windows XP).[65] In addition, owners and operators might not even know that their routers, cameras, lightbulbs, or other devices are part of a botnet (and thus do not know to change their credentials—if possible) because users interact with IoT differently than they do PCs; whereas "an infected PC often malfunctions, slows down, or notifies users," IoT devices are "workhouses that are meant to function indefinitely, with minimal direct user interaction."[66] Because being part of an active botnet does not "noticeably affect" the performance of at least some IoT devices, "there's no reason the average user would even think that their webcam . . . is potentially part of an active botnet."[67]

One of the most infamous IoT botnets to date is known as "Mirai," introduced in the Preface, which first appeared in 2016 but still operates today (some devices have continued to be infected, and attackers have also adapted and continued to use different strains of Mirai's software).[68] The Mirai malware strain has taken over tens of thousands of poorly secured IoT devices, including security cameras, digital video recorders (DVRs),[69] and routers, by scanning the Internet for systems protected by default usernames and passwords (there are just sixty-eight username and password pairs in the botnet source code—many of those are used by dozens of products).[70] The Mirai botnet has received outsized attention in large part because it enabled an "extremely large" DDoS attack against Dyn,[71] a significant provider of the Internet's Domain Name System (DNS) infrastructure (even if that's not what the initial malware creators intended), leaving much of the Internet inaccessible on the US East Coast and bringing down major sites like Etsy, Netflix, and Twitter.[72] DDoS is "a particularly effective type of attack" on a provider like Dyn because the waves of malicious traffic are compounded by "users hitting refresh over and over to summon up an uncooperative page," further overloading its bandwidth.[73] Moreover, this type of attack highlighted "how critical DNS is to maintaining a stable and secure internet presence."[74] Botnets have also "killed" devices they have taken over (as in Brickerbot, so named for "bricking" machines) and been used to shut down the heating of two buildings in Finland.[75]

What if my phone could control a supervisory control and data acquisition (SCADA) system—could I really turn the lights out for a whole city?

Beyond issues related to interconnected home platforms or botnets, some security issues associated with IoT are especially critical because of what is actually connected and potentially at risk—including not only home locks, cars, and medical devices, but also smart guns and SCADA systems. In 2015, Andy Greenberg, a *Wired* reporter, shared that he had volunteered to be a "digital crash-test dummy" for two security researchers testing an exploit of software embedded in a Jeep Cherokee; they remotely took control of the car's air conditioning, radio, windshield wipers—and transmission—all while Andy was driving on a highway outside of St. Louis.[76] In 2016 and 2017, there were confirmed reports of security vulnerabilities in a Johnson & Johnson insulin pump, an Owlet baby heart monitor, and St. Jude Medical's implantable pacemakers and defibrillators, which are used to control heart functions and prevent heart attacks.[77] In 2015, security researchers demonstrated that they could use software vulnerabilities to take control of a TrackerPoint rifle's self-aiming functions remotely—potentially without alerting the shooter (the resulting sudden jump in the scope's view is almost indistinguishable from the recoil of the rifle).[78] While these specialty sniper rifles may not be likely to hit the mainstream soon, more recently police departments have considered allowing their ranks to use "smart" guns that can be operated by an authorized user only.[79] These guns are already being used by militaries.[80]

SCADA systems have also been targeted by security researchers and malicious actors alike. There's even a forum for researchers focused on SCADA security (and, as they proclaim, saving humanity from industrial disaster): SCADA StrangeLove.[81] In 2016, researchers described not only the history of how attacks on SCADA and industrial control systems (ICS) have emerged but also how they created "honeypots"[82] to understand the increasing attack trends.[83] Their honeypot system was subject to significant malicious activity, more than 1,000 attempted attacks ranging from simple probing to more sophisticated behavior, including the shutting down of targeted control systems.[84] That same year, the US Department of Justice announced charges against seven Iranian men for a campaign of attacks, including against a SCADA system controlling the Bowman Dam in Rye, New York.[85] In the energy sector in particular, attackers took down power equipment while attempting to extort money,[86] disrupted uranium enrichment,[87] threatened to cause an explosion at a petrochemical plant,[88] took out safety systems,[89] and left 225,000 people without power for several hours.[90] More specifically, in 2015 and 2016, factions attacked Ukraine's energy grid and took remote control of Ukrainian electricity distribution companies' SCADA systems.[91] Reports have shown that more than twenty US power utilities have been similarly compromised.[92] In 2014, the head of US Cyber Command acknowledged that attackers with the capability "to take down control systems that operate US power grids" had been tracked intruding into ICS;[93] in 2017, Symantec reported that attacks on the energy grid were on the upswing, including those that aim to gain access to operational systems.[94] In 2018, the United States accused Russia of hacking its energy grid and other key infrastructure—and "placing the tools that they would have to place in order to turn the power off" rather than just engaging in reconnaissance efforts—and imposed sanctions.[95]

In other words, it is possible that, by remotely controlling a SCADA system, a malicious actor could turn off the lights for a whole city, and recent efforts by researchers, security companies, and governments demonstrate that attackers are increasingly focusing on such scenarios. Moreover, in 2018, researchers from IOActive and Embedi released a report that outlined 147 cybersecurity vulnerabilities in thirty-four Google Play Store mobile applications used to manage or interact with SCADA systems.[96] The researchers explain that "if the mobile application vulnerabilities identified are exploited, an attacker could disrupt an industrial process or compromise industrial network infrastructure, or cause a SCADA operator to unintentionally perform a harmful action on the system."[97] In other words, mobile applications have vulnerabilities that, if exploited, could "have dire consequences on SCADA systems that operate industrial control systems," including energy grids that keep the lights on.[98]

As is explored further in chapter 7, deterring such attacks is difficult, and in the end rests on either denying access through enhanced cybersecurity measures, or by possessing sufficient offensive capabilities. In other words, we all live in glass houses, and the rocks just keep getting bigger, which has helped to stay the hand of would-be attackers.

What are some of the biggest tech companies and industry groups doing about IoT security? Is the answer sticking our collective head in the Cloud?

IoT security threats and potential consequences ranging from the inconvenient to the truly frightening abound, but as was raised at the outset of this chapter, the future is not entirely bleak; there are opportunities for IoT security to be improved and for the deployment of IoT to help advance security.

A range of providers will contribute to such efforts, including cybersecurity startups focused on IoT,[99] as well as established network providers like Cisco that, in addition to providing other products and services, can deploy security "directly into the network infrastructure so you can use your IoT network as a security sensor and enforcer."[100] Indeed, enhancing IoT security will require that improvements be made by providers with various roles across the IoT ecosystem, including among hardware manufacturers and integrators, software solution developers, IoT solution deployers, and IoT solution operators.[101] Cloud service providers sit at a particularly interesting place in the IoT ecosystem to influence security;[102] as discussed in chapter 1, they often interact with devices as well as apps and other IoT solution software, sometimes acting as an IoT solution's gateway to the Internet.

Each of the dominant global cloud service providers—Amazon Web Services (AWS), Microsoft, Alibaba Cloud, and Google Cloud[103]—integrates security into its IoT platform. Both Alibaba's and Google's cloud-based IoT platforms provide for device authentication and encrypted communication between devices and the IoT platform.[104] AWS's IoT Core also enables users to securely connect devices to the cloud and to other devices, including through end-to-end encryption and authentication and authorization controls as well as audit logging; in addition, AWS's IoT Device Defender is "a fully managed IoT security service" that enables customers to continuously monitor their devices, be alerted of any abnormal device behavior, and get recommendations for actions to mitigate security issues.[105] Microsoft's Azure IoT Hub, Azure IoT Edge, Security Center, and Azure Sentinel solutions also provide authentication, authorization, and encryption features as well as continuous monitoring of security posture and issues, threat detection, recommendations of actions to improve security, and automation of common incident response tasks.[106] In 2018, Microsoft also introduced Azure Sphere, a solution for creating highly secured, Internet-connected microcontroller

(MCU) devices with a custom Linux operating system and built-in security services that enable remote updates,[107] ultimately helping to automate security processes for manufacturers, deployers, and operators.[108] In other words, according to device manufacturers, Azure Sphere takes a holistic approach, addressing security at every layer rather than requiring it to be patched together.[109] Still, as with all cloud providers, disadvantages persist, such as concerns over downtime, security, privacy, limited control, and flexibility, among others.[110]

Beyond the development of products and services, companies and industry groups are also working to identify what design elements, features, and capabilities are critical for IoT solution security, especially considering the low profit margins and, in some cases, minimal incentives to invest significant sums in security differentiators. Azure Sphere, for instance, was built to meet seven properties of highly secure devices, each of which was identified by a small Microsoft Research team that set out to explore how to secure MCU-powered devices in 2015.[111] In 2018, a wireless industry association announced a cybersecurity certification for cellular-connected IoT devices.[112] In early 2019, a number of Washington, DC-based industry coalitions publicized an effort to build cross-sector guidelines for security connected devices,[113] and the Software Alliance announced its Framework for Secure Software, helping to enable industries that are newly integrating software into their devices to evaluate its security.[114] There are also more technical efforts, including among industry standards groups like the Trusted Computing Group (TCG), which, among other things, would help with verifying software updates.[115]

What about experts? What role do security researchers have?

This chapter has made references to "security researchers" that discover vulnerabilities in IoT solutions, test exploits, and use honeypots to understand attacker behavior. These researchers have long played a critical role in improving the security of IT products and services, and numerous major IT companies—including Alibaba, Amazon, Apple, Facebook, Google, IBM, Intel, Microsoft, and Samsung—receive reports about potential vulnerabilities from these researchers and develop patches or mitigations as needed.[116] This process is sometimes referred to as "coordinated vulnerability disclosure," or just vulnerability disclosure. For years, the security community has invested significant effort in promoting cooperation among security researchers and vendors to mitigate vulnerabilities in their products and services.[117] Entities like the Global Forum on Cyber Expertise and European Commission have also aimed to promote best practices among governments that can create an enabling environment for vulnerability disclosure programs and security researcher reporting.[118]

This cooperation has become even more important in the context of IoT as more vendors are managing products and services with vulnerabilities—and they often have fewer resources and less expertise than major technology companies to devote to managing hardware or software vulnerability reports from external experts. Indeed, HackerOne, a company that, like Bugcrowd, helps to facilitate cooperation among security researchers and vendors to get vulnerabilities addressed,[119] has documented that while many non-traditional tech companies, including Caterpillar, Medtronic, and Walmart, have vulnerability disclosure policies in place, 93% of companies on the 2017 Forbes Global 2000 list do not.[120] Without having a policy—or at least a security team point of contact—ready, security researchers will likely struggle to report vulnerabilities to the appropriate person at a vendor. Alternatively, when researchers can share information about the vulnerabilities they find—as the researchers did with the Jeep Cherokee, TrackerPoint Rifle, and smart lightbulb hacks already referenced[121]—the vulnerabilities can get fixed, better protecting both consumers and infrastructure.

As this chapter has shown, there is a seemingly never-ending stream of cybersecurity vulnerabilities in IoT systems, and we have only scratched the surface. In 2017, for example, the US Department of Homeland Security demonstrated that it was possible to remotely hack into a Boeing 757.[122] Printers have also been breached, and, given the rise of 3D and bioprinters, this could have a variety of physical and medical consequences.[123] As Schneier explains, "Everything is becoming vulnerable . . . because everything is becoming a computer. More specifically, a computer on the Internet."[124] This is a challenging situation since, at the same time, attacks on these systems "always get better."[125] To put it bluntly, "It used to be that things had computers in them. Now they *are* computers with things attached to them." As a result it will eventually be the case that "saying 'I'm going on the Internet'" will make about as much sense as plugging in a toaster and saying 'I'm going on the power grid.'"[126] It is unpacking the hopes for and future of privacy in such a hyper-connected world that we turn to next.

4

PROTECTING PRIVACY IN AN INTERNET OF EVERYTHING

As with security, concerns are replete over how best to scale privacy in the emerging Internet of Everything (IoE). How should we define "privacy" in an environment where our thermostats may know more about us than close friends? Is privacy even possible? Or, perhaps even more disturbing, do we care? This chapter digs into some of the innumerable privacy concerns that arise in a world of ubiquitous Internet-connected devices. We begin with the fundamental—and difficult—task of defining privacy in the twenty-first-century technological landscape before moving on to think through how technology has—and will continue to—change our view of this "fragile merchandise." We consider the ethical, and human rights, implications of this transition, and then tee up the governance discussion in chapter 5 with how some leading policymakers from Sacramento to Brussels are trying to help us keep some semblance of privacy in a world where it is increasingly the exception, not the rule.

What is "privacy"?

Privacy as a concept is as old as people's urge to enjoy some measure of solitude, away from the hustle and bustle of the Paleolithic. In many ways, that impulse was easier to satisfy then, in a world with plenty of untamed wilderness; indeed, by most estimates the global population did not surpass one billion until the late nineteenth century.[1] It might not be an accident, then, that the first debates about the contours of a legal right to privacy date back to this time of explosive population growth.[2]

Not only were there suddenly quite a few more people at the turn of the twentieth century, but thanks to the Industrial Revolution they seemed to be boasting an impressive number of gadgets that could impinge more easily than ever before on what privacy people had left. Among the more disturbing of these inventions to many members of the well-heeled cosmopolitan elite, including to two lawyers named Samuel D. Warren and Louis Brandeis, was the mass-produced camera.

Consider the scene in the summer of 1899, when the beaches of Newport, Rhode Island, were full of holiday revelers enjoying their yachts, tennis courts, and privacy. Into that cloistered world stepped a new kind of reporter—a so-called "Kodak fiend"—armed with a powerful new image capturing tool, much to the chagrin of those on holiday.[3] Indeed, public figures of all stripes were rattled by the growing ubiquity of cameras, including President Theodore Roosevelt, who famously chastised a boy who dared to snap his picture upon leaving church, saying, "You ought to be ashamed of yourself. . . . Trying to take a man's picture as he leaves a house of worship. It is a disgrace!"[4]

Warren and Brandeis agreed with Roosevelt's sentiment in their seminal article, *The Right to Privacy*, writing, "Instantaneous photographs and newspaper enterprise have invaded the sacred precincts of private and domestic life; and numerous mechanical devices threaten to make good the prediction that 'what is whispered in the closet shall be proclaimed from the house-tops.' "[5] Distinct from inherent rights to liberty or property,[6] Warren and Brandeis envisioned privacy as "the right to be let alone."[7] Over the following decades, courts unpacked this concept to eventually "give birth" to a constitutional right to privacy in the United States. Even though the

word "privacy" never appears in the US Constitution,[8] the right
to it has paved the way for Supreme Court holdings in seminal
cases like *Roe v. Wade* and *Lawrence v. Texas*, the latter of which
struck down anti-sodomy laws in Texas.[9] Over time, the Court
created three privacy strands, including: (1) decisional privacy
(such as regarding procreation), (2) non-disclosure, and (3) a
reasonable expectation of privacy in the criminal context.[10]

By the twenty-first century, privacy has become a vast concept encompassing (among much else) freedom of thought,
bodily integrity, solitude, information integrity, and freedom
from surveillance, along with the protection of reputation
and personality.[11] Still, there are widely differing views as
to the bounds of privacy rights, including whether it should
be considered a property right (and whether companies like
Facebook, for example, should pay users for their information),[12] and especially how to update core privacy concepts
for the Information Age. A key facet of this debate surrounds
the myriad privacy harms that can arise from information collection (surveillance) and processing (insecurity) to information dissemination (disclosure and distortion) and invasions
(intrusion), as characterized by Professor Peter Solove,[13] each
requiring unique policy responses. Yet there are also a wide
array of benefits that consumers enjoy from these services,
including "free," personalized, and convenient search and
social media that by its nature requires some degree of personal information to appropriately tailor. And there is the fact
that, despite consumer sentiments, relatively few are willing
to pay more for private products and services, and only
roughly half of US adults surveyed trust either social media
sites or the government to protect their data.[14] Some progress
is being made in balancing the costs and benefits of these services, as we will see. In the United States, for example, state-
level efforts such as California's 2018 Consumer Privacy Act
(CCPA) have galvanized interest on the part of civil society,
industry, and policymakers even as Congress has so far stalled
in enacting new protections. But none of these US efforts yet

establish a comprehensive right to privacy of the type enjoyed by Europeans under the 2018 General Data Protection Regulation (GDPR) or that of the more than 100 other nations now enacting similar omnibus privacy laws.

An expanding Internet of Things (IoT) has led many to question whether Warren and Brandeis's definition of privacy still rings true in the twenty-first century. Is it even possible to be "let alone" in an era defined by ubiquitous smart devices that can not only take your picture but record the most intimate moments of daily life? If not, should technology, or the law, change to reflect this new reality? As Henry David Thoreau remarked, "I find it wholesome to be alone the greater part of the time. To be in company, even with the best, is soon wearisome and dissipating. I love to be alone. I never found the companion that was so companionable as solitude."[15]

How has technology changed our views of privacy?

Advancing technology is causing societies around the world to rethink the bounds of privacy rights. For example, technology has made it easier than ever to breach the increasingly sheer veil of privacy—whether by media, private investigation, workplace monitoring, or surveillance.[16] We are surrounded by smart speakers listening for our commands (with the recordings being reviewed by human staff),[17] CCTV cameras watching our every move, and smartphones that could be recording even when they appear powered off.[18] Such a world has led some to argue that "privacy is dead," and that the best we can hope for is a kind of "group privacy" curated by the likes of Google and Facebook.[19] No less than Vint Cerf, a "Father of the Internet," has lamented, "Privacy may actually be an anomaly."[20] Others, such as Professor Alan Westin, have pushed back such an Orwellian end game, defining "privacy" more pragmatically as "the claim of individuals . . . to determine for themselves when, how and to what extent information about them is communicated to others."[21] Under this approach, "privacy enables freedom" by equating it with control, which might be appropriate from a human rights perspective, but that is far from a universal definition, with personal preferences and culture driving different interpretations of privacy rights. Such variance makes policy-making a bit of a challenge, to put it mildly.

Regardless, law alone is a necessary but insufficient force to further this end goal of protecting privacy in the Information Age[22] while, at the same time, it is also true that technology can make user anonymization easier while allowing consumers to choose from a greater range of products than ever before without even having to leave their private residences. As such, it is best to consider technology as both a sword and a shield against the likes of an overly intrusive world. For example, the US National Security Telecommunications Advisory Committee has argued, "The IoT creates opportunities for new thinking on approaches to end-to-end ecosystem security and resiliency, where decisions can be made automatically in a distributed manner."[23]

Still, it remains to be seen both how much control over personal privacy is possible in an IoE, along with how best to safeguard what little remains. In an era in which billions of people are willing to sacrifice their personal privacy online by participating in the explosion of social networking, Facebook has faced waves of criticism from policymakers and from some of its more than two billion users. Such criticism led it at one point to back down from proposed changes to its user agreement that would have made it more difficult to protect private information.[24] In the wake of scandals such as Cambridge Analytica, though, in which the private information of more than 50 million Facebook users was harvested so as to influence the behavior of US voters,[25] no less than the UK Parliament has stated that Facebook has behaved like "Digital Gangsters."[26] And Facebook is not alone. Google, for example, can possess as much as ten times the amount of data on individual users (the equivalent of four million Word docs, according to one researcher) as Facebook, the "everything network."[27] While some individuals wish to promote their freedom of expression even at the expense of their privacy, many others do not. Despite this disparity, the current US legal regime often maximizes freedom of expression at the expense of privacy. The debate about how best and when to protect privacy in a digital world, as encapsulated by the Facebook and Google sagas, is playing out in courtrooms around the world with widely varying results.

Many users remain apathetic about the data collection practices of leading Internet platforms. According to Pew surveys, for example, even as 88% of US respondents aged 18–29 and 78% of those aged 30–49 use social media, only 9% of these users said that they were "very confident" that the firms would adequately safeguard their data.[28] But it should be noted that confidence in the federal government did not rank much higher—only 12% were "very confident" in the ability of the US government to protect their information, which might not be too surprising in the aftermath of the Office of Personnel Management (OPM) and other recent high-profile data breaches.[29]

As sociologist Robert Merton argues, without privacy, "the pressure to live up to the details of all (and often conflicting) social norms would become literally unbearable."[30] In this conceptualization, the main enemy of privacy is community, especially a curious community practicing robust freedom of expression. The more invasive the community norms and the more advanced the technology, the less privacy may flourish. But, so what? Such sentiments presuppose that people still care about their personal privacy, which leads us to the next question—how much is our privacy worth?

How much is your private data worth?

How much would it cost for you to give a company unfettered access to your smartphone? For American teenagers and young adults aged 13–25, the answer was $20/month.[31] As reported by *TechCrunch*, users who chose to download an app entitled "Facebook Research" on either an Apple iPhone or Android device were paid the sum in return for the app "monitor[ing] their phone and web activity" and sending the data back to Facebook.[32] The app was discontinued when Apple objected, arguing that the service violated its data collection guidelines, an assessment to which Facebook later objected.[33]

Perhaps surprisingly, $20/month may be a high-end estimate for the value of private data. The *Financial Times* has since 2013 offered a calculator permitting anyone "to check the worth" of their private information in an effort to shed some light into the opaque data brokerage industry.[34] The methodology of the calculator might not be ironclad, but it does provide some insights on the types of information that make you more or less valuable as a data subject to tech platforms and their clients (e.g., advertisers). For example, if you are engaged, expecting a baby, or have kids, that makes you sought after by a variety of firms given the likely obscene amount of money you are about to spend on honeymoons, diapers, and daycare. Similarly, owning a home increases the worth of your data profile by roughly $0.10, as does regular exercise. Shopping habits—including membership in various loyalty programs—are another important indicator. Still, all this doesn't add up to that much; taking the quiz, your author's data profile was worth a mere $0.40.

Still, taken together, even such small figures really add up, especially given the sheer amount of data being collected. The US Federal Trade Commission (FTC) estimates that a given data broker might have more than 3,000 "data segments" for each US consumer.[35] The value of this industry is difficult to calculate but is likely massive given that an average email address has been reported to be worth $89 to a brand over time. In 2012, for example, the data brokerage industry posted some $150 billion in revenue.[36] Collectively, our data is worth trillions, since it is powering the growth of some of the largest firms in the world, including Google and Facebook. These firms, simply put, would not exist in their current forms but for America's lax approach to personal privacy protections. For example, Amazon draws on its users' search history to recommend products, while Netflix relied on data analytics in making casting decisions.[37] True, some of these services would no longer be "free" in an alternative universe in which Americans enjoyed the same privacy protections as Europeans, but then related questions arise as to the value of maintaining these offerings in their current form.[38]

In reviewing the question of "who should own your data?" at least three options are evident—users, companies, or governments. As we will see, in the European Union, users enjoy relatively more privacy rights over their data than in other jurisdictions such as the United States. In China and a variety of other nations practicing "cyber sovereignty," such information is ultimately in the hands of the State. In the United States, not all private data is created equal—greater protections are built in to protect financial and health information, for example, than someone's IP address. In general, though, companies have a relatively free hand in the United States to collect data largely absent government supervision. Such a state of affairs is in contravention to a recent report from researchers at the Stanford Business School who argue that "[p]eople, not companies, should have rights to their data, and people, not companies, should be able to sell it as they see fit."[39] These sentiments push us in the direction of recognizing privacy as a fundamental human right that is, in essence, priceless.

Is there a human right to privacy? And what does that have to do with my Facebook profile?

In late 2017, it came to light that roughly half of the US population had their personally identifiable information (PII) stolen, including names, dates of birth, and Social Security numbers, thanks to a series of governance failures at Equifax.[40] Shortly thereafter, the news broke that the private firm Cambridge Analytica had gathered information from more than 50 million Facebook users.[41] In response, Facebook founder and CEO Mark Zuckerberg was called upon to testify before Congress as to the importance of protecting both the security and privacy of Facebook's more than 2.2 billion users. Increasingly, people and policymakers around the world are realizing the power of technology companies in their daily lives—and in politics.[42] As a result, what they expect of those companies is changing. Many people, for example, now expect privacy to be protected as part of corporate social responsibility, and even as a human right.[43]

To its credit, Facebook has begun taking some action since its most recent series of blunders has come to light. Zuckerberg has promised the company will apply the protections of the European Union's General Data Protection Regulation to all users around the world,[44] even as it subsequently took steps to move more than 1.5 billion user accounts off of European servers in an apparent effort to skirt the same privacy regulations.[45] It will also require political advertisers to provide additional transparency in future election cycles, as a new weapon in the reported "arms race" Facebook finds itself in with Russian propagandists.[46] And the company is partnering with researchers to better understand its role in elections.[47]

But there are those in Congress and in Europe who do not think Facebook has gone far enough, as seen in the $5 billion fine that the FTC levied against the firm in 2019.[48] European Data Protection Supervisor Giovanni Buttarelli, for example, has suggested Facebook views its users as "experimental rats."[49] They argue that more must be done to ensure that Facebook users' human rights to privacy and security are respected.

It is not enough, in other words, to merely connect people. It is true that Internet access is an emerging human right in itself. Zuckerberg has eagerly embraced this idea, and his company is planning to "connect the next 5 billion people" who have yet to go online.[50] That will, of course, also create plenty more Facebook users just as the company's growth plateaus in the West.[51] Global public opinion seems to overwhelmingly agree with the sentiment that Internet access should be a basic human right, but the issue of what attendant rights and responsibilities go along with it—including privacy and cybersecurity—remains up for debate.[52]

Human rights law, though, is insufficient in and of itself to solve this problem. As Professor Jeffrey Rosen argued, "The problems of protecting privacy are now so daunting that they can't be dealt with by law alone, but require a mix of legal, social and technological solutions."[53] The International Covenant on Civil and Political Rights (ICCPR) already includes a right to privacy, as does the UN's Universal Declaration of Human Rights.[54] But it's not uncommon for countries to shirk their treaty responsibilities. And efforts to clarify the right to privacy in the digital age have been contentious. For example, the UN General Assembly took action on this topic in late 2013, passing a consensus resolution in the wake of NSA revelations that was sponsored by Germany and Brazil on "[t]he right to privacy in the digital age," affirming that human rights, including privacy and freedom of expression, apply online.[55] This move resonates with the UN's High Commissioner for Human Rights (OHCHR) 2011 statement that human rights are equally valid online as offline.[56] The UN's Human Rights Council reinforced that stance in 2012, 2014, and 2016.[57] And in November 2015, the G20, a group of nations with some of the world's largest economies, similarly endorsed privacy, "including in the context of digital communications."[58] However, not all countries agree with this assessment.

One study published in the *Stanford Journal of International Law* by your author, for example, surveyed the national cybersecurity strategies of thirty-four nations in an effort to determine how these countries are defining and operationalizing cybersecurity at the highest level of government.[59] In particular, it looked at references to various human rights (such as privacy). Of the nations surveyed, only two—Turkey and Macedonia—argued that human rights are an integral component to building cyber peace, as explored in chapter 7.[60] Other areas of agreement between the strategies include seventeen countries (47%) referencing "civil rights,"[61] while seven nations (21%) discuss "civil liberties" broadly.[62] In contrast, twenty-one of these nations (62%) discussed the need to safeguard privacy while enhancing their national cybersecurity posture.[63] Such statistics bring to mind Benjamin Franklin's famous observation, "They who can give up essential liberty to obtain a little temporary safety deserve neither liberty nor safety."[64] These data are summarized in Figure 4.1.

The content of these strategies has also evolved over time. For example, by 2018 forty-four nations discussed the importance of privacy in their national cybersecurity strategies, which represents a proportional decrease since 2014 but an absolute increase.[65] However, other Internet freedom trends seem to have reversed course somewhat during this same period. Only Australia, for example, specifically discusses the importance of free speech in its national cybersecurity strategy,

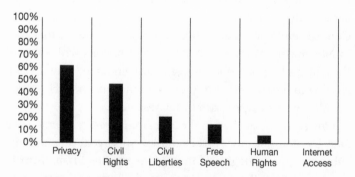

Figure 4.1 Treatment of Human Rights in Surveyed National Cybersecurity Strategies
This figure was originally published in Scott J. Shackelford, *Should Cybersecurity Be a Human Right? Exploring the 'Shared Responsibility' of Cyber Peace*, 55 Stan. J. Int'l L. 155, 171 (2019).

though the broader notion of "freedom" was discussed by thirty-four nations.[66]

Civil society and the private sector, including major Internet platforms like Facebook, could help breathe new life into this effort by modernizing international privacy law. Facebook could also require its vendors and partners to provide world-class cybersecurity protections for users and their information.[67] It could, in short, lead a global race to the top and in the process promote cyber peace. Coordination with other technology companies—mirroring efforts such as the Cybersecurity Tech Accord—would make such efforts more likely to succeed. As part of its early 2019 "pivot to privacy," in which the firm would transition from a global "town square" model to a "digitally secure 'living room,'" Facebook could begin disclosing its cybersecurity and data privacy practices as part of its integrated corporate report.[68] Another logical next step would be for Facebook to provide its users with a *paid subscription option* and thereby allow them to completely opt out of having their personal data packaged and sold for advertising.[69] However, that creates a different ethical problem, because less well-off people would not be able to afford to keep their data private and still use Facebook. The main way to address that problem is to flip the relationship and have Facebook pay people for their data. The National Academies, for example, have estimated the value to be approximately $9 per person per year for the average social media user.[70]

Proposed new laws could also help. The CONSENT Act (Customer Online Notification for Stopping Edge-Provider Network Transgressions Act), for example, would require data-gathering social networks to get clear consent from users before being able to "use, share, or sell any personal information."[71] The FTC would enforce those rules.[72] Lawmakers could go further still and let the FTC impose larger fines for data breaches, make platforms liable for hosting illegal information, or even require companies to establish ethical review boards similar to universities. NIST is also aiding the effort through its standard-setting authority, as seen in the development of a new Privacy Framework,[73] comparable to the NIST Cybersecurity Framework discussed in chapter 5. The OECD Guidelines on the Protection of Privacy and Transborder Flows of Personal Data are also influential given that they address the balance between privacy and freedom of expression, making it a useful foundation on which to build a more global consensus on these issues.[74]

Richard Stolley, founding managing editor of *People* magazine, famously (and somewhat ironically) described privacy as "fragile merchandise."[75] This merchandise, which we have all entrusted to Facebook, once broken, is not easily mended. Zuckerberg told Congress he understands this fact, and that his firm needs to rebuild users' trust. If Facebook declared its support for both privacy and security as inalienable human rights akin to Internet access, that could help the company get started, perhaps before policymakers in the United States and around the world step up to have their say.

How is IoT impacting policy discussions about Big Data and digital privacy?

Of the billions of Internet-connected devices that are already interconnected,[76] how much control do we have over them in protecting our privacy? Researchers in 2018, for example, located a vulnerability in Amazon's Alexa that permitted the investigators to enable the device to "record and transcribe your private conversations."[77] Similarly, Google and Apple Home speakers are reportedly only listening after a prompt such as "Hey, Google," but even though these systems are in some ways more secure than PCs and smartphones, they can still be compromised, especially by actors with deep pockets and patience.[78]

The IoT presents unique challenges in the realms of "Big Data" (e.g., the large volume of both structured and unstructured information that regularly inundates organizations)[79] and digital privacy as many of those subjected to such automated surveillance are unaware of the risk to which they are being exposed.[80] A huge range of devices and sensors is deepening these pools of Big Data, creating an array of business opportunities while simultaneously threatening what remains of personal privacy with estimates of more than 200 billion smart sensors being deployed globally by 2025, as was discussed in chapter 2.[81] This sort of unprecedented real-time surveillance is forcing regulators and policymakers to address how to better protect consumers, a topic returned to in chapter 5.[82]

Big Data is characterized by three primary metrics: volume, variety, and velocity.[83] Although imprecise, these traits underscore the extent to which the IoT is feeding the rush to create ever more robust datasets, which in turn are feeding an array of machine learning and artificial intelligence applications.[84] The overwhelming amount of data being cheaply collected, and its subsequent protection, is concerning even as it also has resulted in myriad benefits for consumers. Yet in a 2015 Trustee survey, 87% of Internet users expressed their alarm about the type of personal information being collected.[85] The threat to digital privacy and the control over personal data are accentuated by widely publicized data breaches from Equifax to Marriott.[86] A key component in the drive for digital privacy reform is standardization,[87] which involves creating and enforcing a certification process in the technology development and digital storage process.[88] Currently, individual companies are often attempting to certify their own devices, which creates a broad spectrum of protection levels.[89] Organizations ranging from *Consumer Reports* to the European Union are trying to standardize such certification schemes, as is explored in chapter 5. However, aside from the protection of digital privacy, the collection of Big Data presents another pressing issue—what are the ethical concerns surrounding the IoE?

*Exploring IoT ethics: is a digital companion for your grandparent
a good thing?*

The benefits of companionship at any age are well documented. According to the US Centers for Disease Control
and Prevention, "Studies have shown that the bond between
people and their pets can increase fitness, lower stress, and
bring happiness to their owners."[90] Sometimes, though, seniors
might not be able to care for a pet. Instead, some are turning
to a slew of robotic companions, such as Hasbro's "Joy for
All" line featuring, among other things, a lifelike Companion
Pet Cat for $99.[91] Unfortunately, though, such digital compan-
ions can contribute to concerns over surveillance and privacy,
which may be particularly problematic to older adults given
their higher propensity to fall victim to identify theft and other
types of cybercrime.[92] In all, researchers and journalists have
documented the vast amount of information being harvested
by the ubiquitous use of IoT devices in our homes, "from when
we brush our teeth, to when we turn our lights on and off,
when we stream music, what we watch on Hulu, and how well
we sleep."[93] In a similar vein, the robot vacuum firm iRobot announced its intention in 2018 to share the maps that its devices
generated of users' homes to the likes of Google, Facebook,
and Apple.[94]

Ethical traditions can help inform the rollout of various IoT
technologies, based on consequences, virtues, and rules. An
example of the first consequences-based approach would be
programming autonomous vehicles to protect a group of pedestrians (perhaps even at the expense of a solo driver), which
is in line with utilitarianism and its modern iteration, cost-
benefit analysis. MIT's Moral Machine represents an effort
to crowdsource such problems, presenting participants with
various scenarios and allowing them to choose how a run-
away autonomous vehicle should behave.[95] Second, IoT firms
could demonstrate virtues (moral character) in their products
and services by ensuring that they comport with traits such
as honesty (i.e., transparency and accuracy in data processing

practices). Third, companies could internalize rules and duties, such as GDPR, which is explored in chapter 5, and work with commercial partners to establish general codes of conduct that might, in time, become global standards.[96]

Considering the vast amount of data being collected, and the near continuous monitoring inherent in the IoT, and putting aside potential legal liability discussed in chapter 5, there are an array of specific ethical concerns surrounding IoT. Most of the issues revolve around the manner in which data is being gathered, whose data is being collected, and who controls the data once it is collected (and for how long).[97] These concepts take shape in the following three broad categories that encapsulate the prevailing ethical concerns: (1) access, (2) control, and (3) privacy.

Access and information use

Increasing connectivity reduces the ability of users to avoid IoT products even if they desired to do so; many of us are wittingly or unwittingly becoming assimilated into an IoE, whether we like it or not.[98] Aside from consent, other ethical concerns revolve around the disproportionate impact that data collection may have on different groups. This includes the concern that older members of society may have a potentially larger amount of resources and data available and are therefore that much more at risk when breaches occur. This is compounded by the fact that they may also have a less sophisticated understanding about how to protect their data, though surveys disagree on this point.[99]

Control and property rights

When everything is connected, who is the end user and who is the collector? Once data is collected by various IoT devices, who is entitled to its use, and for what purpose? As systems become integrated and increasingly autonomous, could the data lead to discrepancies in how different groups are treated?[100] In other words, the well-documented biases of algorithms—whether witting or not—could be fed and further exacerbated by new IoT applications.[101] Such outcomes are of increasing concern as governments begin to integrate data collected from IoT devices into their processes, as highlighted by the fact that those entering the United States for tourism or immigration must submit their phones for examination upon request.[102]

Privacy and information integrity

A related concern revolves around whether data collectors should be required to receive consent prior to information gathering,[103] as well as the scope of the consent that would be given, and how it should best be tailored to specific purposes.[104] For instance, many patients consent to the collection of their medical data for treatment, but should that implicitly include research? What if the hospital shares that information with a third party? Privacy protection advocates rightly question whether any such regime would be effective, given how often notice and consent is failing to safeguard personal privacy.[105] In fact, according to one study, reading all of the policies of the sites visited by the average Internet user in a year would take roughly one full month.[106]

To help address these ethical challenges, some, such as Professors Fred Cate and Viktor Mayer-Schamberger, advocate for updating shared privacy principles, including: collection limitation, data quality, purpose specification, use limitation, security safeguards, openness, individual participation, and accountability.[107] Relatedly, there are concerning issues of user manipulation to consider, which may require the development of ethical codes of conduct.[108] Another option that some companies like Eli Lilly are exploring is not just treating cybersecurity as a cost of doing business, but as a competitive advantage and a corporate social responsibility. The argument goes that it is in the corporate world's own long-term self-interest (as well as that of national security) to take such a wide view of private-sector risk management practices so as to encompass less traditional factors akin to what companies have done with respect to sustainability, as is explored further in chapters 5 and 6.[109]

5

GOVERNING THE INTERNET
OF THINGS

Beginning in 2020, smart devices sold in California that connect "directly or indirectly" to the public Internet have to be equipped with "reasonable" cybersecurity features such as a unique password.[1] But how, exactly, should we define "reasonable" security? More broadly, are we experiencing a market failure in IoT governance necessitating a bigger role for government in setting benchmarks?[2] If so, what role should government play in creating a level playing field, while buttressing lax security and privacy safeguards for consumers? As Professor Andrew Murray of the London School of Economics has argued in the cybersecurity context, "The market functions—but only so far!"[3] Governments also have a role to play to help the private sector meet cybersecurity and privacy challenges, explored in chapters 3 and 4, within the Internet of Things (IoT), but what form should regulation take, and how can any adverse impact to innovation be minimized?[4]

This chapter asks, and answers, fundamental questions of IoT governance in which new technologies—and laws—can cause ripple effects around the world. We begin by taking a high-level approach, looking at the role of the market along with frameworks, standards, and certifications in improving IoT governance. The chapter next turns to how the US government along with other jurisdictions such as the European Union and China are approaching this topic, as well as the role of international law and norms. In general, this chapter reviews the governance landscape, taking note not only of applicable federal, state, and international law but also other "regulatory modalities" popularized by Professors Lawrence Lessig and Yochai Benkler, among others, including architecture and norms that "may be used individually or collectively" by policymakers within a polycentric framework.[5] IoT, as with cyberspace generally, is a dynamic, malleable ecosystem and as such an array of economic, legal, technical, and political tools should be brought to bear to promote good governance in the Internet of Everything (IoE).

How can we regulate the IoT, and even if we could, is that a good idea?

The appropriate role that government should play in regulating the IoT—as with cyberspace generally—largely depends on one's view of governmental power and responsibility. This responsibility exists on a spectrum from purely market-driven to comprehensive government regulation.[6] Real-world solutions are often somewhere in the middle of these extremes, for example, establishing baseline cybersecurity and data privacy standards for IoT providers. Such standards might require "reasonable" security, as in California, or leverage governmental procurement practices as with the proposed IoT Cybersecurity Improvement Act of 2019. In general, jurisdictions around the world are in a difficult place given that they are called upon to be regulators, facilitators, and collaborators (RFC) in cybersecurity risk management. Using this RFC Framework, governments can identify the different factors influencing how the private sector is making security investment decisions and then identify an appropriate combination of tools to either nudge or mandate desired ends. A key concern is that regulation may lead to a culture of check-box compliance, and companies may seek the lowest-cost way of meeting these standards under a reactive mindset and thus not put into place the type of proactive cybersecurity best practices that are so essential in safeguarding vulnerable tech along with critical infrastructure.[7] Relatedly, even finding individuals with the technical ability to work for the public sector—often for just a fraction of the pay of their private sector peers—increases the difficulty for governments, hence the discussion of a Cyber Peace Corps and other workforce development ideas in chapter 7.[8]

Aside from these challenges, jurisdictional confusion may also preclude effective regulatory intervention. As a historical marker, consider the groundbreaking 2001 Yahoo! case mentioned in chapter 1.[9] There, a group in France sued Yahoo! because its auction site was selling Nazi memorabilia in violation of French law.[10] Ultimately, courts in both France and the United States sided with the group, forcing Yahoo! to take down the offending products and, in essence, and according to Professors Jack Goldsmith and Tim Wu, "making French law the effective rule for the world."[11] By 2005, with less confidence and capital, Yahoo! had also bowed to Chinese national laws by censoring search results and monitoring chat rooms.[12]

Yahoo!'s transformation reflects that of the broader Internet "from a technology that resists territorial law to one that facilitates its enforcement."[13] Other more recent but similarly content-related cases reinforce this trend. Take the aftermath of the WikiLeaks episode, in which a combination of political pressure and cyber attacks purportedly incentivized Amazon to stop hosting the WikiLeaks website, forcing it to relocate to servers in Europe.[14] Or consider the 2012 arrest of a Google executive in Brazil for refusing to take down videos from YouTube,[15] or Australia's 2019 law to make social media executives criminally liable for failing to take down violent videos in a timely manner.[16] As these episodes demonstrate, regulatory efforts from Brussels to Beijing, Sacramento to Singapore are shaping this dynamic landscape with significant ramifications for IoT governance. In particular, it makes clear the extent to which decisions made by a particular jurisdiction can have potentially worldwide knock-on effects, as is already being seen with GDPR.

Overcoming these challenges to enable the effective regulation of IoT technologies is no small feat. Data governance alone is an enormous challenge, with some estimates suggesting that IoT devices are generating over 5 quintillion bytes of data from billions of devices *daily* according to Cisco, a figure that is expected to increase exponentially going forward.[17] This level of data accumulation leads to various concerns—including who has access to that data, to what extent they can use it (for analytics, resale, etc.), and also how securely the data should be kept—each requiring various responses at multiple governance levels.[18] For example, in the US context, and depending on the device or application in question, an alphabet soup of agencies have some sort of authority over IoT (FDA, FCC, FTC, etc.).[19] And there is the related issue of too restrictive regulations hurting innovation even as some commentators such as Bruce Schneier have argued that IoT laws can, in fact, spur innovation.[20] For example, buyers express higher confidence in products approved by the FDA.[21] An increase in consumer trust toward IoT technology—perhaps driven by government-backed standards or certification schemes—could similarly boost trust and thereby sales.

Still, despite the difficulties involved, it is no secret that a large majority of consumers today (more than 90% in one 2017 survey) have little confidence in the security of IoT devices.[22] Recent attacks such as the Mirai botnet introduced in the preface and discussed in chapter 3 reinforce the perception (too often accurate) of ubiquitous vulnerabilities in the IoT. In response, there are three predominant approaches to protecting digital privacy and security in the IoT explored throughout the rest of this chapter, namely: (1) allowing free market innovation to help provide a suite of solutions; (2) relying on state, federal, and international regulations to enforce security and privacy standards; or (3) leveraging a combination of the above to ensure adequate protection within a polycentric approach.

As we will see, a market-based approach focuses on educating consumers, encouraging industry best practices, and using current enforcement tools to better protect consumers' data integrity.[23] While the free market encourages innovation, it is unlikely to spawn the comprehensive protection desired by consumers. There is a lack of market mechanisms to effectively incentivize corporations and manufacturers to improve digital security.[24] Witness the failure of the market to adequately punish firms that experience cyber attacks, as documented in a 2018 National Bureau of Economic Research study that found an immediate decrease of only 1% in the stock price of impacted organizations.[25]

No single avenue will be able to manage the full range of threats to the IoT. An all-of-the-above approach is needed to enhance digital privacy and security.[26] There is increasing recognition that such a polycentric approach is the preferable route forward. This multilevel, multipurpose, multifunctional, and multisectoral model, championed by scholars including Nobel laureate Elinor Ostrom and Professor Vincent Ostrom, challenges orthodoxy by demonstrating the benefits of self-organization, networking regulations "at multiple scales,"[27] and examining the extent to which national and private control can coexist with communal management. As originally explained by Professor Vincent Ostrom, "a polycentric political system would be composed of: (1) many autonomous units formally independent of one another, (2) choosing to act in ways that take account of others, (3) through processes of cooperation, competition, conflict, and conflict resolution."[28] In many ways, this governance model—which has been applied to diverse collective action problems ranging from managing inner-city police precincts[29] to adapting to climate change[30] and even mitigating orbital debris[31]—is well situated to addressing dynamic (and oftentimes fragmented) IoT issues given the number of diverse actors and technologies in play. Examples of these applications include issues with the Domain Name System itself, for which the tech community developed a security upgrade that still has not been implemented more than twenty years later owing to the fact that "it requires most sites to adopt it before anyone sees benefits."[32] No governance system is perfect and polycentrism has its disadvantages such as concerns over gridlock and a lack of defined hierarchy.[33] But such an approach could help move the debate regarding the Security of Things in a more productive direction as part of an overarching campaign to promote some measure of cyber peace.[34]

Can self-organization work in the IoT?

One important aspect of polycentric governance is self-regulation.[35] Under certain circumstances, self-regulation has the capacity to adapt better and faster than black letter law to rapidly changing technological and social forces. It can also be more efficient and cost-effective than command-and-control-style regulation,[36] though it is not a panacea given that such efforts are voluntary and are subject to market forces (e.g., changing consumer demands).[37] One need only review Facebook's promises to reform, and its failures to do so, to see why calls for an end to the self-governance of Internet platforms are gaining traction.[38] Still, some regulators such as Maureen Ohlhausen, the former head of the FTC, came out in favor of permitting IoT providers to self-regulate,[39] a perspective mirrored by the US Senate in a resolution that highlighted both the central role of the private sector in developing and regulating IoT applications and the degree of importance accorded this issue by policymakers.[40]

The failure of self-governance is not a foregone conclusion, though. Indeed, some argue that there is not, in fact, a market failure in cybersecurity despite the continued prevalence of data breaches without much in the way of penalties or corrective action.[41] Others point to the lack of sustained stock price dips following breaches, or penalties for repurposing collected data, as examples of the market failing to take account of lax cybersecurity.[42] Much depends on the type of community in question, along with its capacity for effective communication, conflict resolution, norm building, and enforcement of collective rules as are laid out in the Ostrom Design Principles.[43] The varieties of these types of online communities abound—within the IoT context and more generally—as does their potential for successful self-regulation, which depends in large part on the size and scope of the group of IoT manufacturers under consideration.[44] In some of these communities, such as eBay or Facebook—which Professor Murray describes as "Lockean" because users have given over power to a central administrator—some degree of democratic governance can coexist with an established authority such as by empowering users to police and report errant behavior.[45] This state of affairs may be compared to so-called Rousseauean communities in which power remains decentralized; this continues to be the current state of affairs in much of the IoT context.[46] However, such groupings are often ineffective owing to their sheer size and complexity.[47] If, however, such communities could increase collaboration by taking the example of the Internet Engineering Task Force working groups or the EU's General Data Protection Regulation (GDPR) and create industry codes of conduct, then power may not have to be centralized to the degree that it is in Lockean communities such as Facebook. This may be accomplished through forming micro communities to build trust such as in the financial services joint Security Operations Center.

Polycentric theorists, including Professor Elinor Ostrom, have extolled the benefits of small, self-organized communities in the context of managing common resources,[48] and anthropological evidence confirms that groups of humans function more efficiently along certain metrics when they are kept relatively small in scale.[49] However, micro-communities can ignore other interests, stakeholders, and the wider impact of their actions.[50] To overcome such apathy, these communities must have a defined stake in the outcome to effectuate good governance, which can be accomplished by educating users about the cyber threat and their power to help manage it.[51]

The IoT comprises both types of communities, but a hybrid model favoring organic, bottom-up governance composed of small cohorts with a role for centralized coordination that can codify and enforce best practices as well as protect against free riders may be most appropriate to enhance IoT security.[52] Such self-regulation has the flexibility "to adapt to rapid technological progress"[53] arguably better and faster than black letter law, which often changes incrementally. It also has the potential to be relatively more efficient and cost-effective than alternative one-sized-fits-all approaches while instilling civic virtue.[54] Nevertheless, it is only one piece of a very big and complex puzzle, which is why self-governance is but a single component of polycentric governance.[55] Yet as Professor Murray argues, that does not make it any less vital: "In cyberspace the power to decide is, it seems, vested ultimately in the community. We have the power to control our destiny."[56]

One organization that is trying to create such a community is *Consumer Reports*, which has been at the forefront of testing consumer products and advocating for improvements in their safety since it was founded 1936.[57] More recently, in March 2017 *Consumer Reports* launched its Digital Standard, which is designed "to measure the privacy and security of products, apps, and services . . . [to] put consumers in the driver's seat as the digital marketplace evolves."[58] Once it matures, the Digital Standard will empower consumers to be able to select products—including in the IoT context—that meet rigorous privacy and security requirements. Over time, the Standard holds the promise of helping the market function more efficiently. It does so by rewarding those firms that take cybersecurity and data privacy seriously, and penalizing those that do not through lower scores and, as a result, less revenue. Already, these efforts are having an impact, such as when they helped expose privacy risks in the pregnancy and fertility app Glow.[59] As the Digital Standard is continually refined and globalized, it will likely further impact the trajectory and rate of global IoT privacy and security standards.[60] *Consumer Reports* is reportedly working with European colleagues to harmonize its Standard, which could lead to further norm-building efforts around cybersecurity due diligence in the IoT context.[61] However, obstacles remain, given the diverging regulatory stances of the United States and the European Union when it comes to IoT governance.[62]

What is the US approach to regulating the IoT?

The US government has long favored a largely voluntary, sector-specific approach to managing threats to privacy and cybersecurity, unlike other jurisdictions, such as the European Union, discussed next, that prefer more comprehensive measures. IoT governance is no exception to this trend. Overall, federal cybersecurity law is largely unprepared to mitigate security or privacy problems arising in the IoT context.[63] Governance gaps are all too common, only some of which are being filled by relevant state and international law, as we will see.

The demand for a more comprehensive legal framework or regulatory system stems from the importance of protecting consumers while facilitating consumer confidence. There are myriad ways in which consumers can be harmed from security risks and breaches emanating from IoT devices, each potentially requiring a different policy response. For example, granting access to personal information can lead to unfortunate impacts on personal livelihoods, ranging from credit ratings to even personal safety.[64] Furthermore, in addition to consumer confidence, consent is an issue that often arises in the evolving world of IoT, as was introduced in chapter 4.[65] In particular, debates have arisen about the applicability of the "Fair Information Practice Principles (FIPPs), which include such principles as notice, access choice, accuracy, data minimization, security, and accountability, and whether they should apply" to the IoT space.[66] Moreover, consent is connected to aspects of consumer protection law relating to privacy-policy disclosures, which is another realm that is unprepared to address interlinked cybersecurity and privacy issues. For example, sensor devices are, in unique ways, capable of negatively impacting consumer welfare by leading (intentionally or not) to discrimination.[67] This is due to the fact that there is a public desire for new technologies, but consent is unlikely to provide reassurance to consumers.[68]

The US government's response to these IoT privacy and security vulnerabilities has been patchy. As of this writing, there are no federal laws in place mandating IoT cybersecurity and privacy benchmarks, and the likelihood that current proposals will be passed is uncertain at best.[69] Similarly, the notion of a simple solution to this issue such as designating a single three-letter federal agency to take charge is tempting to believe, but difficult to achieve given the sheer breadth of technology sectors, extending from medical devices to traffic lights. Three candidates would be the FTC, the Federal Communications Commission (FCC), and the National Institute for Standards and Technology (NIST), which focus on policing unfair and deceptive trade practices, developing IoT security protocols, and creating cybersecurity and data privacy standards respectively.[70]

The FTC has interpreted its authority in a way that permits it to level penalties against companies whose cybersecurity is not up to par if the company implies or advertises that they use certain cybersecurity practices, or if they operate in at-risk critical infrastructure sectors such as healthcare. The FTC's interpretation has been upheld by the courts.[71] As a result, it has continued to investigate firms with lax cybersecurity standards such as Facebook and Equifax, issuing settlement orders that require the companies to "establish and maintain a comprehensive security program subject to independent audits for the next 20 years." It has issued such orders against the likes of Wyndham Hotel over a data breach, TRENDNet over a security camera flaw, and ASUSTek over issues with its routers and cloud services.[72] The FTC has also issued non-binding guidance to help firms navigate IoT security,[73] encouraging them to:

1. Build security into devices at the outset, rather than as an afterthought in the design process;
2. Train employees about the importance of security, and ensure that security is managed at an appropriate level in the organization;
3. Ensure that when outside service providers are hired, that those providers are capable of maintaining reasonable security, and provide reasonable oversight of the providers;
4. When a security risk is identified, consider a "defense-in-depth" strategy whereby multiple layers of security may be used to defend against a particular risk;
5. Consider measures to keep unauthorized users from accessing a consumer's device, data, or personal information stored on the network;
6. Monitor connected devices throughout their expected life cycle, and where feasible, provide security patches to cover known risks.[74]

It has also recommended that companies adopt the NIST Cybersecurity Framework (CSF).[75] In sum, the FTC recommends "tackling cybersecurity and all consumer-facing software development efforts with a holistic approach that incorporates a 'privacy by design' strategy to address the entire life cycle of data collection, use, access, storage, and ultimately secure data deletion."[76]

In contrast, the FCC has issued IoT-specific regulations, such as in regards to the regulation of IoT device manufacturing.[77] The requirements vary from device to device, but recently the FCC has pushed for regulations that work to close the gap between consumer expectations and actual security features.[78]

Further, the FCC is empowered to levy fines of up to $75,000 for failure to comply.[79]

NIST, on the other hand, which is part of the Department of Commerce, took action on developing cybersecurity and privacy frameworks when, during his 2013 State of the Union address, former president Obama announced an executive order tasking the agency to do so.[80] The original notion was for NIST to work with industry partners to develop a voluntary "Cybersecurity Framework" that firms could adopt to better secure critical infrastructure.[81] The Framework version 1.0, Framework for Improving Critical Infrastructure Cybersecurity (NIST CSF), was released in February 2014, and was designed to harmonize "consensus standard and industry best practices to provide, its proponents argue, a flexible and cost-effective approach to enhancing cybersecurity that assists owners and operators of critical infrastructure in assessing and managing cyber risk."[82] Consisting of three main components (the Framework Core, Profiles, and Tiers),[83] the NIST CSF has proven popular as measured by its more than a half-million downloads since its first publication,[84] and has been influential in clarifying a cybersecurity standard of care in the United States and abroad by helping organizations "identify, implement, and improve cybersecurity practices, and create a common language for internal and external communication of cybersecurity issues."[85] Indeed, increasingly the NIST CSF is "voluntary" in theory but increasingly required in practice, as may be seen by the Trump administration's mandate that all federal agencies use it in 2017.[86] Diverse organizations ranging from Intel to the University of Chicago have utilized the NIST CSF to create enterprise-level heat maps, address known risks, and ensure ongoing accountability.[87] Even the Department of Transportation has utilized the NIST CSF in assessing vehicle cybersecurity, though they found that the Framework had to be significantly adapted to be useful in developing useful security controls for vehicles.

Such cases highlight both the flexibility and impact of the NIST CSF, which prompted NIST to release Version 1.1 of the NIST CSF in April 2018. This, as Secretary of Commerce Wilbur Ross has argued, "should be every company's first line of defense."[88] The new version boasts significant improvements, including with regard to authentication, supply chain cybersecurity, and vulnerability disclosure, though it is still best considered a cybersecurity floor rather than a ceiling.[89] It does not, for example, focus on IoT issues in particular, which is an area that many (including the US Chamber of Commerce) would like NIST to address in more detail beyond its Framework for Cyber-Physical Systems, which is arguably not specific (or user-friendly) enough to make the same impact on IoT as the NIST CSF has had on critical infrastructure protection.[90] Answering the call, NIST put out a draft IoT Cybersecurity Baseline and is gathering feedback on it as of this writing.

Even acting in concert, these agencies do not have the authority to tackle the full range of cyber threats facing the IoT, even by leveraging existing common-law claims such as negligence, breach of contract, and breach of privacy.[91] Reform proposals at the federal level abound, even as there has long been resistance from some corners to IoT-specific legislation.[92] Former FTC chairwoman Edith Ramirez in particular seemed to support the idea that "Internet of Things" is a code word for the self-regulation of things.[93] However, the FTC has encouraged Congress to enact self-regulatory programs intended to incentivize the adoption of privacy and security best practices. These practices would protect against unauthorized access to both personal information and device functionality that are "strong, flexible, and technology neutral" but that include well-defined rules for companies regarding how to provide choices to consumers about data collection and use practices.[94] The FTC has also led a drive, initially in concert with the Obama administration, to provide federal data breach notification regulations to consumers whose information has been compromised as part of a broader revision to the Consumer Privacy Bill of Rights.[95] Other reform proposals include the Internet of Things Cybersecurity Act of 2017, which would require vendors who sell products to the US government to: (1) ensure that their devices "are patchable," (2) that they do not "contain known vulnerabilities," (3) that they "rely on standard protocols," and (4) they "don't contain hard-coded passwords."[96] However, the bill does not take a one-size-fits-all approach to regulating an area as vast as IoT. Indeed, if industry provides "equivalent, or more rigorous, device security requirements," then they may be utilized in lieu of the foregoing.[97] That bill failed to pass, but its bipartisan sponsors, including Mark Warner of Virginia, have refused to give up, introducing the Internet of Things (IoT) Cybersecurity Improvement Act of 2019, which has not been enacted as of this writing but is notable for how it narrows the definition of an "IoT device" (dropping smartphones and personal computers, for example), and moves from establishing minimal standards to directing NIST to make recommendations for "the appropriate use and management" of IoT products "owned or controlled by the Federal Government" to include minimum standards.[98]

Other bills have also been proposed to improve IoT security, including the IoT Consumer TIPS Act of 2017, which is aimed at helping the FTC boost consumer cyber hygiene, as well as the SMART IoT Act, which would mandate that the US Department of Commerce "conduct a study on the state of the industry." The latter act passed the House with a unanimous vote but was not taken up by the Senate.[99] The US General Accountability Office (GAO) has suggested that the US government go even further to reduce vulnerabilities, including by: (1) developing and executing a "more comprehensive" strategy for national and global cyberspace, (2) mitigating global supply chain risks, and (3) ensuring the security of emerging technologies.[100] The GAO has also come out in support of a GDPR-like privacy regime for the United States.[101]

At the state level, California—long a norm entrepreneur in fields as disparate as environmental law and data privacy—is again at the forefront of an urgent matter of national importance, this time in governing the IoE. Specifically, in late 2018 California passed SB-327 ("Security of Connected Devices"), which requires, starting in 2020, that "any manufacturer of a device that connects 'directly or indirectly' to the Internet must equip it with 'reasonable' security features, designed to prevent unauthorized access, modification, or information disclosure."[102] "Reasonable" security features are not explicitly defined, but in general, manufacturers are expected to provide protections from unauthorized access, modification, or information disclosure, such as by requiring unique passwords to avoid attacks like the Mirai botnet.[103] Although some contend that the law does not go far enough in holding IoT manufacturers accountable, or criticize its focus on adding new security features rather than removing insecure ones, it is a step forward in taking a risk-based approach to IoT security and privacy that should be considered in the context of related NIST, FTC, and FCC actions and initiatives.[104] For example, the NIST National Cybersecurity Center of Excellence (NCCoE) has been working with the FIDO Alliance, which is a nonprofit standards group of over two hundred international companies, to eliminate passwords and move on to other more secure means of authentication so as to prevent IoT risks. And California is not alone, as is discussed further in chapter 7—Ohio is incentivizing companies that invest in cybersecurity best practices and frameworks by offering safe harbors from litigation.[105]

Time will tell how popular California's approach to regulating IoT devices becomes, and there are governance challenges to consider especially if other states take competing approaches.[106] But if history is any guide—and especially if Congress continues to be unable to enact reforms like the Internet of Things (IoT) Cybersecurity Improvement Act of 2019—then the centers of IoT governance (as with data privacy) will likely become Sacramento, Beijing, and Brussels.

How are nations regulating the IoT? In particular, how will the EU's General Data Protection Regulation (GDPR) impact IoT governance?

Who owns your data? How you answer that question depends in large part on geography, even your zip code. If you happen to be an EU citizen, then, as we will see, consumers are very much in the driver's seat in determining who can collect, analyze, and profit from their personal information. In other jurisdictions like China, privacy rights remain limited despite a push to expand them through the Personal Information Security Specification.[107] As a result of the doctrine of cyber sovereignty explored in chapter 1, ultimately it is the government that owns the data of Chinese citizens, a fact that was made clear by a new law allowing police to search big data and personal information without due process.[108] In the United States, as lawyers love to say, it depends. Residents of California, for example, will enjoy not only more robust IoT protections starting in 2020 but also arguably the strongest privacy rights in the nation under a transparency statute called the California Consumer Privacy Act (CCPA), which includes at least six distinct privacy rights including: access, portability, deletion, disclosure, easy opt out, and a private right of action when these rights are infringed.[109] Although largely a self-regulatory statute (and one rife with drafting errors and logical inconsistencies when it was first adopted),[110] the law nonetheless already has made waves with more than a half dozen states from Hawaii to Mississippi considering similar legislation, prompting newfound interest in Congress for a federal statute lest the California approach become the national default given its market size.[111] Still, though, even the CCPA falls short of European data privacy and cybersecurity protections, which are having a significant impact not only on the emerging IoE in Europe, but on data governance around the world; more than one hundred nations now have omnibus data protection laws in place.[112] As such, it is worth considering GDPR in some detail.

First, some context is in order. GDPR is designed to replace the 1990s-era EU Data Protection Directive, and to move the EU toward a Digital Single Market (DSM).[113] Similar to the NIST CSF, which "relies on a variety of existing standards, guidelines, and practices to enable critical infrastructure providers to achieve resilience,"[114] the DSM synthesizes initiatives on security and data protection.[115] Most important, the DSM focuses its approach upon considerations of the "data economy (free flow of data, allocation of liability, ownership, interoperability, usability and access), and thus promises to tackle interoperability and standardization," which are critical to boosting the security and privacy of IoT devices.[116]

Building from this foundation, GDPR is an expansive regulatory regime designed to create a consistent EU-wide approach to consumer protection. It features a wide array of requirements, ranging from ensuring data portability and consent to mandating that firms disclose a data breach within seventy-two hours of becoming aware of the incident and then conduct a post mortem to ensure that a similar scenario will not recur.[117] Other requirements include the need to obtain affirmative, "specific, informed, and unambiguous consent"[118] for each type of processing done with personal data (leading to the demise, for example, of long and complex terms of service) as well as to prevent third-party nations without strict enough privacy laws from gathering and transferring data on EU citizens.[119] It also mandates that covered firms appoint a data protection officer to oversee GDPR compliance.[120] The European Commission's reach in enforcing GDPR is also expansive given that it applies to not only EU firms but in fact to all companies that market goods or services to EU residents, regardless of that company's location. Publications including the *Chicago Tribune* and *Los Angeles Times* were initially blocked in the EU for noncompliance with the GDPR.[121] This fact, plus the eye-popping potential fines of non-compliance of up to 4% of total revenue, are already having an impact on the privacy standards of multinationals—some companies like the pharmaceutical giant Eli Lilly, for example, have already announced that they will comply with GDPR globally. Those companies that are not quite so proactive are already feeling the impacts; noncompliance has led to $8.15 billion in fines against companies such as Google, Instagram, WhatsApp, and Facebook as of 2018, and GDPR has also caused some smaller firms that are unable to comply with the GDPR to close.[122]

As groundbreaking as these regulations are, though, they were not drafted with IoT in mind, despite a 2017 finding by the European Union Agency for Network and Information Security (ENISA) "that there were no 'legal guidelines for IoT device and service trust.' Nor any 'level zero defined for the security and privacy of connected and smart devices.'"[123] Yet it is true that GDPR protections are impacting, and will continue to impact, the rate of IoT innovation given that covered organizations must be able to supply user data on demand. This may be particularly challenging in situations ranging from the use of smart doorbells that record visitors without first getting consent, to closed-circuit television (CCTV) cameras in cities. Further, European-level regulation is slow, and a blunt instrument—GDPR, as one example, took more than four years to be adopted after having been proposed in 2012.[124] And, in some (limited) ways, US privacy and cybersecurity standards are, in fact, stronger given that there is no expectation of credit monitoring, no walls of shame for organizations that experience data breaches, and the data breach notification requirement is narrower in Europe than is common in the United States.[125] Still, GDPR provides a foundation on which to build a more secure (and private) IoE, especially when coupled with other initiatives, such as the EU's Network and Information Security (NIS) Directive (which is "the first piece of EU-wide legislation on cybersecurity" and focuses on critical infrastructure protection), the EU Cybersecurity Act, and the decision to make the European Agency for Network and Information Security (ENISA) a permanent EU agency.[126] Yet it should also be noted that the drive to protect consumer privacy, however

laudable, must also be balanced against the need for innovation and economic development.[127]

Other nations are also increasingly taking their privacy
and cybersecurity cues from the EU, not the United States,
as seen in the Brazilian General Data Privacy Law and
Japan's decision to similarly update its privacy regime to ensure compliance with the GDPR.[128] According to the United
Nations Conference on Trade and Development (UNCTAD),
57% of countries had data protection and privacy legislation
as of 2018.[129] India maintains the Aadhaar biometric database
with 1.3 billion users and has no comprehensive data protection law, but the Indian Supreme Court recently did rule
that the Indian Constitution guarantees the right to privacy
as "part of Article 21 that protects life and liberty," permitting Indians, for example, to refuse to give up their biometric
information if they so choose.[130] Additionally, in 2018, a draft
Personal Data Protection bill was introduced that borrows
significantly from GDPR.[131] Still, though, such privacy initiatives as GDPR and CCPA help to ensure the confidentiality
of personal data collected by IoT devices but do not directly
address cyber threats to the integrity or availability of such
IoT systems, such as breaching autonomous systems, as described in chapter 3.

Nations within the EU have been innovating, treating
GDPR as a floor, and not a ceiling, including in the realm of
IoT certification. The UK's Cyber Essentials Program, for example, is designed to "incentivize widespread adoption of
basic security controls that will help to protect organizations
against the commonest kind of Internet attack."[132] It has two
schemes: *Cyber Essentials* and *Cyber Essentials Plus*.[133] Cyber
Essentials' requirements involve self-certification for basic organizational cyber hygiene practices, such as firewalls, secured
configuration, user access control, and patch management.[134]
The Cyber Essentials Assurance Framework is intended for
supplementation of existing organizational approaches to
risk management,[135] with plans for a mandatory IoT labeling

scheme being introduced in 2019.[136] Such schemes have helped British firms market cybersecurity as a competitive advantage, instead of merely a cost of doing business.[137] There are plans to spread such certification schemes throughout the EU to help better inform consumers about the relative safety of IoT products, though compliance will likely remain voluntary for the foreseeable future.[138] Some EU jurisdictions are considering whether to go further still, though. The French government, for example, is weighing whether to mandate strict liability for security lapses on the part of IoT manufacturers.[139] Such a move could boost security and privacy even as it risks hampering innovation. Still, such steps are Band-Aids, given the global scale and myriad technical challenges we face in the IoT. Moreover, they raise concerns about the impact of outliers, as seen with companies moving their data out of Australia due to its controversial new encryption law mandating backdoors for law enforcement.[140] As such, instead of national and regional policymakers, perhaps international law can help safeguard our hyper-connected future?

How can we modernize, and enforce, the international rights to privacy and security within the IoT?

It should come as little surprise that, as of this writing, there is no comprehensive Treaty to Secure the Internet of Things, just as there is no Treaty for Cyberspace in the guise of the Outer Space Treaty or UN Convention on the Law of the Sea, and likely will not be for the foreseeable future. Still, that does not mean that established international law is useless on the topic of IoT governance. For example, organizations like the NATO Cooperative Cyber Defense Centre of Excellence (CCDCOE) have declared that attacks through IoT like the one performed by Russia on Ukraine may "be understood as internationally wrongful acts and violations of state sovereignty under both customary international law and the UN Charter."[141] There are also useful insights that might be gleaned in both the cybersecurity and privacy contexts by investigating emerging norms and established accords respectively.[142]

There is a huge range of international law applicable to cybersecurity short of the armed attack threshold that activates the law of war, even though dedicated cybersecurity treaties such as the Council of Europe Convention on Cybercrime remain rare. These range from trade and investment treaties to mutual legal assistance and extradition accords. It is beyond the scope of this book to go into these treaties in detail since this has already been done elsewhere,[143] but of particular relevance here is critical infrastructure and cybersecurity due diligence. In the private-sector transactional context, cybersecurity due diligence has been defined as "the review of the governance, processes and controls that are used to secure information assets."[144] Put more simply, due diligence refers to activities to identify and understand the various risks facing an organization. Cybersecurity due diligence, then, refers to the international obligations of both state and non-state actors to help identify and instill cybersecurity best practices so as to promote the security of IoT devices.[145]

The international community has increasingly taken note of the necessity of securing critical infrastructure generally. This includes various IoT applications, given the extent to which smart sensors and devices are embedded in electrical, water, and financial systems, making them vulnerable to a range of cyber attacks as exemplified by the Mirai botnet.[146] The G7 Declaration on Responsible States Behavior in Cyberspace, for example, maintains that "[s]tates should not knowingly allow their territory to be used for internationally wrongful acts using ICTs."[147] The UN Group of Government Experts (GGE) has reiterated this norm.[148] The *Tallinn Manual* Rule 6 maintains that "a State must exercise due diligence in not allowing its territory, or territory or cyber infrastructure under its governmental control, to be used for cyber operations that affect the rights of, and produce serious adverse consequences for, other States."[149] Other stakeholders, including China, Kazakhstan, Kyrgyzstan, the Russian

Federation, Tajikistan, and Uzbekistan, have also maintained that nations should not "use information and communications technologies and information and communications networks to carry out activities which run counter to the task of maintaining international peace and security."[150] Eventually, such harmonization could lead to new international agreements on the scope and meaning of cybersecurity due diligence in the IoT context. However, such a day remains distant at present, given the extent to which such statements paper over significant differences in what exactly constitutes due diligence, especially in the context of censorship and cyber sovereignty.

Similarly, efforts are under way to upgrade global data privacy standards. For example, it is arguably past time to update the right to privacy mentioned in the 1948 Universal Declaration of Human Rights. The Declaration was expanded upon by the 1966 International Covenant on Civil and Political Rights (ICCPR), which was signed by more than 160 nations, including the United States. In particular, Article 17 of the ICCPR states, "No one shall be subjected to arbitrary or unlawful interference with his privacy, family, home or correspondence, nor to unlawful attacks on his honor and reputation."[151] For example, a new protocol could be drafted to include the "digital sphere" so as to create "globally applicable standards for data protection and the protection of privacy in accordance with the rule of law." The German government—notably German Federal Data Protection Officer Peter Schaar—has pushed this approach,[152] which was approved by the International Conference of Data Protection and Privacy Commissioners in 2013.[153] Without clarification, the utility of the ICCPR and human rights law generally to advancing global privacy law will continue to be undermined by spy agencies and private industry. But with renewed support, several ICCPR provisions—including Article 17 (protecting the right to privacy) and Article 19 (protecting the right to seek information)—would have new life as applied to enabling data privacy in the IoT.[154]

Government intervention may indeed be vital to help clean up the "current sloppy state of Internet+ security," which Schneier asserts "is the result of poorly aligned business incentives, a government that prioritizes offensive use of the Internet over defense, collective action problems, and market failures that require intervention to fix."[155] But we need not approach such a task in a vacuum; instead, it is wise to learn from other analogies and historical precedents, which is the topic of chapter 6.

6

ANALOGIZING THE INTERNET
OF THINGS

As any new frontier opens or industry matures, it's natural to search for analogies and historical precedents to guide both our actions and perceptions. President Kennedy famously compared space exploration to seafaring.[1] The rise of artificial intelligence and machine learning discussed further in chapter 7 has drawn parallels to a "fourth industrial revolution,"[2] while "Big Data" has been described as a "flood" or even "a natural resource that must be harnessed."[3] Cyberspace has not been immune from this propensity, from "surfing" the 1990s web to getting on the "information superhighway"[4] (the latter being a loaded example, given that governments can and do regulate highways rather closely, evoking the discussion of governing IoT in chapter 5). More recently, Twitter has been referred to as a digital "town square."[5] According to Harvard fellow Judith Donath, "Information is fairly formless, so almost everything we do online we do with some kind of metaphor."[6] With the increasing interconnection of our world, though, the "digital dualism" (as the social media theorist Nathan Jurgenson describes it) that gives rise to the concept of "cyberspace" as a distinct reality is breaking down.[7] As chief executive of the National Endowment for Science Technology and the Arts (NESTA) Geoff Mulgan has said, "As the Internet of Things advances, the very notion of clear dividing line between reality and virtual reality becomes blurred, sometimes in creative ways."[8] In short, "the internet is everywhere now, so it's harder to use totalizing metaphors that describe the it [sic] as a separate space."[9] Indeed, the search for a suitable lens through which to better understand the contours of the Internet of Things (IoT) has long bedeviled academics and policymakers alike. Still, despite the lack of effective metaphors, there are still lessons from other contexts in which humanity has faced complex problems, such as public health emergencies and climate change, that are worth exploring.[10] This chapter takes on that task, beginning with public health and ecosystem-based approaches for analyzing the IoE, before moving on to corporate social responsibility and exploring other lessons and tools from the green movement.

What can public health teach us about securing the IoT?

Each of us is walking around at the helm of an incredibly complex ecosystem. The human body is composed of more than 37 trillion cells.[11] But that's far from the whole story—the best estimates are that there are more than *ten times* as many bacteria and other microbes living in us than the cells that compose muscle, fat, organs, and bone;[12] that's right, by this accounting, each of us is only 10% "human," though of course there is variation from person to person. (When you think about it, that fact might explain rather an awful lot really.) And the complexity only grows exponentially from there when considering the myriad electrochemical signals traveling between these cells, to say nothing of how they interact with external pathogens. Really, it's not so surprising that we misplace our keys (or forget our passwords), but that we manage to remember them most of the time.

The quest to keep such a complicated organism functioning— for example, improving healthcare for individuals, and public health for communities—then might have something to teach us in our quest to better secure and govern the IoT, and more broadly the Internet of Everything (IoE). After all, by some estimates, the number of Internet-connected devices will top 125 billion by 2030 and could grow exponentially from there.[13]

In trying to treat chronic conditions and cure diseases, the medical community creates medications, just as software vendors create new programs and patches. Some medications are available over the counter, and some medications require a prescription because you need guidance from your doctor, just as some software updates are available for free, while others require a subscription or even access to a specialized information sharing organization. Also, some medications can only be administered in the hospital because they're very specialized or dangerous, just as in the cybersecurity context, in which certain systems are so vital that they must be air gapped from the public Internet for security reasons (though this is a far from perfect solution).[14] In short, we have a whole social and policy framework to govern the use and administration of medicine—even if it doesn't work perfectly—whose purpose is to keep you safe and promote both individual and public health.[15]

Public health has long grappled with governance best practices for managing a wide range of communicable and noncommunicable diseases, along with risky behaviors such as poor hygiene and issues with toxic environmental exposures.[16] The parallels with cybersecurity are obvious, such as the need to quarantine infected systems and to maintain proper "cyber hygiene" such as not reusing passwords, requiring VPNs for remote access, and installing firewalls and antivirus software.[17] Such preventative acts can help ensure that cyber attacks such as the WannaCry ransomware do not spread so quickly, especially when coupled with proactive techniques to minimize damage.[18] Yet others are critical of this approach, such as Amit Mital of Symantec, who argues that "IoT devices hardware and processing constraints make current endpoint protection models ('vaccination') impossible."[19] Instead, he argues in favor of "security by design. To continue with our

public health analogy, think about this as genetically engin-
eered immunity instead of vaccination."[20]

The governance regimes of public health and IoT are also
similar in some ways. Consider the National Institutes of
Health (NIH) model, which consists of more than twenty-seven
different component centers, each "focusing on particular diseases or body systems."[21] Such an approach jives well with the
findings from polycentric governance discussed in chapter 5,
including the desirability of "loosely coupled" institutions
designed to manage particular problems at multiple levels.[22]
The same may be said for the complex, multi-stakeholder approach to Internet governance discussed in chapter 1.[23] Indeed,
the FTC recommends that the long-standing Fair Information
Practice Principles should apply to the IoT, with a primary
challenge being "the sheer number of stakeholders involved,"
according to IT governance expert Chris Moschovitis.[24] Such
a fragmented approach can lead to a digital Tower of Babel,
underscoring the need for a dynamic "framework that is very
flexible and accepted internationally."[25]

Healthcare generally has also been a test bed for developing
and deploying various cybersecurity best practices, even as
it has also been a victim of cyber attackers. On the positive
side, the inclusion of IoT in the medical field is revolutionizing modern medicine, such as may be seen by the adoption
of innovations like the Electronic Health Records,[26] and even
blockchain to help safeguard the supply chains for connected
medical devices.[27] Yet, on the other hand, cyber attacks remain endemic. One variety, known as "Locky," was among the
"most prolific types of ransomware" infecting, for example, the
Hollywood Presbyterian Medical Center, resulting in "an 'internal emergency.'"[28] A related problem made national news
in 2017 when the FDA mandated a recall of more than 400,000
vulnerable pacemakers, as was discussed in chapter 2.[29] The
healthcare sector has made strides to improve its cybersecurity
posture, but could do more by implementing these lessons
from public health.[30] Still, as David Bray, the former CIO for

the FCC, has argued, "Public health exists because even with our best efforts, infectious disease outbreaks do occur in the real world, and we have to rapidly detect, respond, and help treat those effected [sic]."[31] What is needed, according to Bray, is a "mashup of cyber personal hygiene and cyber epidemiology" along with enhanced information sharing as to the health of IoT devices.[32] Small acts, like washing your hands or not reusing passwords, can have an outsized, cumulative impact that raises the overall level of hygiene, as is discussed further in chapter 7.

What if we took an ecosystem-based approach to IoT governance?

In the 1960s, a British scientist named James Lovelock, who was working at NASA, was tasked with examining the possibility of finding life on Mars. As part of his mission, Dr. Lovelock began thinking about how diverse ecosystems influence one another at a planetary scale, a line of thought that ultimately gave birth to the "Gaia Theory."[33] In short, this notion asserts "that living organisms and their inorganic surroundings have evolved together as a single living system that greatly affects the chemistry and conditions of Earth's surface."[34] Considering the Earth as a conjoined planetary ecosystem, in which climatic fluctuations or species extinctions in one region can resonate across the globe, may also hold lessons for managing risks in another rapidly expanding network of networks—the IoE.

It is common practice to refer to the "IoT ecosystem" in discussing the evolution of Internet-connected technologies and how they interact with and shape our wider world. NIST, for example, has called out the IoT ecosystem for its security concerns and has worked on various governance frameworks to better manage them, as was discussed in chapter 5.[35] Similar, groups, such as the IoT Cybersecurity Alliance, note that Internet-connected technologies "can introduce risk across the entire ecosystem, via multiple threat vectors."[36] Because of the complexity inherent in IoT systems, which might be considered at another level of magnitude than the issues inherent in traditional cybersecurity domains, such as protecting data centers, there is not a one-size-fits-all approach to managing the problem. Rather, as has been discussed, it is vital to undertake a bottom-up effort to securing the IoE that is built on proactivity.[37] As one commentator noted, "The only solution is to take a security-first approach, embedding it to leverage the network itself, both to enable real-time monitoring, and to provide defense and protection."[38] But how useful is this analogy really in furthering IoE security?

The growth of a global, Digital Ecosystem of Everything, to coin a term, is not a foregone conclusion. In fact, it is fairly unlikely in the foreseeable future, since, after all, many IoT systems are essentially collections of isolated "Intranets of Things," also referred to as "vertical silos," which cannot easily and efficiently interact with one another. Really, it's a state of affairs not dissimilar from the early days of the Internet itself discussed in chapter 1. An important prerequisite for a successful open IoT ecosystem is to create a solid technological, economic, and legal foundation upon which to build, such as by ensuring the provision of secure and trustable devices and services by creating trusted marks, leveraging supply chains, and fostering an exchange through which end users can trade personal data and/or services.[39] From there, it might be possible to create a single software and communication framework-based approach to unify disparate IoT systems.[40]

Yet, would such a future, if it were to come to pass, of a fully realized IoE be an unparalleled boon to innovation spawning industries undreamed of today, or be the ultimate enabler of a dystopian future in which surveillance is the norm and privacy the exception?[41] We have already seen cyber attacks cause physical damage, and the opportunities for such cyber-enabled calamities will increase exponentially in an increasingly interconnected world, from "smart" door locks being hacked to let in intruders to cars being hit with ransomware.

In response, as Bruce Schneier points out, we need updated regulations, as was discussed in chapter 5, along with an "entire ecosystem that supports people bridging the gap between technology and law."[42] But even with a trained workforce and sector-specific regimes in place, there is still a persistent danger of institutional fragmentation due to a lack of coordinated governance.[43] This points to the need for local, national, and international laws that practice ecosystem-based management, like the 1980 Convention on the Conservation of Antarctic Marine Living Resources, a point that is returned to in chapter 7.[44] Such an integrated approach that pays attention to not only particular sectors and systems but the interconnections between them would seem to better match the complexity in the Digital Ecosystem of Everything that is increasingly spanning the world, mirroring the Gaian philosophy. Scholars including Professor Charlotte Hess predicted this outcome in the mid-1990s, arguing that cyberspace is a shared common pool resource that should be approached as a collectively managed ecosystem.[45] A central player in this movement is the firm, which is the topic we turn to next.

How much would it help matters if more firms began treating cybersecurity as a corporate social responsibility?

The 2017 NotPetya ransomware attack underscored both the extent to which businesses around the world are going online, and how vital it is to take proactive steps to manage cyber threats in the broader Internet ecosystem before they spread unabated.[46] By the time the digital dust settled, NotPetya, which made use of leaked NSA hacking tools to penetrate Windows systems and has been called by *Wired* "the most devastating cyberattack in history," resulted in more than $10 billion in damages at diverse firms, including power utilities, banks, and tech firms.[47] Especially hard hit were FedEx ($400 million), the pharmaceutical firm Merck ($870 million), and the shipping giant Maersk, which reportedly lost $300 million and had to use WhatsApp, Gmail, Excel spreadsheets, and Post-It notes to communicate and take orders.[48] One Maersk employee commented in the aftermath, "I can tell you it's a fairly bizarre experience to find yourself booking 500 shipping containers via WhatsApp, but that's what we did"—it took two weeks for the firm to be able to begin reissuing systems.[49] NotPetya was a big deal not just for these particular companies, though, but for their thousands of vendors and millions of customers. Many were left without power and other crucial services, in part because the companies did not make the necessary proactive investments to better protect themselves and their employees.

Following on the heels of WannaCry, which used the same vulnerability and impacted more than 200,000 computers spread across 150 nations earlier the same year, the NotPetya episode revealed the extent to which privately owned and operated corporate information systems are interconnected, as well as how much we have all become reliant on the proper functioning of these networks. When a company like Equifax or an organization like the UK's National Health Service fails to keep its operating systems and software up to date, ultimately all of us pay the price, which can be steep, as we have seen. Yet few boards seem to be getting the message. According to research conducted by Bay Dynamics, 97% of board members report that they know what to do with the information provided to them by cybersecurity experts, but only one-third of those experts "believe the board comprehends the cyber security information provided to them," highlighting an important disconnect and corporate communication breakdown,[50] one that has been fueled by US government decisions to stockpile certain vulnerabilities for use as cyber weapons rather than turning them over to vendors for patching. Through this program, known as the Vulnerabilities Equities Process (VEP), the US government is one of the few nations in the world to publicly discuss how vulnerabilities are managed, including roughly how many are kept or disclosed.[51] There are risks at both extremes; publicly disclosing all vulnerabilities, for example, makes both users and criminals aware of unpatched systems at the same time. Similarly, if too many vulnerabilities are stockpiled, then they become a tempting target, such as when the NSA's vault of such weapons was broken into by a group calling themselves the Shadow Brokers. The city of Baltimore grappled with a series of prolonged cyber attacks that were fueled by this breach,[52] showcasing the need for finding a middle-ground of coordinated disclosure.

Rather than just a cost of doing business, increasingly firms are treating cybersecurity as a competitive advantage, and even a corporate social responsibility (CSR). The overall idea is that companies should make corporate decisions that reflect obligations not just to owners and shareholders, customers, and employees, but to society at large, the natural environment, and cyberspace. There are myriad approaches to analyzing CSR, such as that taken by Archie Carroll, who postulates a pyramid composed of four layers: economic, legal, ethical, and philanthropic obligations.[53] Yet such an approach to conceptualizing CSR has its limits. Cyber threats do not easily fit into such classifications, given that they can pose economic, legal, and ethical quandaries (the last as seen in the active defense context). Moreover, under Carroll's definition of ethical responsibilities, it is unclear how to go about balancing needs such as rigorously protecting sensitive customer data with the centralization of security practices that could negatively impact privacy rights.[54]

Part of this tension lies in differing conceptions about the nature of the firm, that is, whether it should be conceptualized as a "nexus of contracts" or as a distinct "legal entity" enjoying some of the same rights and responsibilities as natural persons.[55] Both views have their strengths and weaknesses,[56] but the latter generally lends itself to a broader view of the firm and its societal obligations,[57] including with regards to managing cyber risk.

An assortment of policymakers and managers around the world have noted the trend toward taking a wider view of cybersecurity risk management, with the US Department of Homeland Security referencing the "shared responsibility" of businesses to protect themselves and their customers from cyber attacks.[58] After all, end users cannot be expected to safeguard their power utility or bank accounts on their own; cybersecurity is by necessity a shared enterprise, or a team sport. Some companies are embracing this understanding. The energy utility EDP, for example, boasts a high Dow Jones Sustainability Index score even as it has taken steps to recognize and proactively manage the cyber risk endemic in its extended supply chain.[59]

If more companies get serious about cybersecurity, the Internet ecosystem will be safer for everyone. The concept is much like vaccinating people against disease: if enough people are protected, other unvaccinated people benefit too, a process known as "herd immunity."[60] In terms of deterring hackers, the number of vulnerable targets will drop (a doctrine known as "deterrence by denial"), making it harder for hackers to find them, and less worthwhile to even look. And more companies will have defenses ready when cyber attackers come calling. This isn't a perfect solution: with enough time and resources, any system is vulnerable, as was discussed in chapter 4. But this change in corporate perception is an important step in developing a global culture of cybersecurity.

Such an evolution of CSR to widen the lens of risk management has historical precedent. In fact, as Professor Reuven Avi-Yonah has argued, corporate governance dates back to Roman times when firms were considered primarily "to be non-profit organizations motivated toward promoting the public good."[61] It was only in modern times that companies evolved into entities with shared management structures, eventually becoming the multinational for-profit corporations driving so much of the evolution of the IoE today.[62] More than 2,000 companies, such as Etsy and Kickstarter, have reincorporated as benefit corporations that are focused not just on profit but on furthering social goods. This is emblematic of the trend toward managers seeking a middle ground between completely for-profit and nonprofit enterprise.[63] If more IoT providers fol-lowed suit, it might help press these organizations to consider the wider impact of their often lax security investments and privacy policies.

Customers can also get involved in this effort, demanding better cybersecurity from companies they do business with, as is discussed further in chapter 7. Such companies can include online retailers, whether small specialized sellers or giants like Amazon. But local brick-and-mortar stores that have built their brands on trust can also be susceptible to consumer pressure. To date, it's been hard to know which companies have the best cybersecurity practices. But with civil society efforts like the Consumer Reports Digital Standard discussed in chapter 5, along with various trust mark and certification schemes, there is hope that things will start to change. Concerned consumers can also get active in advocacy groups like the Internet Society to pressure firms to include cybersecurity efforts in their re-ports to regulators and shareholders. Similarly, government agencies could develop voluntary programs modeled after the EPA's Energy Star appliance-efficiency rating system.

Ultimately, companies will play a huge role in shaping the future of our shared experience online. More firms are increas-ingly interested in CSR and have learned that "doing good" can often translate to "doing well" for their customers, the en-vironment, and digital ecosystems.[64] Unaddressed vulnerabil-ities threaten the sustainability of the Internet ecosystem, while the rise of walled gardens to isolate networks threatens the in-teroperability that lies at the heart of the IoE's transformative potential. Cybersecurity and data privacy are key forces at the heart of this conundrum, and are integral even to attaining the United Nations' seventeen Sustainable Development Goals.[65] It is time consumers demand corporations treat them as the twenty-first-century social responsibilities they are, perhaps fueled by some of the same tools that have sparked the green revolution.

Sustainable cybersecurity: could leveraging tools from the green revolution lead to a new era of secure IoT devices?

The environmental situation facing businesses specifically and the international community generally in the mid-to-late twentieth century was bleak.[66] Industrial waste caused the Cuyahoga river in Cleveland to catch fire in 1969.[67] The Rhine was long one of the most polluted waterways in Europe, similarly catching fire in 1986.[68] Schoolchildren in Japan were dying from mercury poisoning at around the same time.[69] Problems associated with drought and desertification were already underway in China during this period, a process that has only quickened in the early twenty-first century.[70] Into this world stepped seminal figures, including the marine biologist Rachel Carson, whose 1962 book *Silent Spring* documented the effects of widespread pesticide use in the United States and is credited with jumpstarting the modern global environmental movement.[71] Much like that time, the twenty-first-century cybersecurity landscape is littered with failed attempts to manage and unintended consequences of managing security and privacy concerns in the IoE. Banning DDT was important for environmental quality, for example, but arguably contributed to a spike in malaria-related deaths worldwide, just like enacting the Communications Decency Act provided the protections that permitted the likes of Google and Facebook to flourish, even as it also has undermined democratic institutions such as by permitting the spread of disinformation. But we are still waiting for our cyber *Silent Spring*.

In the search for analogies to get a better handle on the multifaceted cyber threat facing the IoE, we should not ignore the green movement, given that it deals with similar issues of complex systems, interoperability, and scale. Consider the Aria hotel in Las Vegas, which became famous for more than its slot machines—it is also known for its wet towels.[72] " 'We say, if you want us to wash your towels every day, we will do it, just let us know,' says Cindy Ortega, chief sustainability officer for MGM Resorts, which owns Aria, 'but other than that, we're just going to hang the towels up every night.'"[73] Such measures may seem small, but they add up to Aria's being a pioneer in sustainability. It is saving a bundle, and generating business in the process. Large multinationals such as IBM provide questionnaires to Aria that ask about everything from waste recycling to water use (hence the wet towels).[74] If Aria elected not to make investments in sustainability, it would be at a competitive disadvantage to its competitors that were.

The example of Aria is illuminating as applied to promoting sustainable cybersecurity for at least three reasons. First, it demonstrates that furthering a company's sustainability by promoting CSR is not necessarily at odds with the bottom line; it can be a strategic advantage to firms in distinguishing themselves and adding value to what they do. The same may be said of investments to enhance cybersecurity, be they technological or organizational, allowing firms with best-in-class cybersecurity to charge a premium for services to increasingly demanding corporate partners and customers.[75] Second, the Aria example illustrates the cost savings that can come from investing in sustainability initiatives with a short return on investment. This tactical advantage is not isolated to the hospitality industry; in fact, after a $20 million investment, BP wound up saving more than $2 billion.[76] Although it is difficult to quantify the dollars saved from an avoided cyber attack, or where to put that next euro of investment, firms with more proactive cybersecurity investments have been shown to save in the event of cyber attacks.[77] The third dimension to the Aria tale is the power of leveraging supply chains through information sharing to attain a corporate goal and even build trust. In this case, "IBM encourages MGM. MGM encourages its vendors. And more and more businesses feel pressure to go green."[78] If more companies used the power of their supply chains to signal the need to invest in cybersecurity best practices rather than focusing on "perimeter defense," then the cause of sustainable cybersecurity could be greatly enhanced.[79]

Along with the growth of the sustainability movement in the private sector, there has been a concomitant evolution of tools designed to better inform managers about the various impacts of their business decisions. Among the most prevalent sustainability reporting tools today, especially in Western Europe and the United States, is the Global Reporting Initiative (GRI).[80] More than 13,000 organizations have submitted some 53,000 Reports as of May 2019 (a more than 300% increase since 2014), making the framework the dominant sustainability-reporting standard for international business.[81] The GRI framework itself is designed to be flexible so as to be useful to firms operating across an array of industry sectors. It has sections focusing on firm profile and governance, as well as the social, economic, and environmental impacts of a firm's operations, along with a statement of product responsibility.[82] Although submitting a report does not compel a given business decision, protagonists argue that the act of compiling and disclosing the information can have an impact on firm decision making.

The movement for a more robust disclosure regime for sustainability mirrors the clamoring by investors for more information regarding cyber attacks.[83] In fact, it has been reported that "almost 80% [of surveyed firms] would likely not consider investing in a company with a history of attacks."[84] The Securities and Exchange Commission (SEC) published its views on disclosure requirements in 2011, and although it stopped short of requiring publicly traded firms to disclose all cyber attacks, it interpreted existing regulations broadly, for example, in requiring disclosure of "material" attacks leading to financial losses.[85] It also hinted that additional reporting requirements may be coming.[86] Indeed, in 2018 the SEC issued a Commission Statement and Guidance underscoring that it is "crucial for public companies to inform investors about relevant cybersecurity risks and incidents in a timely fashion."[87] Among other things, the 2018 SEC guidance lowered the threshold for "materiality" to "known trends and uncertainties" by referencing "the nature, extent and potential magnitude of the event," which in the IoT context, as we have seen, can be widespread and unpredictable, along with encouraging tailored (i.e., not boilerplate) disclosures.[88] And the SEC backed up this guidance with action, fining a firm $35 million "for failing to disclose a substantial data breach and cyberattack."[89] As such, companies would be well advised to get ahead of both the sustainability and cybersecurity regulatory curves and begin integrated reporting that combines a firm's impact on the environment, economy, and surrounding communities with its cybersecurity footprint.

Other tools drawn from the sustainability movement beyond integrated reporting may also have some application to enhancing cybersecurity. In addition to Energy Star, elements within the private sector could also, for example, begin developing the digital equivalent of Leadership in Energy and Environmental Design (LEED) standards,[90] which would help identify IoE firms with best-in-class cybersecurity. The program is a "voluntary, consensus-based, marketdriven program that provides third-party verification of green buildings."[91] It provides a flexible framework to rank various types of projects along multiple dimensions, including everything from building design and construction to maintenance and neighborhood development.[92] The NIST Cybersecurity and Privacy Frameworks could provide a foundation on which to build a LEED-type cybersecurity certification scheme for IoT devices, and are similar to the type of impact assessments and risk management frameworks common in the environmental context. Already, a number of firms, including Bank of America and IBM, are requiring their vendors to rely on the NIST CSF as a guide for improving their cybersecurity postures.[93] After all, the negative impact of a major data breach on a firm in terms of direct and indirect costs can mirror that of an environmental disaster, yet too often cybersecurity is still treated as an IT, and not a C-Suite, problem.[94]

Rachel Carson's *Silent Spring* was not written overnight, and it took years before the first Earth Day and decades more before tools matured for companies to more effectively measure and improve their long-term sustainability goals. Unfortunately, we have not yet had our cyber *Silent Spring*, but nor do we have decades to wait. The time for action is now, and the path forward includes learning from what has worked and what has not in other contexts, including the green movement, to pave a path toward sustainable cybersecurity in the IoE, as is explored further in chapter 7.

7

HOW CAN WE DO BETTER? FINDING CYBER PEACE IN THE INTERNET OF THINGS

Making predictions is generally a somewhat foolhardy endeavor, especially in a field as dynamic as the Internet of Things (IoT), but history can be a useful guide. After all, according to George Savile, Marquis of Halifax, "The best qualification of a prophet is to have a good memory."[1] As such, this final chapter calls upon us to take out the crystal ball (however opaque it may be) to look into where our hyperconnected world may be headed, but also to look back to see how we can bend the curves by using old tools like insurance, and new technologies like blockchain and machine learning, to help ensure some measure of cyber peace. We conclude with a call to action for what more we all can do to help ensure that a fully realized Internet of Everything (IoE) is a future in which we can live, and even thrive.

What is "cyber peace," and how does it apply to the IoT?

Headlines regularly attest to a seemingly constant, and deepening, state of cyber insecurity. From the 2019 Marriott breach, to North Korean–sponsored ransomware, Chinese espionage against Airbus, and Hamas-organized cyber attacks against Israel, in all, humanity does not seem to be doing a particularly good job at managing cyber attacks.[2] The news is not all bad, though. There are reports that efforts such as the

National Initiative for Cybersecurity Education (NICE) have led to improved cyber hygiene, as have more robust behavior-based threat analytics.[3] More boards of directors also seem to be taking their cybersecurity oversight responsibilities seriously,[4] while omnibus privacy regulations like GDPR, discussed in chapter 5, are forcing more firms to re-examine their data governance practices worldwide.[5] Yet the cybersecurity talent crisis is continuing, and IoT threats remain acute with more nation states, for example, exploiting vulnerabilities to launch cyber attacks.[6] What hope is there, then, for peace in such an uncertain and fast-evolving Internet ecosystem?

As has been argued, only limited efforts have been made to date at defining "cyber peace."[7] One example of such an effort is the International Telecommunication Union, which defined the term in part as "a universal order of cyberspace" built on a "wholesome state of tranquility, [i.e.] the absence of disorder or disturbance and violence."[8] Although certainly desirable, such an outcome is politically and technically unlikely, at least in the near term. Nor can cyber peace (sometimes also called "digital peace")[9] be understood merely as the "absence of violence" online, which was the starting point for how Professor Johan Galtung described the field of peace studies he helped to create in 1969.[10] As such, cyber peace is not defined here as the absence of conflict online, a state of affairs that may be called *negative* cyber peace.[11] Rather, by working together through polycentric partnerships of the kind described in chapter 5, we can mitigate the risk of cyber conflict by laying the groundwork for a *positive* cyber peace that respects human rights, spreads Internet access along with cybersecurity best practices, promotes stability, and strengthens governance mechanisms by fostering multi-stakeholder collaboration.[12]

All this is (needless to say) easier said than done, and as such, promoting cyber peace requires tackling a host of thorny governance challenges discussed throughout this book, from incentivizing manufacturers to harden their Internet-connected devices against cyber attacks to defining and operationalizing concepts like corporate social responsibility, sustainability, and international norms such as due diligence. An all-of-the-above approach is needed to meet this challenge. The effort needs to embrace polycentric principles, including subsidiarity, which is the notion that "a central authority should have a subsidiary function, performing only those tasks which cannot be performed effectively at a more immediate or local level."[13]

Consider the 2018 Paris Call for Trust and Security in Cyberspace, which was a broad statement of principles designed to help guide the international community toward greater cyber stability and, perhaps one day, cyber peace. It was signed by more than 50 nations (with the notable exception of the United States), and over "130 companies and 90 universities and nongovernmental groups."[14] The Call was criticized for how it papered over continuing concerns over cyber sovereignty,[15] as seen in French president Emmanuel Macron's accompanying remarks that "giant platforms could become not just gateways but also gatekeepers."[16] Nevertheless, the Call has had an impact in catalyzing and shaping the conversation around the scope and meaning of cyber peace. For example, it focuses on improving "cyber hygiene," along with "the security of digital products and services," and the "integrity of the Internet,"[17] all of which are integral to enhancing IoT security. And it is just one of myriad private sector initiatives to promote cybersecurity.[18]

Under this framing, our goal, in other words, should not be to reach some predetermined finish line, but rather to promote progress along a cyber peace spectrum and toward a more robust and sustainable Digital Ecosystem of Everything. Such a spectrum would include systems in place to "deter hostile or malicious activity in cyberspace"[19] and in so doing promote stability, human rights, and international security both online and offline.[20] To realize this vision of an "open, interoperable, reliable, and secure"[21] IoE, it will be necessary to leverage civil society, academia, and, yes, put into place appropriate regulations. There is a regime complex of organizations engaged in this effort from which to draw, including the Online Trust Alliance,[22] Cyber Peace Alliance,[23] ICT4Peace,[24] and the Ostrom Workshop's Cyber Peace Working Group, to name just a few.[25] There is even growing support for movements such as a Cyber Peace Corps, building from successful programs like the Peace Corps and AmeriCorps.[26] Fostering such efforts can help ensure that, to paraphrase Dr. Martin Luther King Jr., the moral arc of the universe is long, but that it bends toward cyber peace.[27]

Taking out the crystal ball—let's envision the state of the IoT in 2050; what do current trend lines reveal?

By some estimates, in the late 2000s, something of a milestone was reached—for the first time in history, the total number of Internet-connected devices outnumbered humans on the planet.[28] Estimates vary, as was discussed in chapter 1, but using this data, the ratio between people to smart devices went from 0.08 in 2003 to 3.47 by 2015 to 6.58 by 2020, the same year that consumers are projected to spend some $3 trillion on such devices.[29] If these trends continue, there could be a 400:1 ratio by 2050.

Similarly, even though to date most of the IoT installed base is in North America, Europe, and China, the geographic spread of these technologies also looks likely to diffuse further across both the private and public sectors.[30] Intelligent, ultra-high-speed networks will fuel the advent of truly smart cities replete with smart streetlights and sidewalks, changing the way we live, work, and love. We are already seeing the beginnings of this long-term trend in various countries around the world, such as the United Arab Emirates' "Vision 2021 Smart Dubai"[31] and Singapore's "Smart Nation" initiative.[32] We are also seeing pushback from this development, such as privacy concerns surrounding Toronto's Quayside project, and broader issues involving the growing reach of Huawei—and with it some argue the Chinese government—across cities in more than sixty-five nations.[33] Fully autonomous vehicles (AV) will help fuel this rise; by 2050, McKinsey estimates that AVs will be the primary mode of transport for the consumer and industrial sectors, leading to enhanced efficiency and safety while driving (pun intended) dramatic changes in related industries like insurance.[34]

In other words, the cyberspace of 2050 will look far different from how cyberspace was envisioned in 2000 when LG announced the world's first Internet-enabled refrigerator.[35] We will likely be surrounded by ubiquitous sensors, screens, and other stuff that is designed to interact with us, predict our desires, and respond to our fears. Whether such a future will be an Orwellian dystopia in which the ancestors of the "digital gangsters" of Facebook will know us better than our closest friends and family is uncertain.[36] We are already seeing efforts in various jurisdictions, including the EU and Australia, to rein in the worst abuses of social media, even as responses have been slower in other jurisdictions, such as the United States. But more needs to be done to hold companies accountable for breaches of consumer trust and to protect against spread of disinformation of the type that has stoked civil unrest and violence in diverse communities from Myanmar to Sri Lanka. The power of these firms, including Google, left unchecked, is only set to increase without countervailing forces applied, particularly in the United States, given its long history of relatively lax and sector-specific privacy and security standards. Such reforms could include enhancing the power of the US Federal Trade Commission to investigate and levy fines against firms that fail to make adequate cybersecurity investments, establishing ethics review boards, revamping antitrust laws, and/or revising Section 230 of the 1996 Communications Decency Act to permit some degree of liability to hold tech firms accountable for the content spread on their platforms.[37]

The potential for governmental abuse of the emerging IoT is also present. As VP at GuideSpark Parker Trewin has said, "The Internet of Things is big news because it ups the ante: 'Reach out and touch somebody' is becoming 'reach out and touch everything.'"[38] For example, China became the first nation to recognize IoT as a key sector in 2010,[39] and since then has been working to ensure that Chinese firms dominate the coming IoT revolution (for example, through influencing the foundational standards and technology, like 5G, on which these system will be built).[40] When augmented by other technologies, such as artificial intelligence (AI) making use of ever Bigger Data provided by IoT sensors, China could perfect a surveillance society pioneered against the Muslim-minority Uighurs. It has, for example, more than 200 million cameras already in place as of early 2019.[41] Such technologies are enabling its "Social Credit Score" system, which tracks "non-compliance with legally prescribed social and economic obligations and contractual commitments . . . to determine the trustworthiness of companies and individuals."[42] Good deeds like charitable donations or paying your bills on time increase your score, while breaking norms or laws—such as by breaching a contract, speeding, or perhaps protesting—decrease it. By 2020, the Chinese government plans on releasing the scores for all 1.4 billion Chinese citizens. Ultimately, the Chinese Communist Party "intends the social credit score system to 'allow the trustworthy to roam freely under heaven while making it hard for the discredited to take a single step.'"[43]

It is easy to see how such technology might not only become widespread in China, but could potentially migrate to many other nations through China's Belt and Road Initiative, which permits the tracking of individuals globally from cradle to grave.[44] It is important to note, though, despite the popularity of the Credit System in mainland China (it is being viewed as a tool to enhance social safety), it remains to be seen whether the same would prove true in other cultures.[45]

Underlying these trends are three related developments that will dramatically shape the IoE through 2050 and beyond: edge computing (the "practice of processing data near the edge of your network [such as in IoT devices], where the data is being generated"[46]), the mesh network ("gives every IoT device a local network to understand and connect with the world around it"[47]), and the brain-computer interface. Right now, most of the computing power on the Internet is idle. Your Alexa is capable of doing a lot more. We can imagine a future, then, in which consumers will no longer need high-powered computers because all of their networked devices will be able to distribute the workload between them. But that is just one, futurist, prediction about edge computing. Edge computing more practically refers to devices that do much of the computational work themselves and then ship the most useful data to the cloud for analysis and storage. Consider the self-driving car, which can generate 6GB of data per second.[48] It needs to make decisions in nanoseconds. It may not have time to send the data to the cloud for a decision, receive the decision, and execute the action. It likely needs to perform all of that locally, and quickly—lives could be at stake. Edge computing in the self-driving car context will generate, analyze, and act on data in real time and then send the most important bits back to the cloud for analysis. The same model can be mapped on to more or less any industrial system from manufacturing to agriculture.[49]

The mesh network operates on a similar concept to the edge computer—in short, rather than a central router, in a mesh network every device is connected to every other device.[50] This means that these networks are self-healing; if one node of the network goes down, the traffic gets rerouted seamlessly. They are also generally cheaper, smaller, and last longer than traditional hub-and-spoke networks. A futurist prediction of the interaction between mesh networks and edge computing is "unlimited" bandwidth, storage, and computing power for users. Traffic on the mesh can travel along any available route to its destination, so bandwidth constraints by centralized ISP data lines can be eliminated. Computational work can be outsourced to any idle device the user has access to on the network, and data can be stored anywhere there is excess capacity. Mesh networks and edge computing are one of the core conceits of the sci-fi futurist setting for the popular role-playing game Eclipse Phase.

The third and final area that IoT tech will likely advance are in implanted computing and the Brain-Computer Interface (BCI). Companies are already implanting volunteer employees with chips that do things like mediate access, unlock doors, log in to computers, or pay for items in vending machines.[51] In 2018, researchers were able to use BCI chips to control off-the-shelf tablets. Paralyzed users have been able to manipulate apps,[52] while others have used brainwaves as a means to authenticate their identity.[53] With the use of sensors and edge computing, a simple EEG reading was enough to allow a user to control a wheelchair using signals directly from his brain.[54]

Looking ahead, your brainwaves could be used to unlock your devices, or control them directly, potentially leading to a form of embodied cognition that has some parallels with the race of cyborgs called the Borg from *Star Trek* who shared a collective consciousness. Perhaps we could one day make use of the collective cognitive surplus in our brains that is sitting idle in the same way that edge computing and mesh networks are helping us take advantage of unused processing power.[55] Although there would be obvious benefits to not having to go to the trouble of vocalizing commands to Alexa and just thinking about the laundry detergent that you need today (delivered via drone, or transporter, of course), resistance to such a fate is certainly not futile. We next examine an array of technologies such as blockchain to help build trust, and security, in the IoT.

Deus ex Machina—can technology save us from our hyperconnected fate?

Technology is a double-edged sword. Just as some IoE innovations hold the promise to dramatically remake our world, and ourselves, from the way we learn (think universal on-demand predictive-based education) to how we eat (with farmers using IoT tech to help monitor and track their crops, thereby moving to in-vitro food production and lessening carbon footprints),[56] others can challenge our most fundamental values, even leading to the death of privacy, as was explored in chapter 4. Yet, on balance, there is cause for hope. Automated sensors and machine learning (ML) applications, like those used in the edge computing context, can help firms better manage their cyber risk (though, in adversarial machine-learning, attackers can compromise ML systems by feeding them with misinformation).[57] In particular, such technologies permit: (1) the correlation of vast amounts of threat intelligence;[58] (2) the deployment of countermeasures right on the edge of the network, in real time, to react to spreading attacks (imagine if Equifax's systems had been able to notice unusual data exfiltration, trace it back to a vulnerability in an unpatched Apache Struts package, and fix it, in real time, without operator intervention); and (3) improved identification of existing infections (by some estimates, the average breach goes undetected for more than 200 days[59]). Such automated systems would allow defenders to look backward through their mountains of audit logs more easily, or forward to make predictions and search for suspicious behavior.

In a related vein, AI can be used to more proactively manage cyber threats by detecting malware,[60] even as it also risks setting off a cyber arms race.[61] AI can aid cybersecurity risk management and real-time customer protection, especially through the automation of basic analytics. The International Data Corporation predicted that by 2019, AI will support "all effective" IoT efforts, and that without AI, data from the deployments will only have "limited value."[62] Applications are widespread, including using AI to detect "fraudulent behavior at bank ATMs, predicting auto insurance premiums based on driving patterns, identifying potentially hazardous stress conditions for factory workers, and monitoring law enforcement surveillance data to proactively identify likely crime scenes."[63]

And because many of the devices in the future IoE will likely not have individualized security protocols, AI can be used on a network-wide basis to identify and eliminate threats in our smart homes and cities.[64]

The potentially transformative power of blockchain is now also being better recognized.[65] At its root, a blockchain is a "shared, trusted, distributed ledger that everyone can inspect, but which no single user controls."[66] The participants in a given blockchain system work together to keep the ledger updated; it may be amended only by strict rules and consensus.[67] From making businesses more efficient to recording property deeds to engendering the growth of "smart" contracts, blockchain technology is now being investigated by a huge range of organizations and is attracting billions in venture funding.[68] And it is increasingly being deployed in the IoT context; a Russian drone, for example, was controlled by the Etherium blockchain in 2016.[69] By moving away from centralized operators, blockchain applications hold the potential not only to speed up the collection, processing, and storage of data, but also to improve security such that vulnerabilities in just a few operators would no longer be able to lead to the potential for catastrophic systemic failures.[70] By not relying on third parties to oversee transactions, a Blockchain of Things would also permit secure communication between devices manufactured by different firms, though it is still important to note that no system is infallible and, as such, blockchains can be hacked.[71] Still, the technology has sufficient promise that the likes of IBM and Samsung have partnered on a blockchain-powered IoT platform, likely the first of many.[72]

What more should companies, governments, and the international community be doing to safeguard the IoT?

It is a well-known refrain that the job of president of the United States is tough—impossible, really. In fact, a group of mathematicians at the New England Complex Systems

Institute have argued that it might be better for everyone if the position no longer existed, at least not in its current form.[73] This group (which predicted the Arab Spring and identified a correlation between the food price index and rioting) makes the case that traditional hierarchical decision-making is increasingly ill-suited to a complex society. Simply put, they argue that no one individual, or even group of individuals, can possibly be sufficiently informed about the possible consequences of various actions to make effective decisions. Instead, they suggest a move toward a more lateral approach to governance to improve focus and coherence.[74]

As with democracy, so too possibly with the IoE. An interconnected worldwide network composed of billions of devices, humans, and organizations of all sizes is nearly impossible to conceive, to say nothing of govern. Yet the cost of pervasive insecurity is already being felt in many ways, from the personal to the global. For example, some smart devices, purchased for their convenience, are increasingly being used by domestic abusers as a means to harass, monitor, and control their victims.[75] The issue is becoming more pressing, as cybersecurity guru Bruce Schneier has argued, since "with the advent of the Internet of Things and cyber-physical systems in general, we've given the Internet hands and feet: the ability to directly affect the physical world. What used to be attacks against data and information have become attacks against flesh, steel, and concrete."[76]

In response, a full array of polycentric action is needed, and it's needed now. As FTC Commissioner Rebecca Kelly Slaughter argued:

> We are at a critical point in the IoT era in terms of getting privacy and security right. At the precipice of exponential growth, we have the opportunity both to thoughtfully develop products that start and stay secure, and to educate consumers early on about how to assess the

risks of connected devices, how to choose brands that take privacy and security seriously, and how to maintain device security with patches over the lifespan of the product. I cannot overstate the importance of getting this right, now.[77]

In response to this call for action, an array of international norm-building efforts are being pursued to help harden the IoE. These include: public-private partnerships—such as the NIST CSF and Privacy Frameworks—as well as efforts by civil society, such as the *Consumer Reports* Digital Standard discussed in chapter 5, and national governments such as the UK's proposed IoT labeling system,[78] along with EU schemes like the "ce" mark on products already being sold in Europe that include a provision for "responsible vulnerability disclosure."[79] Space constraints prohibit a thorough exploration of the benefits and drawbacks of each of these approaches,[80] but in short, both pure voluntary and overly regulatory approaches contain significant downsides.[81] An inflexible, comprehensive regime could actually stifle innovation by crowding out smaller-scale efforts, even as voluntary efforts alone will likely prove insufficient to address these collective action challenges, given the difficulties of coordination between such disparate stakeholders.[82] Instead, both individual and elective cybersecurity expenditures should be boosted.[83] That is in part why Professor Elinor Ostrom argued that polycentric regulation is "the best way to address transboundary problems . . . since the complexity of these problems lends itself well to many small, issue-specific units working autonomously as part of a network that is addressing collective action problems. It is an application of the maxim, 'think globally, but act locally.' "[84] Suffice it to say, what is needed is an "all-of-the-above" approach to promote cyber peace in the IoE.

Enterprises acting as norm entrepreneurs can play an important role in improving IoE safety by helping to pioneer and spread standards and norms,[85] and even organizing rating and labeling systems that clearly "explain the user's security re-sponsibilities."[86] Cyber risk-mitigation strategies favored by factions of the US Congress, such as cyber risk insurance, can help firms limit their exposure in the event of a data breach,[87] but they may do little to enhance overall cybersecurity ab-sent a proactive strategy that infuses best practices from the beginning.[88] Other concerns must also be overcome, such as the "war exclusion," which may limit recovery due to cov-ered entities being classified as "collateral damage" in a cyber war.[89] Further, the type and extent of investment must be ana-lyzed using robust information-sharing mechanisms to instill technical, budgetary, and organizational best practices.[90] More also needs to be done to clarify liability structures and, in so doing, boundaries of responsibility and accountability,[91] in-cluding on the part of Internet Service Providers (ISPs) that serve as gatekeepers "sit[ting] between our homes and the rest of the Internet."[92] Above all, tech firms should practice the pre-cautionary principle, which states that "when the potential of harm is great, we should err on the side of not deploying new technology without proof of security."[93]

At the next level up, governments can do more to promote cybersecurity due diligence in the IoE, such as by establishing a Cyber Peace Corps, National Cybersecurity Safety Board,[94] or even an International Criminal Tribunal for Cyberspace.[95] States are already getting into the game. Aside from California (discussed in chapter 5), Ohio is incentivizing companies that invest in cybersecurity best practices and frameworks by pro-viding them with a safe harbor.[96] Twenty-five states have also passed anti-DDoS laws, with another five focusing on the urgent problem of ransomware with a five-fold increase in ransomware variants in 2016 alone.[97] Other states are focusing on removing insecure features from IoT devices and bolstering incident re-sponse plans.[98] Similarly, more than twenty-five nations are ex-perimenting with various bottom-up approaches to cybersecurity risk management modeled after the NIST CSF.[99] The federal gov-ernment also has an invaluable role in solving collective action and free-riding problems discussed throughout this book.[100] For example, it could create baseline standards, outcome-based rules, norms, and organizing agencies.[101] The courts could also help foster cybersecurity due diligence, up to and including holding executives responsible for data breaches happening on their watch.[102] Of course, none of this is simple,[103] and it's easy to go too far; as Schneier points out, "If computers were subject to the same product liability regulations as stepladders, they probably wouldn't be available on the market yet."[104] But given the stakes, the US government can and must do more to lead on IoT governance,[105] or others will step into the void.

Globally, the G7 continued its work on cybersecurity in 2016, publishing its view that "no country should conduct or knowingly support ICT (information and communication technology)-enabled theft of intellectual property" and that all G7 nations should work to "preserve the global nature of the Internet" including the free flow of information in a nod to the notion of cyberspace as a "global networked commons."[106] Bilateral relationships such as the G2 (United States and China), minilateral clubs (including the Five Eyes [FVEY] and NATO), and ultimately the international community must also be proactive in this polycentric effort to spread cybersecurity due diligence and promote cyber peace. In part because of the perception that cyber risk is "escalating out of control,"[107] there exists an opportunity to engage in constructive international dialogue on norm building. One idea is to build from the 2015 Paris Agreement model, in which individual nations and clubs could announce "Cyber Peace Pledges" at annual Conference of the Parties (COP) gatherings to help build momentum toward global agreements on IoT governance, which would include clarifying how existing international law applies to the IoT. All this could set the stage for an eventual, if still fanciful, UN Framework Convention on Cyber Peace. Even this outcome, though, would not be the finish line, but just another mile marker—successfully governing the IoE requires all of us to do our part.

What can I do? We need you! Take control, demand better,
and be a responsible netizen.

In the 1970s, there were widespread concerns about food safety. The British scientist Sir Albert Howard was making the case about returning nutrients to the soil, helping to jump-start the organic movement.[108] However, just as we are now seeing with IoT certification schemes, the first consumer-facing organic food programs were decentralized, largely state-by-state, affairs. It took nearly twenty years, until 1990, for Congress to pass the Organic Foods Production Act (OFPA) and finally usher in national organic food standards. Final regulations defining the production and handling of organic food were not enacted until 2002.[109] In all, the quest to adequately label organic food took nearly a quarter century, which is blazingly fast compared to, for example, automobile safety. One of the first popular reports pushing for improving car safety was published by *Popular Science* in 1950.[110] But it then took nearly two decades before the crash test results were published to inform consumers of the variable safety performances of cars. The first US law mandating the use of seat belts was not passed until 1984.

As these examples testify, consumers should not wait for government to regulate our way to a safe and secure IoT. After all, these issues were, in comparison, relatively straightforward to the billions of devices spread across myriad product categories, industries, sectors, and nations that compose this emerging digital global ecosystem. Instead, consumers should get active in civil society groups like *Consumer Reports* and push for a right to repair their IoT devices.[111] They should also look to academic hubs like Citizen Lab and their Security Planner tool,[112] industry groups like Cyber Peace Alliance,[113] and ICT4Peace.[114] Consumers can, in short, use their hard-earned dollars to demand better from IoT manufacturers. They can also change default passwords and stop using "free" services that do not adequately respect their privacy rights. Moreover, you can submit comments to regulatory bodies like the Federal Trade Commission (FTC) encouraging more robust cybersecurity regulations—and cast your ballot for candidates who promise to take consumer privacy seriously. Progress is possible—even though approximately half of the email sent daily is spam, 99.9% of it is blocked.[115] And there is increasing evidence that the word is getting out. For example, according to a 2019 McKinsey report, cybersecurity is now the top concern among surveyed participants when deciding between IoT products.[116]

More also needs to be done to address the severe cybersecurity workforce shortage that is, as of this writing, estimated at up to six million open positions in the coming years.[117] Yet even though cybersecurity may be one of the hottest career tickets around today, surprisingly few students are choosing it as a focus for their undergraduate studies or graduate degrees. In one 2013 survey sponsored by Raytheon with adults ages eighteen to twenty-six, for example, only 24% said they were interested in a cybersecurity career.[118] That is despite the fact that demand is strong;[119] in fact, by some estimates the cybersecurity shortage is on par with, if not greater than, the nursing shortage.[120] The Bureau of Labor Statistics similarly ranks Cybersecurity as a *Top Occupation*.[121] Moreover, the number of scholarships and programs such as the National Science Foundation's CyberCorps Scholarship for Service initiative are growing rapidly,[122] and the pay is good—the average salary is almost $90,000 per year.[123]

So, what's going on? Why the low interest? Part of the problem seems to be that many students still see cybersecurity as primarily a technical field, and they may not be that keen on managing information systems (incorrectly equating the field, for example, to fixing printers).[124] But that perspective is outdated and inaccurate. In fact, an understanding of core technical cybersecurity skills such as basic coding is a useful but by itself insufficient component for success in both the public- and private-sector cybersecurity workforce. Many cybersecurity professionals have nothing to do with stopping botnets or recovering from ransomware attacks; rather, they are working at the intersection of security, privacy, and risk management on such topics as cyber risk insurance, due diligence, civil rights, and CSR.[125] Some are even members of the C-Suite, one of a whole range of new career paths that include Chief Privacy Officers, Chief Information Officers, Chief Information Security Officers, and even Chief Information Governance Officers.

To increase interest, we need to engage students from diverse backgrounds to pursue cybersecurity education and career opportunities, especially underrepresented minorities and women, given that the latter of which makes up only a dismal 10% of the US cybersecurity workforce; African Americans compose another 7%, and 5% is Hispanic American.[126] To tackle this problem, we need to show that cybersecurity matters—whether it is protecting people from identity theft, safeguarding intellectual property, picking the next president of the United States free from foreign influence, or securing the IoE. We then need to give students the tools, and the funding, to join the fight. Cybersecurity is a calling, one that is increasingly vital both to US national security and to the private sector.[127] Multidisciplinary for-credit and not-for-credit offerings should be seeded, along with clinical and service-learning opportunities to provide more students the chance to hone their craft, and help out under-resourced stakeholders like local governments, small business, and school corporations in the process. Basic cyber hygiene ideally should be taught in K-12, just as it is now in parts of Europe, with ongoing training and well-funded public education programs for all ages, including Cybersecurity Awareness Month (which happens to be every October, though few seem to be aware of that fact).

Continuing the green analogy from chapter 6, it is good for consumers to adopt sustainable habits. Safe and secure IoT devices are the organic foods of the twenty-first century. By taking action, you can help promote cyber peace, and help yourself in the process, such as by making it less likely that you do not become one of the more than 13 million annual US victims of fraud or identity theft.[128] So, to that end, use strong, unique passwords, and even password managers like LastPass or Keychain to help keep track of them. Also be sure to change default passwords on smart devices, and patch them often; keep your antivirus, antispyware, firewalls, and other software up to date; use flash drives cautiously, or better yet not at all; be wary of the information you share on social media; encrypt sensitive information; treat unsolicited emails prudently, especially those including attachments or links; avoid public Wi-Fi hotspots whenever possible without using a VPN or a private brower like DuckDuckGo; and check your credit report regularly for fraudulent activity (you might even consider freezing your credit until you need it).[129]

By taking these steps, we can all help make it harder to launch the kinds of attacks that led to WannaCry and NotPetya. Together, these are vital components of the polycentric partnerships necessary to promote cyber peace. The sci-fi author William Gibson coined the term "cyberspace" in his novel *Neuromancer* in 1984, in which he described "a consensual hallucination experienced daily by billions."[130] One need only view pedestrians staring at their smartphones while walking down the street, often with headphones in, to know that Gibson was on to something. The hallucination will not end anytime soon; in fact, as we have argued, if anything there likely will be such blurring between the "virtual" and "real" worlds that even the term "cyberspace" may seem as antiquated as "Information Superhighway" is today. Regardless of what we call it, though, and how "real" it seems, it will be our world. Let's make it a good one.

Conclusion

Just as none of us can wall ourselves away from the natural world, in the twenty-first century we will be increasingly enmeshed (wittingly or not) in the IoT. Achieving a sustainable level of cybersecurity and privacy in this hyperconnected future demands novel methodologies, standards, and regimes. As Schneier has observed, "The internet is no longer a web that we connect to. Instead, it's a computerized, networked, and interconnected world that we live in. This is the future, and what we're calling the Internet of Things."[131] And as the IoT matures, disparate commercial and governmental networks will be able to communicate with one another, creating smart (and potentially more resilient) things, homes, factories, cities, and societies. Such an ultimate, macro-level outcome echoes the early days of networking discussed in chapter 2, when Cisco used multi-protocol routing to join dissimilar networks. This eventually led to the widespread adoption of a common networking standard called the Internet Protocol, which we all rely on today every time we go online.

IoT standards, potentially powered by various blockchain, AI, and ML applications, are set to follow a similar route, albeit on a larger scale, spanning myriad sectors and industries. In response, polycentric governance systems should be adapted and improved to better keep pace with these changes,[132] particularly with regards to data regulations monitoring private firms and public-sector organizations that transfer personally identifiable information (PII).[133] This includes using frameworks and standards, along with the use of corporate governance structures, such as sustainability, and international norms, like due diligence. Such an all-of-the-above polycentric approach is essential to addressing governance gaps in the ever-expanding IoE.

There is no technological or policy panacea for hardening the IoT. Instead, a thousand large and small actions at nearly as many governance levels are required to address the issues raised throughout this book. But that should not be seen as a recipe for inaction; far from it. All that is needed is the will to act, the desire to experiment with new models of governance, and the recognition that we should learn from history. As President Franklin D. Roosevelt famously said, "The country needs and, unless I mistake its temper, the country demands bold, persistent experimentation. It is common sense to take a method and try it: If it fails, admit it frankly and try another. But above all, try something."[134] It is time for us to experiment—to set up a Cyber Peace Corps, a National Cybersecurity Safety Board, offer IoT trust marks and certification schemes, consider extending products liability to IoT the way France already has, leverage disclosure laws, and incentivize IoT manufacturers to take data privacy and cybersecurity seriously, such as through R&D tax credits and reforming corporate governance.

Many of these ideas may well indeed fail. But some might not. Human beings are fallible, but we are also at the very center of the IoT. That makes us the problem, true. Yet as Rachel Carson noted in the introduction to *Silent Spring* in referring to a once idyllic US town now blighted by a "white granular powder."[135] It was not caused by "witchcraft. . . . The people had done it to themselves."[136] That is equally true in sustainability as cybersecurity; we are to blame, and we are the solution.

NOTES

Preface

* This book summarizes a wide swath of research previously undertaken by the author. As such, sections of this preface, along with other portions of the preceding text, have been previously published in long form. These are indicated where appropriate at the beginning of each chapter, and include in reverse chronological order: Scott J. Shackelford, *Smart Factories, Dumb Policy? Managing Cybersecurity and Data Privacy Risks in the Industrial Internet of Things*, 21 MINN. J. OF L., SCI., & TECH. 1 (2019); Scott J. Shackelford et al., *When Toasters Attack: Enhancing the "Security of Things" through Polycentric Governance*, 2017 U. ILL. L. REV. 415 (2017).

1. *See, e.g.*, Mike Elgan, *Mind-Reading Tech Is Here (and More Useful Than You Think!)*, COMPUTER WORLD (Apr. 7, 2018), https://www.computerworld.com/article/3268132/mind-reading-tech-is-here-and-more-useful-than-you-think.html.

2. Margaret Rouse, *IoT Gateway*, TECHTARGET, https://whatis.techtarget.com/definition/IoT-gateway; *see also* Overview of Internet of Things, GOOGLE, https://cloud.google.com/solutions/iot-overview; *What Is Azure IoT Hub?* MICROSOFT Azure, https://docs.microsoft.com/en-us/azure/iot-hub/about-iot-hub.

3. *See* Samantha Murphy Kelly, *Pampers Is Making a 'Smart' Diaper. Yes, Really*, CNN (July 19, 2019), https://www.cnn.com/2019/07/19/tech/pampers-smart-diapers/index.html.

4. *See* Daniel Burrus, *The Internet of Things Is Far Bigger Than Anyone Realizes*, WIRED (Nov. 2014), http://www.wired.com/2014/11/the-internet-of-things-bigger/; Lawrence J. Trautman, *Cybersecurity: What About US Policy?*, 2015 U. ILL. J.L. TECH. & POL'Y 341, 348 (2015).

5. *See* Dave Evans, *The Internet of Everything: How More Relevant and Valuable Connections Will Change the World*, CISCO, at 2 (2012), https://www.cisco.com/c/dam/global/en_my/assets/ciscoinnovate/pdfs/IoE.pdf ("As these 'things' add capabilities like context awareness, increased processing power, and energy independence, and as more people and new types of information are connected, we will quickly enter the Internet of Everything (IoE)—a network of networks where billions or even trillions of connections create unprecedented opportunities as well as new risks.").

6. Ahmed Banafa, *The Internet of Everything (IoE)*, OPEN MIND (Aug. 29, 2016), https://www.bbvaopenmind.com/en/the-internet-of-everything-ioe/.

7. Bernard Marr, *Big Data: 20 Mind-Boggling Facts Everyone Must Read*, FORBES (Sept. 30, 2015), https://www.forbes.com/sites/bernardmarr/2015/09/30/big-data-20-mind-boggling-facts-everyone-must-read/#5234b4cd17b1.

8. Martin Giles, *For Safety's Sake, We Must Slow Innovation in Internet-Connected Things*, MIT TECH. REV. (Sept. 6, 2018), https://www.technologyreview.com/s/611948/for-safetys-sake-we-must-slow-innovation-in-internet-connected-things/.

9. Christina Medici Scolaro, *Why Google's Eric Schmidt Says the "Internet will Disappear,"* CNBC (Jan. 23, 2015), https://www.cnbc.com/2015/01/23/why-googles-eric-schmidt-says-the-internet-will-disappear.html.

10. *See* Chris Welch, *Tesla's Model S Will Add Self-Driving 'Autopilot' Mode in Three Months*, VERGE (Mar. 19, 2015), http://www.theverge.com/2015/3/19/8257933/tesla-model-s-autopilot-release-date.

11. *See* Richard Baguley & Colin McDonald, *Appliance Science: The Internet of Toasters (and Other Things)*, CNET (Mar. 2, 2015), http://www.cnet.com/news/appliance-science-the-internet-of-toasters-and-other-things/.

12. Richard D. Taylor, *The Next Stage of US Communications Policy: The Emerging Embedded Infosphere*, 41 TELECOM POL'Y 1039, 1040 (2017)

(arguing that "the United States needs to reimagine the basic principles of its telecommunications and information policy to fit an emerging society in which networking and intelligence are embedded into an increasing number of everyday things which constantly monitor and measure our lives. This emerging environment is an always-on, ubiquitous, integrated system comprised of the Internet of Things, Big Data, Artificial Intelligence/Intelligent Systems and the Intercloud, which act together as a single system, referred to here as the 'Embedded Infosphere' (EI).").

13. Jeffrey Voas, *Demystifying the Internet of Things*, 49 IEEE COMPUTER SOC. 40, 42 (2016), http://wmcyberintrusion.info/wp-content/uploads/2017/11/DemystifyingIoT2016.pdf.

14. Chunka Mui, *Thinking Big About the Industrial Internet of Things*, FORBES (Mar. 4, 2016), https://www.forbes.com/sites/chunkamui/2016/03/04/thinking-big-about-industrial-iot/#7f1e54066220.

15. T. C. Sottek, *The Internet of Things Is Going to Be a Legal Nightmare*, VERGE (Jan. 27, 2015), http://www.theverge.com/2015/1/27/7921025/will-self-regulation-be-a-huge-problem-for-privacy-in-the-internet-of.

16. *See Mobile Fact Sheet*, PEW RESEARCH CTR. (Feb. 5, 2018), http://www.pewinternet.org/fact-sheet/mobile/; Susan Engleson, *Smart Speaker Penetration Hits 20% of U.S. Wi-Fi Households*, COMSCORE (Apr. 11, 2018), https://www.comscore.com/Insights/Blog/Smart-Speaker-Penetration-Hits-20-Percent-of-US-Wi-Fi-Households.

17. Hazim Almuhimedi, Forian Schaub, Norman Sadeh, Idris Adjerid, Alessandro Acquisti, Joshua Gluck, Lorrie Cranor, & Yuvraj Agarwal, *Your Location Has Been Shared 5,398 Times! A Field Study on Mobile App Privacy Nudging* (2015), http://www.cs.cmu.edu/~halmuhim/MobileAppPrivacyNudging_CHI2015.pdf.

18. Manisha Priyadarshini, *Which Sensors Do I Have in My Smartphone? How Do They Work?* FOSSBYTES (Sept. 25, 2018), https://fossbytes.com/which-smartphone-sensors-how-work/.

19. *See, e.g.*, David Nield, *All the Ways Your Smarthphone and Its Apps Can Track You*, GIZMODO (Jan. 4, 2018), https://gizmodo.com/all-the-ways-your-smartphone-and-its-apps-can-track-you-1821213704; Cathy Cunningham, *Help Squad: Smartphone Apps Collect and Share Lots of User Data, but How and with Whom?*

CHI. TRIBUNE (June 6, 2018), https://www.chicagotribune.
com/suburbs/ct-ahp-column-help-squad-tl-0614-story.html.
Information may also be shared among app providers. *See* Sam
Schechner and Mark Secada, *You Give Apps Sensitive Personal
Information: Then They Tell Facebook.* WALL ST. J. (Feb. 22, 2019),
https://www.wsj.com/articles/you-give-apps-sensitive-
personal-information-then-they-tell-facebook-11550851636.

20. *See* Harriet Sherwood, *Alexa, Say Grace: C of E Launches Prayer
Skill for Smart-Home Devices,* GUARDIAN (May 24, 2018), https://
www.theguardian.com/world/2018/may/24/alexa-say-grace-
church-of-england-launches-skill-for-smart-home-devices.

21. *See* Ashley Carman, *Hands-On with Nike's Self-Lacing App-
Controlled Sneaker of the Future,* VERGE (Jan. 15, 2019), https://
www.theverge.com/2019/1/15/18167388/nike-self-lacing-
shoes-adapt-bb-smart-bluetooth-app-features-battery-life-price-
release-date.

22. Matt Day, *Google, Amazon Expanding Smart Home Device
Data Gathering,* INSURANCE J. (Feb. 12, 2019), https://www.
insurancejournal.com/news/national/2019/02/12/517456.htm.

23. *See, e.g.,* INSIDE THE SMART HOME (Richard Harper ed., 2006).

24. *Making Buildings Smarter, Starting with Goodwin Hall,* VIRG. TECH.
(Feb. 27, 2018), https://vtnews.vt.edu/articles/2018/02/eng-
rodrigosarlo.html.

25. *See* Jennifer Weingart, *These Smart Sewers Are Part of a Growing Trend
Connecting Infrastructure to the Internet,* NPR (May 8, 2018), https://
www.npr.org/2018/05/08/609493403/these-smart-sewers-are-
part-of-a-growing-trend-connecting-infrastructure-to-the-.

26. *See, e.g., Oceans 2.0: An Internet of Things for the Ocean,* OCEAN
NETWORKS CANADA (Feb. 9, 2018), http://www.oceannetworks.
ca/oceans-20-internet-things-ocean; Jon Gold, *IoT Roundup: Outer
Space, the Building Is Getting Smart, and Trucking,* NETWORK
WORLD (Feb. 22, 2019), https://www.networkworld.com/
article/3343059/iot-roundup-outer-space-the-building-is-getting-
smart-and-trucking.html.

27. PLATO, APOLOGY, PLATO IN TWELVE VOLUMES, V.1 (translated by
Harold North Fowler, 1966).

28. *See* Neena Kapur, *The Rise of IoT Botnets,* AM. SEC. PROJECT (Jan.
13, 2017), https://www.americansecurityproject.org/the-rise-
of-iot-botnets/ ("A bot is defined as a computer or internet-
connected device that is infected with malware and controlled by

a central command-and-control (C2) server. A botnet is the term used for all devices controlled by the C2 server, and they can be used to carry out large scale distributed denial of service (DDoS) attacks against websites, resulting in an overload of traffic on the website that renders it unusable.").

29. Garrett M. Graff, *How a Dorm Room Minecraft Scam Brought Down the Internet*, WIRED (Dec. 13, 2017), https://www.wired.com/story/mirai-botnet-minecraft-scam-brought-down-the-internet/; Constantinos Kolias et al., *DDoS in the IoT: Mirai and Other Botnets*, CARNEGIE MELLON UNIV. (2017), https://cs.gmu.edu/~astavrou/research/DDoS_Mirai.pdf.

30. Graff, *supra* note 29.

31. *See, e.g., IBM Study: Hidden Costs of Data Breaches Increase Expenses for Businesses*, IBM (July 11, 2018), https://newsroom.ibm.com/2018-07-10-IBM-Study-Hidden-Costs-of-Data-Breaches-Increase-Expenses-for-Businesses; *Microsoft Security Intelligence Report: Volume 24*, MICROSOFT (2019), https://clouddamcdnprodep.azureedge.net/gdc/gdc09FrGq/original.

32. *Are Your Company's IoT Devices Secure? Internet of Things Breaches Are Common, Costly for US Firms*, ALTMAN VILANDRIE & COMPANY (2017), www.altvil.com/wp-content/uploads/2017/06/AVCo.-IoT-Security-White-Paper-June-2017.pdf.

33. BRUCE SCHNEIER, CLICK HERE TO KILL EVERYBODY: SECURITY AND SURVIVAL IN A HYPER-CONNECTED WORLD 16 (2018).

34. The first such episode was Stuxnet. *See* Kim Zetter, *An Unprecedented Look at Stuxnet, the World's First Digital Weapon*, WIRED (Nov. 3, 2014), https://www.wired.com/2014/11/countdown-to-zero-day-stuxnet/.

35. Kim Zetter, *A Cyberattack Has Caused Confirmed Physical Damage for the Second Time Ever*, WIRED (Jan. 8, 2015), https://www.wired.com/2015/01/german-steel-mill-hack-destruction/.

36. *See How the Coffee-Machine Took Down a Factories Control Room*, REDDIT (2017), https://www.reddit.com/r/talesfromtechsupport/comments/6ovy0h/how_the_coffeemachine_took_down_a_factories/. An earlier version of this research was first published as Shackelford, *Smart Factories, Dumb Policy?, supra* note *.

37. *See* Selena Larson, *A Smart Fish Tank Left a Casino Vulnerable to Hackers*, CNN (July 19, 2017), https://money.cnn.com/2017/07/19/technology/fish-tank-hack-darktrace/index.html.

38. SCHNEIER, *supra* note 33, at 103.

39. Derek Hawkins, *The Cybersecurity 202: Pence Takes Tough Tone on Russia in First Cybersecurity Speech*, WASH. POST (Aug. 1, 2018), https://www.washingtonpost.com/news/powerpost/paloma/ the-cybersecurity-202/2018/08/01/the-cybersecurity-202- pence-takes-tough-tone-on-russia-in-first-cybersecurity-speech/ 5b608b381b326b0207955e81/?utm_term=.9555763d46d0.

40. This is an industry term for the legacy costs of rolling out new products without first improving security. *See There Are 3 Main Types of Technical Debt. Here's How to Manage Them,* HACKERNOON (Jan. 25, 2018), https://hackernoon.com/there- are-3-main-types-of-technical-debt-heres-how-to-manage-them- 4a3328a4c50c.

41. *See Cyber Timeline*, NATO REV. MAG., http://www.nato.int/ docu/review/2013/Cyber/timeline/EN/index.htm (last visited Jan. 16, 2014); JONATHAN ZITTRAIN, THE FUTURE OF THE INTERNET AND HOW TO STOP IT 36–37 (2008).

42. *See* Scott R. Peppet, *Regulating the Internet of Things: First Steps toward Managing Discrimination, Privacy, Security, and Consent*, 93 TEX. L. REV. 85, 94–95 (2014).

43. For more on how these debates are playing out across the frontiers of international relations, including the global commons, see SCOTT J. SHACKELFORD, GOVERNING NEW FRONTIERS IN THE INFORMATION AGE: TOWARD CYBER PEACE (forthcoming 2020).

44. *See* Chris Merriman, *87 Percent of Consumers Haven't Heard of the Internet of Things*, INQUIRER (Aug. 22, 2014), https://www.theinquirer.net/inquirer/news/2361672/ 87-percent-of-consumers-havent-heard-of-the-internet-of-things.

45. 2017 Unisys Security Index US, UNISYS, http://www.app5. unisys.com/library/cmsmail/USI/Unisys%20Security%20 Index_United%20States_Supplemental.pdf (e.g., most Americans support sharing their location with police via an emergency button on a smart watch but don't support police accessing data from a wearable fitness monitor at their discretion to determine your location).

46. 2018 Unisys Security Index: Global Report, UNISYS, https:// www.app5.unisys.com/library/cmsmail/USI2018/2018%20 Unisys%20Security%20Index%20Global%20Report.pdf.

47. *Id.*; 2017 Unisys Security Index US, *supra* note 45.

48. *Survey Finds Majority of Consumers Are Comfortable with IoT Products*, CEPro (Feb. 29, 2019), https://www.cepro.com/article/survey_consumers_comfortable_iot_products.

49. *The Trust Opportunity: Exploring Consumer Attitudes to the Internet of Things*, Internet Society (May 1, 2019), https://www.internetsociety.org/resources/doc/2019/trust-opportunity-exploring-consumer-attitudes-to-iot/.

50. *See* Charlie Osborne, *The Future of IoT? State-Sponsored Attacks, Say Security Professionals*, ZDNet (Aug. 13, 2018), https://www.zdnet.com/article/the-future-of-iot-state-sponsored-attacks-say-security-professionals/; *see also* chapter 7.

51. Lesli White, *50 King Quotes*, BeliefNet, https://www.beliefnet.com/love-family/holidays/martin-luther-king-jr-day/50-king-quotes.aspx (last visited Mar. 5, 2019).

Chapter 1

* This chapter is based on years of distilled research in the field of cybersecurity and Internet governance. As such, earlier versions of selections from this chapter have previously been published in reverse chronological order as follows: Scott J. Shackelford, Managing Cyber Attacks in International Law, Business, and Relations: In Search of Cyber Peace (2014); Scott J. Shackelford, *Toward Cyberpeace: Managing Cyber Attacks through Polycentric Governance*, 62 Am. U. L. Rev. 1273 (2013). Readers are encouraged to consult these sources for additional discussion of the covered topics.

1. *Internet Time: Will the 'Beat' Go On?* CNN (Feb. 26, 1999), http://www.cnn.com/TECH/computing/9902/26/t_t/internet.time/.

2. *What Is the Origin of "Cyber"?*, Oxford Dictionaries, https://blog.oxforddictionaries.com/2015/03/05/cyborgs-cyberspace-csi-cyber/ (last visited Mar. 5, 2019).

3. *Id.*

4. Stephen J. Lukasik, *Protecting the Global Information Commons*, 24 Telecomm. Pol'y 519, 525 (2000).

5. Milton Mueller, *Internet Fragmentation Exists, but Not in the Way That You Think*, Council on Foreign Rel. (June 12, 2017), https://www.cfr.org/blog/internet-fragmentation-exists-not-way-you-think.

6. F. J. Baker, *Core Protocols in the Internet Protocol Suite*, IETF (2009), https://tools.ietf.org/id/draft-baker-ietf-core-04.html.

7. *See* Jesus Diaz, *Google's New AI Puts Us One Step Closer to Star Trek's Universal Translator*, TOM'S GUIDE (May 17, 2019), https://www.tomsguide.com/us/google-translatotron-universal-translation,news-30104.html.

8. *Architecture of the World Wide Web, Volume One* (2004), https://www.w3.org/TR/webarch/.

9. HTTPS is an encrypted version of HTTP. Consumers should be on the lookout for https-enabled sites, especially when entering their financial information, as such sites better protect their data, making it less likely that they will become a victim of cybercrime.

10. BRUCE SCHNEIER, CLICK HERE TO KILL EVERYBODY: SECURITY AND SURVIVAL IN A HYPER-CONNECTED WORLD 22 (2018).

11. WILLIAM GIBSON, NEUROMANCER (1984).

12. For an early look at mapping cyberspace, see MARTIN DODGE & ROB KITCHIN, ATLAS OF CYBERSPACE (2001).

13. *See, e.g.*, BISHOP FOX CYBERSECURITY STYLE GUIDE (2018) ("Industry professionals don't use this prefix, but it's helpful when informing the public, as in the title of this document. For many users, 'cyber' on its own invokes cybersex, not hacking.").

14. WHITE HOUSE, NATIONAL STRATEGY TO SECURE CYBERSPACE vii (2003), https://www.us-cert.gov/sites/default/files/publications/cyberspace_strategy.pdf.

15. Noah Shachtman, *26 Years after Gibson, Pentagon Defines "Cyberspace,"* WIRED (May 23, 2008), https://www.wired.com/2008/05/pentagon-define/.

16. *Id.*

17. *See, e.g.*, DAVID BELL, AN INTRODUCTION TO CYBERCULTURES 6–7 (2001).

18. Damir Rajnovic, *Cyberspace—What Is It?*, CISCO (July 26, 2012), https://blogs.cisco.com/security/cyberspace-what-is-it.

19. *See, e.g.*, *Army Cyber*, U.S. ARMY CYBER COMMAND, https://www.arcyber.army.mil/ (last visited May 17, 2019); Robert A. Miller & Daniel T. Kuehl, *Cyberspace and the "First Battle" in 21st-Century War*, 68 DEF. HORIZONS 1, 1–3 (2009), http://www.au.af.mil/au/awc/awcgate/ndu/defhoriz_68.pdf.

20. *Estonian President Addresses National Defense University Students*, NAT'L DEF. U. (Aug. 29, 2013), https://www.ndu.edu/News/Press-Releases/Article/572587/estonian-president-addresses-national-defense-university-students/.

21. *See, e.g.*, MICHAEL E. WHITMAN & HERBERT J. MATTORD, PRINCIPLES OF INFORMATION SECURITY 9–15 (2011); D. Stepanova,

S. E. Parkin, & A. van Moorsel, *Computing Science: A Knowledge Base for Justified Information Security Decision-Making* (Newcastle Univ., Working Paper No. CS-TR-1137, 2009).

22. *See, e.g.*, Bishop Fox Cybersecurity Style Guide (2018) (defining "cybersecurity" as "defense contractors and government officials use this term or 'infosec.' Industry professionals do not prefer this term, but it is used for clarity with the public, as in the title of this document. We prefer the term information security." It then defines "information security" as, "This industry is also called infosec, cybersecurity, and internet security.").

23. This group is the International Organization for Standardization (ISO)/International Electrotechnical Commission (IEC) Joint Technical Committee 1 Subcommittee 27. *See* ISO/IEC JTC1/ SC27, https://www.iso.org/committee/45306.html.

24. *See* Gerry Smith, *State Department Official Accuses Russia and China of Seeking Greater Internet Control*, Huff. Post (Sept. 28, 2011), http://www.huffingtonpost.com/2011/09/27/russia-china-internet-control_n_984223.html.

25. For example, the US government has published and used National Institute of Standards and Technology (NIST) Special Publication 800-53, entitled Security and Privacy Controls for Information Systems and Organizations, as well as the Framework for Improving Critical Infrastructure Cybersecurity (also developed by NIST in coordination with industry, civil society, and other government stakeholders). In 2016 and 2019, the European Parliament, Council, and Commission passed the Directive on security of network and information systems as well as the Cybersecurity Act.

26. Nicholas Negroponte, Being Digital (1995), at 131–33; *The Best Books on the Internet—Recommended by David Soskin*, Five Books, https://fivebooks.com/best-books/david-soskin-internet/ (last visited June 6, 2019).

27. *Secretary-General's High-Level Panel on Digital Cooperation*, United Nations, https://www.un.org/en/digital-cooperation-panel/ (last visited May 17, 2019).

28. *Developments in the Field of Information and Telecommunications in the Context of International Security*, U.N. Doc. A/C.1/73/L.27/ Rev.1 (Oct. 29, 2018), https://undocs.org/A/C.1/73/L.27/Rev.1; *Advancing Responsible State Behaviour in Cyberspace in the Context of International Security*, U.N. Doc. A/C.1/73/L.37 (Oct. 18, 2018), https://undocs.org/A/C.1/73/L.37.

29. *How a Simple "Hello" Became the First Message Sent via the Internet*, PBS (Feb. 9, 2015), https://www.pbs.org/newshour/science/internet-got-started-simple-hello.

30. *Id.*

31. David Clark, *Characterizing Cyberspace: Past, Present, and Future*, MIT CSAIL (2010), https://ecir.mit.edu/sites/default/files/documents/%5BClark%5D%20Characterizing%20Cyberspace-%20Past%2C%20Present%20and%20Future.pdf (characterizing cyberspace using a model with four layers: the top layer—people, the information layer, the logical layer, and the physical layer).

32. *Brief History of the Internet*, Internet Soc'y, https://www.internetsociety.org/internet/history-internet/brief-history-internet/.

33. *Individuals Using the Internet (% of Population)*, World Bank, https://data.worldbank.org/indicator/it.net.user.zs?end=2017&start=1960&view=chart (last visited May 18, 2019).

34. Simon Kemp, *Digital 2019: Global Internet Use Accelerates*, We Are Social (Jan. 30, 2019), https://wearesocial.com/blog/2019/01/digital-2019-global-internet-use-accelerates.

35. *Statistics*, ITU, https://www.itu.int/en/ITU-D/Statistics/Pages/stat/default.aspx (showing increase in connectivity from 2001–18 alongside increases in mobile phone and broadband subscriptions).

36. Nina Czernich, Oliver Falck, Tobias Kretschmer, & Ludger Woessmann, *Broadband Infrastructure and Economic Growth* (2009), https://www.isto.bwl.uni-muenchen.de/download/forschung/ictcm/czernich_et_al.pdf.

37. Four Years of Broadband Growth, Off. of Sci. & Tech. Pol'y & Nat'l Econ. Council (June 2013), https://obamawhitehouse.archives.gov/sites/default/files/broadband_report_final.pdf.

38. Gil Press, *A Very Short History of Big Data*, Forbes (May 9, 2013), https://www.forbes.com/sites/gilpress/2013/05/09/a-very-short-history-of-big-data/#19b99acb65a1.

39. *Data Never Sleeps 6.0*, DOMO, https://www.domo.com/learn/data-never-sleeps-6.

40. *Id.*

41. Bernard Marr, *Big Data: 20 Mind-Boggling Facts Everyone Must Read*, Forbes (Sept. 30, 2015), https://www.forbes.com/sites/bernardmarr/2015/09/30/big-data-20-mind-boggling-facts-everyone-must-read/#5234b4cd17b1.

42. Rita Sharma, *Top 15 Sensor Types Being Used in IoT*, FINOIT, https://www.finoit.com/blog/top-15-sensor-types-used-iot/ (last visited Dec. 12, 2019).

43. JONATHAN ZITTRAIN, THE FUTURE OF THE INTERNET AND HOW TO STOP IT 3 (2008) (discussing the "rise and stall" of the generative Internet).

44. Chris Anderson & Michael Wolff, *The Web Is Dead: Long Live the Internet*, WIRED (Aug. 17, 2010), https://www.wired.com/2010/08/ff-webrip/.

45. *30 Most Visited Websites on the Internet in 2018*, MEDIUM (Aug. 22, 2018), https://medium.com/@hotinsocialmedia/30-most-visited-websites-on-the-internet-in-2018-523be3aca0df.

46. Anderson & Wolff, *supra* note 44.

47. *Id.*

48. The U.N. Secretary-General's High-Level Panel on Digital Cooperation noted that "access is a necessary, but insufficient, step forward. To capture the power of digital technologies we need to cooperate on the broader ecosystems that enable digital technologies to be used in an inclusive manner." UNITED NATIONS, THE AGE OF DIGITAL INTERDEPENDENCE 4 (2019), https://digitalcooperation.org/wp-content/uploads/2019/06/DigitalCooperation-report-for-web.pdf.

49. For instance, consider the Internet penetration rate for these nations in 2017: Afghanistan, 11%; Bahrain, 96%; Bangladesh, 18%; Burundi, 6%; Canada, 93%; Central African Republic, 4%; Chad, 6%; Denmark, 97%; Eritrea, 1%; Haiti, 12%; Iceland, 98%; Liberia, 8%; Japan, 91%; Mongolia, 24%; Nepal, 21%; Netherlands, 93%; New Zealand, 91%; Norway, 97%; Pakistan, 16%; Papua New Guinea, 11%; Qatar, 96%; Sierra Leone, 13%; Switzerland, 94%; Turkmenistan, 21%; and Yemen, 27%. Press Release, More and More Governments Now Benchmark Broadband Status in Their National Plans, Says New Global Report, ITU (Sept. 11, 2018), https://www.itu.int/en/mediacentre/Pages/2018-PR25.aspx (noting that "the challenge of connecting people living in rural and remote areas to the Internet persists in many countries).

50. *Individuals Using the Internet (% of Population)*, WORLD BANK, https://data.worldbank.org/indicator/it.net.user.zs?end=2017&name_desc=false&start=1960&view=chart.

51. Czernich, Falck, Kretschmer, & Woessmann, *supra* note 36.

52. Press Release, *supra* note 49.

53. *See, e.g.*, Chris Brook, *What Is Cyber Hygiene? A Definition of Cyber Hygiene, Benefits, Best Practices, and More*, DIGITAL GUARDIAN (Dec. 5, 2018), https://digitalguardian.com/blog/what-cyber-hygiene-definition-cyber-hygiene-benefits-best-practices-and-more.

54. *See* Marthie Grobler & Joey Jansen van Vuuren, *Broadband Broadens Scope for Cyber Crime in Africa, in* INFORMATION SECURITY SOUTH AFRICA CONFERENCE PROC. (Hein S. Venter et al. eds., 2010), http://icsa.cs.up.ac.za/issa/2010/Proceedings/Full/28_Paper.pdf; *Cybercriminals in Developing Nations Targeted*, BBC NEWS (July 20, 2012), http://www.bbc.co.uk/news/technology-18930953 (pointing out that enhanced interconnectivity often means increased criminal activity); Tamisin Ford, *Ivory Coast Cracks Down on Cyber Crime*, BBC (Jan. 16, 2014), http://www.bbc.co.uk/news/business-25735305 ("According to the Ivorian government, it received more complaints about cyber criminality in the first half of 2013 than any other country on the continent, making it Africa's unlikely capital of "brouteurs"—Ivorian slang for cyber criminals.").

55. *Internet Access Is "a Fundamental Right,"* BBC NEWS (Mar. 8, 2010), http://news.bbc.co.uk/2/hi/8548190.stm.

56. *See* Vinton G. Cerf, Op-Ed, *Internet Access Is Not a Human Right*, N.Y. TIMES, Jan. 5, 2012, at A25 (arguing that the Internet enables people to seek their human rights, but access to the Internet in and of itself is not a human right). For a discussion of the link between spreading Internet access, human rights, and the promotion of positive cyber peace, see Henning Wegener, *Government Internet Censorship: Cyber Repression, in* THE QUEST FOR CYBER PEACE 43, 51 n.85 (Int'l Telecomm. Union & Permanent Monitoring Panel on Info. Sec. eds., 2011) (citing Recommendations Concerning the Promotion and Use of Multilingualism and Universal Access to Cyberspace, UNESCO ¶ 6 (Oct. 15, 2003), http://portal.unesco.org/ci/en/ev.php-URL_ID=13475&URL_DO=DO_TOPIC&URL_SECTION=201.html (arguing for "universal access to the Internet as an instrument for promoting the realization of the human rights")); Geneva Declaration of Principles, World Summit on the Information Society, Dec. 12, 2003, ¶ 4, www.itu.int/dms_pub/itu-s/md/03/wsis/doc/S03-WSIS-DOC-0004!!PDF-E.pdf (reaffirming "that everyone has the right to freedom of opinion and expression").

57. Press Release, *supra* note 49.

58. Press Release, USDA Launches New Program to Create High Speed Internet e-Connectivity in Rural America, US Dep't of Agriculture (Dec. 13, 2018), https://www.usda.gov/media/press-releases/2018/12/13/usda-launches-new-program-create-high-speed-internet-e-connectivity.

59. Laura Lorenzetti, *Microsoft Makes Its First Grants to Promote Global Internet Access*, Fortune (May 24, 2016), http://fortune.com/2016/05/24/microsoft-makes-its-first-grants-to-promote-global-internet-access/ (announcing grants of $70,000 to $150,000 to twelve organizations based across five continents in eleven countries); *Dynamic Spectrum and TV White Spaces*, Microsoft, https://www.microsoft.com/en-us/research/project/dynamic-spectrum-and-tv-white-spaces/; *Airband Initiative*, Microsoft, https://www.microsoft.com/en-us/airband.

60. Press Release, *supra* note 58.

61. Richard Waters & Patti Waldmeir, *Yahoo Loses Nazi Memorabilia Case*, Fin. Times (Jan. 12, 2006), https://www.ft.com/content/81127f12-83cb-11da-9017-0000779e2340.

62. *Yahoo! Loses Nazi Auction Case*, CNN (Nov. 20, 2000), http://www.cnn.com/2000/TECH/computing/11/20/france.yahoo.02/.

63. Charles Arthur, *Egypt Cuts Off Internet Access*, Guardian (Jan. 28, 2011), https://www.theguardian.com/technology/2011/jan/28/egypt-cuts-off-internet-access.

64. Elizabeth C. Economy, *The Great Firewall of China: Xi Jinping's Internet Shutdown*, Guardian (June 29, 2018), https://www.theguardian.com/news/2018/jun/29/the-great-firewall-of-china-xi-jinpings-internet-shutdown; Scott J. Shackelford, *Welcome to the 'Managed' Internet: Unpacking Cyber-Sovereignty in China's New Cybersecurity Law*, Asia & Pacific Soc'y Pol'y F. (June 15, 2017), https://www.policyforum.net/welcome-managed-internet/.

65. Kate Fazzini, *A New Russian Law Will Further Separate the Country from the Global Internet*, CNBC (Apr. 18, 2019), https://www.cnbc.com/2019/04/18/russia-stable-runet-law-will-further-separate-country-from-internet.html.

66. *See* chapters 1 and 2 in Shackelford, Managing Cyber Attacks in International Law, Business, and Relations, *supra* note *. These organizations include: the Internet Engineering Task Force

(IETF), the Internet Assigned Numbers Authority (IANA), and the Internet Corporation for Assigned Names and Numbers (ICANN). For a history of the IETF and other early Internet governance issues, see David G. Post, In Search of Jefferson's Moose: Notes on the State of Cyberspace (2009).

67. *Stewardship of IANA Functions Transitions to Global Internet Community as Contract with U.S. Government Ends*, ICANN (Oct. 1, 2016), https://www.icann.org/news/announcement-2016-10-01-en. As a graduate student in the 1970s, Jon Postel was enlisted as the caretaker of the master copy of the "hosts.txt" file, which listed ARPANET's IP addresses and corresponding domain names. *See* Richard Pearson, *Jon Postel, Pioneer of Internet Technology, Dies at 55*, Wash. Post (Oct. 19, 1998), https://www.washingtonpost.com/archive/local/1998/10/19/jon-postel-pioneer-of-internet-technology-dies-at-55/96b27812-6b71-4a04-abba-d5c49a2664df/?utm_term=.b883b2d1fee1; *Sci/Tech 'God of the Internet' Is Dead*, BBC News (Oct. 19, 1998), http://news.bbc.co.uk/2/hi/science/nature/196487.stm.

68. *See, e.g.*, Richard Bennett, *The Gathering Storm: WCIT and the Global Regulation of the Internet*, Info. Tech. & Innovation Found. (2012), http://www2.itif.org/2012-gathering-storm-wcit-regulations.pdf; *A Digital Cold War?*, Economist (Dec. 14, 2014), https://www.economist.com/babbage/2012/12/14/a-digital-cold-war; Gus Rossi, *ITU's Plenipot: What Happened*, Pub. Knowledge (Nov. 18, 2018), https://www.publicknowledge.org/news-blog/blogs/itus-plenipot-what-happened/.

69. *See, e.g.*, Richard A. Clarke, Cyber War: The Next Threat to National Security and What to Do about It (2010).

70. *See, e.g.*, Taylor Armerding, *Cybercrime: Much More Organized*, CSO Online (June 23, 2015), https://www.csoonline.com/article/2938529/cybercrime-much-more-organized.html.

71. For example, whereas a 2007 conflict between Russia and Estonia was confined to cyberspace, a 2008 conflict between Russia and Georgia involved both cyber and conventional battles (though whether these cyber conflicts should be understood as "war" is debatable). *See, e.g.*, Joshua Davis, *Hackers Take Down the Most Wired Country in Europe*, Wired (Aug. 21, 2007), https://www.wired.com/2007/08/ff-estonia/; Josh Markoff, *Georgia Takes a Beating in the Cyberwar with Russia*, N.Y. Times (Aug. 11, 2008), https://bits.blogs.nytimes.com/2008/08/11/georgia-takes-a-beating-in-the-cyberwar-with-russia/.

72. *Tallinn Manual 2.0*, NATO Cooperative Cyber Def. Ctr. of Excellence, https://ccdcoe.org/research/tallinn-manual/; Scott J. Shackelford, *The Law of Cyber Peace*, 18 Chi. J. Int'l L. 1, 2 (2017).

73. *See, e.g.*, James Andrew Lewis, *How Much Have the Chinese Actually Taken?* Ctr. for Strategic & Int'l Stud. (Mar. 22, 2018), https://www.csis.org/analysis/how-much-have-chinese-actually-taken (estimating that US economic loss from Chinese cyber espionage may reach $600 billion).

74. *See* Teri Robinson, *U.S., China Agree to Cybersecurity Code of Conduct*, SC Mag. (June 26, 2015), https://perma.cc/K9GQ-FZPT.

75. M. J. Warren, *Terrorism and the Internet, in* Cyber Warfare and Cyber Terrorism 42, 42 (Leah Janczewski ed., 2008) (citing Paul Wilkinson, Political Terrorism (1976)).

76. *Id.* at 49; *see also* Computer Sci. & Telecomm. Bd., Nat'l Res. Council, Info. Tech. for Counterterrorism: Immediate Actions and Future Possibilities 1–2 (John L. Hennessy et al. eds., 2003) [hereinafter Information Technology for Counterterrorism] (defining cyber terrorism).

77. Daniel R. Coats, *Statement for the Record: Worldwide Threat Assessment of the US Intelligence Community*, at 6 (Feb. 13, 2018), https://www.dni.gov/files/documents/Newsroom/Testimonies/2018-ATA---Unclassified-SSCI.pdf ("Terrorist groups will continue to use the Internet to organize, recruit, spread propaganda, raise funds, collect intelligence, inspire action by followers, and coordinate operations. Given their current capabilities, cyber operations by terrorist groups [most] likely would result in personally identifiable information (PII) disclosures, website defacements, and denial-of-service [i.e., disruptive] attacks against poorly protected networks.").

78. Schneier, *supra* note 10, at 54 (noting the challenge of attribution, the fact that it "takes time," often has to "rely on classified evidence" making it difficult to offer public proof, and that the know-how is widely diffused to non-state actors).

79. Lesley Stahl, *The Growing Partnership between Russia's Government and Cybercriminals*, 60 Minutes (Apr. 21, 2019), https://www.cbsnews.com/news/evgeniy-mikhailovich-bogachev-the-growing-partnership-between-russia-government-and-cybercriminals-60-minutes/.

Chapter 2

* This chapter is based on years of distilled research in the field of IoT governance. As such, earlier versions of selections from this chapter have previously been published in reverse chronological order as follows: Scott J. Shackelford, *Smart Factories, Dumb Policy? Managing Cybersecurity and Data Privacy Risks in the Industrial Internet of Things*, 21 MINN. OF L., SCI., & TECH. 1 (2019); Scott J. Shackelford, *Securing the Internet of Healthcare*, 19 MINN. OF L., SCI., & TECH. 405 (2018); Scott J. Shackelford, *When Toasters Attack: Enhancing the 'Security of Things' through Polycentric Governance*, 2017 U. ILL. L. REV. 415 (2017); Scott J. Shackelford, *Toward Cyberpeace: Managing Cyber Attacks through Polycentric Governance*, 62 AM. U. L. REV. 1273 (2013). Readers are encouraged to consult these sources for additional discussion of the covered topics, particularly SCOTT J. SHACKELFORD, MANAGING CYBER ATTACKS IN INTERNATIONAL LAW, BUSINESS, AND RELATIONS: IN SEARCH OF CYBER PEACE (2014).

1. *Resistance Is Futile*, NPR: THROUGHLINE (Apr. 25, 2019), https://www.npr.org/2019/04/23/716521520/resistance-is-futile (describing the disruptive innovation of tractors).
2. *See* CHARLES POSTEL, THE POPULIST VISION (2009).
3. *See* BRUCE SCHNEIER, CLICK HERE TO KILL EVERYBODY: SECURITY AND SURVIVAL IN A HYPER-CONNECTED WORLD 6 (2018).
4. Table 2.1 is reproduced from Shackelford et al., *When Toasters Attack, supra* note *.
5. Michael Raynor, *Strategy and the Internet of Things*, TM FORUM (Keynote Address, June 2, 2015).
6. *Id.*
7. *Id.*
8. *See* Casey Newton, *Tim Cook: Silicon Valley's Most Successful Companies Are Selling You Out*, VERGE (June 2, 2015), http://www.theverge.com/2015/6/2/8714345/tim-cook-epic-award-privacy-security.
9. Raynor, *supra* note 5.
10. *See, e.g.,* SAMUEL GEORGE & FELIPE BUITRAGO, THE NO COLLAR ECONOMY: EXPONENTIAL CHANGE AND THE DIGITAL REVOLUTION, BERTELSMANN FOUNDATION (2018).
11. Dave Smith, *Google Chairman: "The Internet Will Disappear,"* BUS. INSIDER (Jan. 25, 2015), https://www.businessinsider.com/google-chief-eric-schmidt-the-internet-will-disappear-2015-1.

12. *See* Chris Greer, *The Intersection of IoT and CPS*, NIST (June 19, 2015), http://www.picasso-project.eu/wp-content/uploads/2017/06/2017-06-19-9h15_Keynote_Greer.pdf.

13. Kevin Ashton, *That 'Internet of Things' Thing*, RFID J. (June 22, 2009), www.rfidjournal.com/articles/view?4986.

14. *Id.*

15. Gil Press, *A Very Short History of the Internet of Things*, Forbes (June 18, 2014), http://www.forbes.com/sites/gilpress/2014/06/18/a-very-short-history-of-the-internet-of-things/. ARPANET first existed as a closed four-node network, connecting computers at the University of California, Los Angeles; Stanford University; the University of California, Santa Barbara; and the University of Utah. Eventually, it linked with other networks, adopted a common set of design protocols called Transmission Control Protocol and the Internet Protocol (TCP/IP) that allowed diverse networks to talk to one another—giving rise to many security implications—and became *the* Internet. Andrew D. Murray, The Regulation of Cyberspace: Control in the Online Environment 63 (2006); *see also* chapter 1.

16. Jackie Fenn & Hung LeHong, *Hype Cycle for Emerging Technologies*, Gartner (July 28, 2011), https://www.gartner.com/doc/1754719/hype-cycle-emerging-technologies-2011.

17. *NSTAC Report to the President on the Internet of Things*, Nat'l Sec. Telecomm. Advisory Comm., at 4. (Nov. 19, 2014), https://www.dhs.gov/sites/default/files/publications/NSTAC%20Report%20to%20the%20President%20on%20the%20Internet%20of%20Things%20Nov%202014%20%28updat%20%20%20.pdf.

18. *See The Internet of Things: Groundbreaking Tech with Security Risks*, WeLiveSec. (Oct. 29, 2015), http://www.welivesecurity.com/2015/10/29/internet-things-groundbreaking-tech-security-risks/ ("Researchers at Carnegie Mellon University first came up with an internet-connected Coke vending machine in 1982.").

19. Jim Chase, *The Evolution of the Internet of Things*, TX. Instruments (Sept. 2013), www.ti.com/lit/ml/swrb028/swrb028.pdf; *see also* Jeffrey Voas, *Demystifying the Internet of Things*, NIST (2016), http://wmcyberintrusion.info/wp-content/uploads/2017/11/DemystifyingIoT2016.pdf (discussing trends in IoT governance).

20. Jacob Morgan, *A Simple Explanation of 'The Internet of Things,'* Forbes (May 13, 2014), http://www.forbes.com/sites/

jacobmorgan/2014/05/13/simple-explanation-internet-things-that-anyone-can-understand/.

21. *Id.* Continuing digital divides persist between developed and developing nations with regards to Internet connectivity, meaning that the IoT has not evolved at the same rate globally. *See, e.g.*, David Bolton, *Developing Countries Will Drive the Growth of the Internet of Things*, APPLAUSE (Dec. 2, 2015), http:// arc.applause.com/2015/12/02/internet-of-things-growth-developing-countries/ ("Developing countries have not really had the opportunity to interact or engage with the IoT thus far"). See also chapter 1 for more on issues and efforts related to global broadband access.

22. *See* Morgan, *supra* note 20.

23. *Id.*

24. *See, e.g.*, David Oro, *Gartner Identifies the Top 10 Internet of Things Technologies for 2017 and 2018*, IoTCENTRAL (Mar. 1, 2016), https://www.iotcentral.io/blog/gartner-identifies-the-top-10-internet-of-things-technologies-for (identifying IoT analytics, networks, and processes among the most in-demand technologies); *see also Gartner Identifies Top 10 Strategic IoT Technologies and Trends*, GARTNER (Nov. 7, 2018), https:// www.gartner.com/en/newsroom/press-releases/2018-11-07-gartner-identifies-top-10-strategic-iot-technologies-and-trends (identifying artificial intelligence and new wireless networking technologies among the ten trends).

25. SCHNEIER, *supra* note 3, at 7.

26. Benedikt Abendroth, Aaron Kleiner, & Paul Nicholas, *Cybersecurity Policy for the Internet of Things*, MICROSOFT (2017).

27. NSTAC report, *supra* note 17, at 3 (noting that IoT is distinct from previous advancements with "intelligent" devices because of "its explosive proliferation in three dimensions: first, the scale of deployment eclipses anything ever seen before in terms of pace of adoption . . .; second, the scope of deployment ranges from the most complex system to the simplest device, from manufacturing facilities and control centers to consumers; and third, the demographic span of these deployments is spreading rapidly, leaving no aspect of infrastructure untouched by this phenomenon").

28. Roberto Minerva, Abyi Biru, & Domenico Rotondi, *Toward a Definition of the Internet of Things (IoT)*, IEEE at 11 (May 27, 2015),

https://iot.ieee.org/images/files/pdf/IEEE_IoT_Towards_
Definition_Internet_of_Things_Revision1_27MAY15.pdf.

29. Calum McClelland, *IoT Explained—How Does an IoT System Actually
Work?*, Medium (Nov. 20, 2017), https://medium.com/iotforall/
iot-explained-how-does-an-iot-system-actually-work-e90e2c435fe7.

30. *Id.*

31. Steve Ranger, *What Is the IoT? Everything You Need to Know
about the Internet of Things Right Now*, ZDNet (Aug. 21, 2018),
https://www.zdnet.com/article/what-is-the-internet-of-things-
everything-you-need-to-know-about-the-iot-right-now/.

32. *See, e.g.*, Dave Evans, *The Internet of Things: How the Next
Evolution of the Internet Is Changing Everything* (Cisco Whitepaper,
Apr. 2011).

33. *See* Minerva, Biru, & Rotondi, *supra* note 28, at 73 (distinguishing
between "small environment" and "large environment"
scenarios).

34. *See, e.g.*, Mary Wollerton, *12 Smart Thermostats to Make Your
Home the Right Temperature*, CNET (May 15, 2019), https://
www.cnet.com/news/smart-thermostat-roundup/; Mary-
Kerstin Hassiotis, *Beyond Next: 9 Ways IoT Is Reshaping the HVAC
Industry* (Mar. 31, 2016), https://news.ewmfg.com/blog/
beyond-nest-9-ways-iot-is-reshaping-the-hvac-industry.

35. *See, e.g.*, *Smart Cities*, Sensus, https://sensus.com/internet-of-
things/smart-cities/.

36. *Samsung Delivers Vision for Open and Intelligent IoT Experiences
to Simplify Everyday Life*, Samsung (Jan. 8, 2018), https://news.
samsung.com/uk/samsung-delivers-vision-for-open-and-
intelligent-iot-experiences-to-simplify-everyday-life. This caused
some consternation in Washington and elsewhere, given ongoing
concerns about smart-TV manufacturers "tracking consumers'
viewing behavior without their knowledge." Sapna Maheshwari,
Two Senators Call for Investigation of Smart TV Industry, N.Y. Times
(July 12, 2018), https://www.nytimes.com/2018/07/12/business/
media/senators-smart-tv-investigation.html. Concerns seemed
warranted when the firm announced multiple SmartThings Hub
security flaws and patches in 2018. *See* Mariaella Moon, *Samsung
Patches Multiple SmartThings Hub Security Flaws*, Engadget (July
28, 2018), https://tinyurl.com/yxk33xhu.

37. Smith, *supra* note 11 (quoting Google's chairman and ex-CEO
Eric Schmidt during a panel at the World Economic Forum).

38. Galen Hunt, *Introducing Microsoft Azure Sphere: Secure and Power the Intelligent Edge*, Microsoft (Apr. 16, 2018), https://azure. microsoft.com/en-us/blog/introducing-microsoft-azure-sphere-secure-and-power-the-intelligent-edge/.

39. Alfonso Velosa, Nathan Nuttall, W. Roy Schulte, & Benoit Lheureux, *Hype Cycle for the Internet of Things, 2018*, Gartner (2018); *Garter Hype Cycle*, Gartner, https://www.gartner.com/ en/research/methodologies/gartner-hype-cycle.

40. In 2011, Cisco forecasted that more than 50 billion devices would be connected to the Internet by 2020; that figure has been widely cited but is considered outdated today. Evans, *supra* note 32.

41. *Gartner Says 8.4 Billion Connected "Things" Will Be in Use in 2017, Up 31 Percent from 2016*, Gartner (Feb. 7, 2017), https://www. gartner.com/en/newsroom/press-releases/2017-02-07-gartner-says-8-billion-connected-things-will-be-in-use-in-2017-up-31-percent-from-2016; *Population, Total*, World Bank, https://data. worldbank.org/indicator/SP.POP.TOTL (indicating the total world population was about 7.5 billion in 2017).

42. Knud Lasse Lueth, *State of the IoT 2018: Number of IoT Devices Now at 7B—Market Accelerating*, IoT Analytics (Aug. 8, 2018), https://iot-analytics.com/state-of-the-iot-update-q1-q2-2018-number-of-iot-devices-now-7b/.

43. Oro, *supra* note 24.

44. *Internet of Things Forecast*, Ericsson, https://www.ericsson.com/ en/mobility-report/internet-of-things-forecast.

45. Schneier, *supra* note 3, at 5.

46. *Internet of Things (IoT) Analytics Market: Global Forecast to 2020*, MarketsandMarkets (2015) (highlighting IoT analytics market size in 2015 and projected compound annual growth rate (CAGR) to 2020 as: North America—2,375.7 and 23.23%; Europe—859.5 and 25.33%; and APAC—836.9 and 37.28%); *IoT Analytics Market 2019 Global Recent Trends, Competitive Landscape, Size, Segments, Emerging Technology, and Industry Growth by Forecast to 2022*, RFDTV (Apr. 11, 2019), https://www.rfdtv.com/ story/40291846/iot-analytics-market-2019-global-recent-trends-competitive-landscape-size-segments-emerging-technologies-and-industry-growth-by-forecast-to-2022 (reporting that the global IoT Analytics market report assessed that North America has the biggest market share and that the Asia Pacific region is expected to grow rapidly relative to others).

47. Gartner, *supra* note 41.

48. See chapter 1 for a discussion of Internet access issues and efforts.

49. Oro, *supra* note 24 ("The shift from centralized and cloud to edge architectures is well under way in the IoT space. However, this is not the end point because the neat set of layers associated with edge architecture will evolve to a more unstructured architecture comprising of a wide range of 'things' and services connected in a dynamic mesh. These mesh architectures will enable more flexible, intelligent and responsive IoT systems . . . [and] additional complexities.").

50. Lueth, *supra* note 42; NSTAC report, *supra* note 17.

51. David Reinsel, John Gantz, & John Rydning, *The Digitization of the World: From Edge to Core*, IDC, at 13 (Nov. 2018), https://www.seagate.com/files/www-content/our-story/trends/files/idc-seagate-dataage-whitepaper.pdf.

52. Louis Columbus, *The State of IoT Intelligence, 2018*, FORBES (Nov. 4, 2018), https://www.forbes.com/sites/louiscolumbus/2018/11/04/the-state-of-iot-intelligence-2018/#25dfb304db00 (reporting on the Dresner Advisory Services 2018 IoT Intelligence Market Study).

53. Gartner, *supra* note 41; Louis Columbus, *2018 Roundup of Internet of Things Forecasts and Market Estimates*, FORBES (Dec. 13, 2018), https://www.forbes.com/sites/louiscolumbus/2018/12/13/2018-roundup-of-internet-of-things-forecasts-and-market-estimates/#64c3a0a7d838.

54. *Internet of Things (IoT) Analytics Market: Global Forecast to 2020, supra* note 46; *IDC Forecasts Worldwide Technology Spending on the Internet of Things to Reach $1.2 Trillion in 2022*, IDC (June 18, 2018), https://www.idc.com/getdoc.jsp?containerId=prUS43994118 (highlighting that the two largest industries for IoT spending are manufacturing and transportation); Columbus, *supra* note 53.

55. Kasey Panetta, *Technologies Underpin the Hype Cycle for the Internet of Things*, GARTNER (Nov. 2, 2016), https://www.gartner.com/smarterwithgartner/7-technologies-underpin-the-hype-cycle-for-the-internet-of-things-2016/?cm_mmc=social-_-rm-_-gart-_-swg; Gartner, *supra* note 41.

56. Ezra Gottheil & Daniel Callahan, *2019 Devices & Internet of Things Predictions*, TECH. BUS. RES., INC. (Nov. 2018).

57. *Id.*; Columbus, *supra* note 53.

58. *See, e.g.*, Bernard Marr, *What Is Digital Twin Technology—And Why Is It So Important?*, FORBES (Mar. 6, 2017), https://www.forbes.com/sites/bernardmarr/2017/03/06/what-is-digital-twin-technology-and-why-is-it-so-important/#16e7ebf32e2a; Digital Twins, MICROSOFT, https://azure.microsoft.com/en-us/services/digital-twins/.

59. *See, e.g.*, Brian Buntz, *The Top 20 Industrial IoT Applications*, IoT WORLD TODAY (Sept. 20, 2017), https://www.iotworldtoday.com/2017/09/20/top-20-industrial-iot-applications/.

60. *See, e.g.*, Xiao-Feng Xie, *Key Applications of the Smart IoT to Transform Transportation*, WIOMAX (Feb. 8, 2019), www.wiomax.com/what-can-the-smart-iot-transform-transportation-and-smart-cities/.

61. *See, e.g.*, Jim Eckenrode, *Future Scenarios for IoT in Financial Services*, DELOITTE and THE WALL STREET J. (2016), https://deloitte.wsj.com/cio/2016/01/06/future-scenarios-for-iot-in-financial-services/.

62. *See, e.g.*, *Intel's Grid Intelligence*, INTEL, https://www.intel.com/content/www/us/en/energy/energy-iot.html; *Intel in Energy*, INTEL, https://www.intel.com/content/www/us/en/energy/energy-overview.html; *See the Amazing Things People Are Doing with Azure*, MICROSOFT, https://azure.microsoft.com/en-us/case-studies/?term=iot&industry=energy.

63. *Internet of Things (IoT) Analytics Market: Global Forecast to 2020*, *supra* note 46.

64. *See, e.g.*, Nikki Baird, *Five Retail IoT Use Cases, When Retailers Finally Get Around to IoT*, FORBES (Apr. 24, 2017), https://www.forbes.com/sites/nikkibaird/2017/04/24/five-retail-iot-use-cases-when-retailers-finally-get-around-to-iot/#71bb3dfd6255; *see also* Dan Mitchell, *5 IoT Applications Retailers Are Using Today*, SAS, https://www.sas.com/en_us/insights/articles/big-data/five-iot-applications-retailers-are-using-today.html.

65. Table 2.2 is reproduced from Shackelford et al., *When Toasters Attack, supra* note *.

66. *See, e.g.*, *The Future of Smart Parking in the Cities of Tomorrow*, IoT INNOVATION, https://internet-of-things-innovation.com/insights/the-blog/smart-parking/ (last visited June 7, 2019).

67. Andrea M. Matwyshyn, *The "Internet of Bodies" Is Here: Are Courts and Regulators Ready?*, WALL ST. J. (Nov. 12, 2018), https://www.wsj.com/articles/

the-internet-of-bodies-is-here-are-courts-and-regulators-ready-1542039566.

68. *See, e.g.*, Meghan Neal, *The Internet of Bodies Is Coming, and You Could Get Hacked*, MOTHERBOARD (Mar. 13, 2014), https://motherboard.vice.com/en_us/article/gvyqgm/the-internet-of-bodies-is-coming-and-you-could-get-hacked.

69. Laurel Wamsley, *FDA Approves First Digital Pill That Can Track Whether You've Taken It*, NPR (Nov. 14, 2017), www.npr.org/sections/thetwo-way/2017/11/14/564112345/fda-approves-first-digital-pill-that-can-track-if-youve-taken-it; Maddy Kennedy, *U of M Doctors Use "Smart Pills" to Monitor Health of Cancer Patients*, MINNEINNO (Jan. 23, 2019), www.americaninno.com/minne/twin-cities-startup/u-of-m-doctors-use-smart-pills-to-monitor-health-of-cancer-patients/.

70. *Medtronic Launches Mobile App That Communicates Directly with World's First Smartphone-Connected Pacemakers*, CATH LAB DIGEST (Jan. 25, 2019), www.cathlabdigest.com/content/medtronic-launches-mobile-app-communicates-directly-worlds-first-smartphone-connected-pacemakers.

71. *The Smart Bimodal Hearing Solution*, COCHLEAR, www.cochlear.com/au/home/discover/cochlear-implants/smart-bimodal-solution (last visited June 9, 2019).

72. *The Miracle of an Artificial Pancreas*, NIH MEDLINEPLUS (2017), medlineplus.gov/magazine/issues/spring17/articles/spring17pg15-16.html.

73. *Introducing Our Smart Contact Lens Project*, GOOGLE (Jan. 16, 2014), https://googleblog.blogspot.com/2014/01/introducing-our-smart-contact-lens.html.

74. Sandra Levy, *Google Seeks Patent for Implantable, Smart Intraocular Device*, MED CITY NEWS (May 5, 2016), https://medcitynews.com/2016/05/google-implantable-intraocular/.

75. *See Firmware Update to Address Cybersecurity Vulnerabilities Identified in Abbott's (Formerly St. Jude Medical's) Implantable Cardiac Pacemakers: FDA Safety Communication*, FED. DRUG ADMIN. (Aug. 29, 2017), https://www.fda.gov/MedicalDevices/Safety/AlertsandNotices/ucm573669.htm.

76. *See, e.g.*, Statement by FDA Commissioner Scott Gottlieb, M.D., on FDA Ushering in New Era of 3D Printing of Medical Products; Provides Guidance to Manufacturers of Medical Devices, FDA Stmt. (Dec. 4, 2017), https://www.fda.gov/NewsEvents/

Newsroom/PressAnnouncements/ucm587547.htm. For more on this topic, see Scott J. Shackelford et al., *Securing the Internet of Healthcare*, *supra* note *.

77. Charlie Osborne, *The Best IoT, Smart Home Gadgets in 2018*, ZDNet (Apr. 24, 2018), https://www.zdnet.com/pictures/the-best-iot-smart-home-gadgets-in-2018/.

78. *Ring Video Doorbells*, Ring, https://shop.ring.com/pages/doorbells.

79. Osborne, *supra* note 77.

80. *An Important (and Difficult) Announcement*, Kuri (July 25, 2018), https://www.heykuri.com/blog/important_difficult_announcement/.

81. Sharon Shea, *Use Cases and Benefits of Smart Sensors for IoT*, IoT Agenda, https://internetofthingsagenda.techtarget.com/opinion/How-smart-sensors-are-transforming-the-Internet-of-Things.

82. Sharma, *supra* note 42. Others categorize sensors differently, such as by physics domains: light and electromagnetism sensors; thermal sensors; vibration and sound sensors; matter and materials sensors.

83. *Id.*

84. Schneier, *supra* note 3, at 29.

85. Sharma, *supra* note 42.

86. *Id.*

87. Stacey Higginbotham, *The 6 Reasons Consumers Buy Connected Devices*, Stacey on IoT (Aug. 27, 2018), https://staceyoniot.com/the-6-reasons-consumers-buy-connected-devices/.

88. *How to Make Your Home a Smart Home*, Direct Energy, https://www.directenergy.com/learning-center/modern-home/advantages-smart-home.

89. Steven Brand, *The Role of Smart Sensors in Manufacturing*, CMTC Manufacturing Blog, https://www.cmtc.com/blog/the-new-role-of-sensors-in-manufacturing.

90. *Id.*

91. *See How Has the Internet of Things Helped Provide a Better Service for Compressed-Air Customers at a Lower Price?*, SAP (2018), https://www.sap.com/documents/2018/08/ead5f0e7-167d-0010-87a3-c30de2ffd8ff.html.

92. Shea, *supra* note 81.

93. Brand, *supra* note 89.

94. *Internet of Things: Privacy and Security in a Connected World*, FTC REP. (Jan. 2015), https://www.ftc.gov/system/files/ documents/reports/federal-trade-commission-staff-report-november-2013-workshop-entitled-internet-things-privacy/ 150127iotrpt.pdf; *see also* Bernie Magkilat, *Critical Gov't Infrastructures Become Targets*, MANILA BULLETIN (Nov. 21, 2015), http://www.mb.com.ph/critical-govt-infrastructures-become-targets/ (noting that "[as] the Internet of Things advances, Trend Micro said, smart devices or innovations that are used for public-facing technologies can be exploited, potentially causing virtual and physical destruction").

95. *FTC Report on Internet of Things Urges Companies to Adopt Best Practices to Address Consumer Privacy and Security Risks*, FED. TRADE COMM'N (Jan. 27, 2015), https:// www.ftc.gov/news-events/press-releases/2015/01/ ftc-report-internet-things-urges-companies-adopt-best-practices.

96. *Safeguarding the Internet of Things: Being Secure, Vigilant, and Resilient in the Connected Age*, DELOITTE REV. 17 (July 27, 2015), http://dupress.com/articles/internet-of-things-data-security-and-privacy [hereinafter "Safeguarding IoT"].

97. Rich Quinell, *10 Top Challenges Industrial IoT Must Overcome in 2015*, EE TIMES (Dec. 24, 2014), http://www.eetimes.com/ document.asp?doc_id=1325067&page_number=2.

98. Jonathan Gregory, *The Internet of Things: Revolutionizing the Retail Industry*, Accenture Strategy (n.d.), https://www.accenture. com/_acnmedia/Accenture/Conversion-Assets/DotCom/ Documents/Global/PDF/Dualpub_14/Accenture-The-Internet-Of-Things.pdf

99. *Id.*

100. Eric Topol, *The Future of Medicine Is in Your Smartphone*, WALL ST. J. (Jan. 9, 2015), http://www.wsj.com/articles/ the-future-of-medicine-is-in-your-smartphone-1420828632.

101. *The Internet of Things for Health Care: A Comprehensive Survey*, IEEE ACCESS (June 1, 2015), http://ieeexplore.ieee.org/stamp/stamp. jsp?arnumber=7113786.

102. Brett Jurgens, *How IoT Will Change Your Relationship with Insurance*, TECH. CRUNCH (Aug. 17, 2015), http://techcrunch. com/2015/08/17/how-iot-will-change-your-relationship-with-insurance/#.u6joyyv:3zq5.

103. *Id.*

104. Jeff John, *Smart Grid's Latest Cloud: Honeywell's Cloud-Connected Thermostats*, GREENTECH MEDIA (Nov. 3, 2011), http://www. greentechmedia.com/articles/read/smart-grids-latest-cloud-honeywells-cloud-connected-thermostats.
105. *Id.*
106. Jill Hayden, *Embracing Automated and Connected Vehicles*, INFRASTRUCTURE-INTELLIGENCE (May 27, 2015), http:// www.infrastructure-intelligence.com/article/may-2015/ embracing-automated-and-connected-vehicles.
107. *Id.*

Chapter 3

* This chapter is based on years of distilled research in the field of cybersecurity and Internet governance. As such, earlier versions of selections from this chapter have previously been published in reverse chronological order as follows: Scott J. Shackelford, *Smart Factories, Dumb Policy? Managing Cybersecurity and Data Privacy Risks in the Industrial Internet of Things*, 21 MINN. OF L., SCI., & TECH. 1 (2019); Scott J. Shackelford, *When Toasters Attack: Enhancing the 'Security of Things' through Polycentric Governance*, 2017 U. ILL. L. REV. 415 (2017). Readers are encouraged to consult these sources for additional discussion of the covered topics.

1. *See, e.g.*, SCOTT J. SHACKELFORD, MANAGING CYBER ATTACKS IN INTERNATIONAL LAW, BUSINESS, AND RELATIONS: IN SEARCH OF CYBER PEACE (2014).
2. *See, e.g.*, Marshall Brain & Wesley Fenlon, *How Computer Viruses Work*, HOWSTUFFWORKS, https://computer.howstuffworks.com/ virus6.htm (last visited June 9, 2019); *see also There Are 3 Main Types of Technical Debt: Here's How to Manage Them*, HACKERNOON (Jan. 25, 2018), https://hackernoon.com/there-are-3-main-types-of-technical-debt-heres-how-to-manage-them-4a3328a4c50c.
3. *See Space IoT Takes Off*, PHYS.ORG (July 10, 2018), https://phys. org/news/2018-07-space-iot.html.
4. *See, e.g.*, Dave Piscitello, *Threats, Vulnerabilities, and Exploits—Oh My!*, ICANN (Aug. 10, 2015), https://www.icann.org/news/ blog/threats-vulnerabilities-and-exploits-oh-my; *Hardware vs. Software Vulnerabilities*, INSIDE BATTELLE (Jan. 18, 2018), https://inside.battelle.org/blog-details/hardware-vs.-software-vulnerabilities; *Types of Security Vulnerabilities*, APPLE, https://

developer.apple.com/library/archive/documentation/Security/
Conceptual/SecureCodingGuide/Articles/TypesSecVuln.
html; *National Vulnerability Database*, NIST, https://nvd.nist.
gov/general/visualizations/vulnerability-visualizations/
cwe-over-time.

5. *See, e.g.*, Chris Brook, *What Is Cyber Hygiene? A Definition of Cyber Hygiene, Benefits, Best Practices, and More*, Digital Guardian (Dec. 5, 2018), https://digitalguardian.com/blog/what-cyber-hygiene-definition-cyber-hygiene-benefits-best-practices-and-more; Bill Bradley, *Practicing Good Cyber Hygiene: Avoid the Dangers of Phishing*, Forbes (July 19, 2017), https://www.forbes.com/sites/centurylink/2017/07/19/practicing-good-cyber-hygiene-avoid-the-dangers-of-phishing/#511c00213ae5.

6. Bruce Schneier, Click Here to Kill Everybody: Security and Survival in a Hyper-Connected World 27 (2018); Pam Baker, *IoT and the Looming Mobile Tidal Wave*, Info. Wk. (Apr. 28, 2015), http://www.informationweek.com/mobile/mobile-business/iot-and-the-looming-mobile-tidal-wave/a/d-id/1320182.

7. Schneier, *supra* note 6.

8. *Id.*

9. *Mobile Computing and Internet of Things*, TXT Gp., http://www.txtgroup.com/corporateresearch/Style%20Library/docs/TXT%20NEXT%20for%20Mobile%20Computing%20and%20Internet%20of%20Things.pdf (last visited Nov. 23, 2015).

10. Jon Oltsik, *The Internet of Things: A CISO and Network Security Perspective*, Enterprise Strategy Gp. (2014), https://www.cisco.com/web/strategy/docs/energy/network-security-perspective.pdf. Still, the parallels are not perfect; one of the major differences between mobile technologies and IoT, for example, lies in the desired functionality for which these technologies were developed. Mobile technologies were designed to enhance user interaction with portable devices, while IoT is designed primarily to enable devices to communicate with each other directly, without human intervention. *Mobile Computing and Internet of Things*, TXT Gp., http://www.txtgroup.com/corporateresearch/Style%20Library/docs/TXT%20NEXT%20for%20Mobile%20Computing%20and%20Internet%20of%20Things.pdf (last visited Nov. 23, 2015).

11. Michael Raynor, *Strategy and the Internet of Things*, TM Forum (Keynote Address, June 2, 2015).

12. Eric A. Fischer, *Cybersecurity Issues and Challenges: In Brief*, Cong. Res. Serv. (Aug. 12, 2016), https://pdfs.semanticscholar.org/ 65e3/4c9bb7330fcfec378394b5d308b6a323947d.pdf (highlighting that "developers have traditionally focused more on features than security, for economic reasons" and that "the structure of economic incentives for cybersecurity has been called distorted or even perverse. Cybercrime is regarded as cheap, profitable, and comparatively safe for the criminals. In contrast, cybersecurity can be expensive, is by its nature imperfect, and the economic returns on investments are often unsure.").

13. *See, e.g.*, Bruce Schneier, *The Internet of Things Will Turn Large-Scale Hacks into Real World Disasters*, Schneier on Sec. (July 25, 2016), https://www.schneier.com/essays/archives/2016/ 07/the_internet_of_thin_3.html (arguing that the increased risks associated with IoT come from three factors, including software control as well as "interconnections" and "autonomy." Specifically, "what might seem benign to the designers of a particular system becomes harmful when it's combined with some other system," and "autonomy is great for all sorts of reasons, but from a security perspective it means that the effects of attacks can take effect immediately, automatically, and ubiquitously.").

14. Bernard Marr, *19 Astonishing Quotes about the Internet of Things Everyone Should Read*, Forbes (Sept. 12, 2018), https://www. forbes.com/sites/bernardmarr/2018/09/12/19-astonishing-quotes-about-the-internet-of-things-everyone-should-read/ #1be607a1e1db. For more information on Robert Cannon, see Amy Adams, *Robert Cannon, Stanford Engineer Who Set the Course for Future Robots, Dies at 93*, Stan. News (Aug. 24, 2017), https:// news.stanford.edu/2017/08/24/robert-cannon-engineer-set-course-future-robots-dies-93/.

15. Marr, *supra* note 14 (highlighting challenges with patch and update systems for IoT).

16. Steve Ranger, *Windows XP: Why Hospitals Are Still Using Microsoft's Antique Operating System*, ZDNet (Dec. 8, 2016), https://www.zdnet.com/article/windows-xp-why-hospitals-are-still-using-microsofts-antique-operating-system/.

17. *See, e.g.*, Stacey Higginbotham, *6 Reasons Why IoT Security Is Terrible*, IEEE (June 20, 2018), https://qa.spectrum.ieee.org/ telecom/security/6-reasons-why-iot-security-is-terrible (citing

Josh Corman regarding his six reasons why IoT security is different from traditional IT security, including the first reason, which is that: "the consequences of failure are more dire. We've raised the stakes by connecting more physical systems and facilities to wireless networks.").

18. *See, e.g.,* Margaret Rouse, *Confidentiality, Integrity, and Availability (CIA Triad)*, TECHTARGET (Nov. 2014), https://whatis.techtarget.com/definition/Confidentiality-integrity-and-availability-CIA.

19. Schneier, *supra* note 13.

20. SCHNEIER, *supra* note 6, at 90.

21. Bruce Schneier, *Real-World Security and the Internet of Things*, SCHNEIER ON SEC; (July 28, 2016), https://www.schneier.com/blog/archives/2016/07/real-world_secu.html.

22. *See, e.g., Top Security Threats and Management Issues Facing Corporate America: 2016 Survey of Fortune 1000 Companies*, SECURITAS (2016), http://www.scisusa.com/wp-content/uploads/2018/05/2016-Top-Security-Threats.pdf.

23. *See, e.g., Managing Cybersecurity: The Cyber Risk Protection Story*, MARSH & MCLENNAN AGENCY (2018), http://bit.ly/2VoRijF.

24. *Speeches*, FED. BUREAU OF INVESTIGATION (Mar. 1, 2012), https://archives.fbi.gov/archives/news/speeches/combating-threats-in-the-cyber-world-outsmarting-terrorists-hackers-and-spies.

25. For instance, in 2017, Microsoft announced that it invests over $1 billion per year on cybersecurity. Tova Cohen, *Microsoft to Continue to Invest over $1 Billion a Year on Cyber Security*, REUTERS (Jan. 26, 2017), https://www.reuters.com/article/us-tech-cyber-microsoft-idUSKBN15A1GA.

26. *NSTAC Report to the President on the Internet of Things*, NAT'L SEC. TELECOMM. ADVISORY COMM., at 10–11 (Nov. 19, 2014), https://www.dhs.gov/sites/default/files/publications/NSTAC%20Report%20to%20the%20President%20on%20the%20Internet%20of%20Things%20Nov%202014%20%28updat%20%20%20.pdf.

27. Lily Hay Newman, *AI Can Help Cybersecurity—If It Can Fight through the Hype,* WIRED (Apr. 29. 2018), https://www.wired.com/story/ai-machine-learning-cybersecurity/; *see also NSTAC Report to the President on the Internet of Things, supra* note 26, at 36–37 (describing how near-term AI may be applied to advance cybersecurity, especially if human and machine intelligence is combined).

28. *NSTAC Report to the President on the Internet of Things, supra* note 26, at 11.
29. *Id.*
30. *Id.* at 37.
31. See more in the below question: "How does the scale of insecure IoT devices create new risks?"
32. *NSTAC Report to the President on the Internet of Things, supra* note 26, at 11.
33. Alex Chapman, *Hacking into Internet Connected Light Bulbs*, CONTEXT (July 4, 2014), https://www.contextis.com/en/blog/hacking-into-internet-connected-light-bulbs.
34. Ian Paul, *Researchers Hack Philips Hue Smart Bulbs from the Sky*, PCWORLD (Nov. 7, 2016), https://www.pcworld.com/article/3138872/researchers-hack-philips-hue-smart-bulbs-from-the-sky.html.
35. *Id.*
36. *Id.*
37. Daniel Oberhaus, *This Hacker Showed How a Smart Lightbulb Could Leak Your Wi-Fi Password*, MOTHERBOARD (Jan. 31, 2019), https://www.vice.com/en_us/article/kzdwp9/this-hacker-showed-how-a-smart-lightbulb-could-leak-your-wi-fi-password.
38. SCHNEIER, *supra* note 6, at 36.
39. Prices may need to be kept low to be competitive with "dumb" device counterparts. For instance, in May 2019, a four-pack of Philips Hue White LED 60W-Equivalent Dimmable Smart Wireless bulbs was $42.47 at Home Depot (and the four-pack with the bridge was $149.15 at Home Deport). By comparison, an eight-pack of the EcoSmart Soft White LED 60W-Equivalent bulbs was $9.94 at Home Depot.
40. Bruce Schneier, *Security Economics of the Internet of Things*, SCHNEIER ON SEC. (Oct. 10, 2016), https://www.schneier.com/blog/archives/2016/10/security_econom_1.html.
41. *See, e.g.*, Alex Colon, *The Best Smart Light Bulbs for 2019*, PCMAG (Oct. 5, 2018), https://www.pcmag.com/roundup/334096/the-best-smart-light-bulbs; Christopher Null, *Best Smart Bulbs for Your Connected Home*, TECHHIVE (June 3, 2019), https://www.techhive.com/article/3129887/best-smart-bulbs.html.
42. *See Bulbs*, PHILIPS, https://www2.meethue.com/en-us/products.bulbs#filters=BULBS_SU&sliders=&support=&price=&priceBoxes=&page=&layout=12.subcategory.p-grid-icon; *LIFX*

Wi-Fi LED Smart Lights, LIFX, https://www.lifx.com/ (neither page mentions security). Note that only an exemplary but not exhaustive search among product reviews and marketing pages was done.

43. *See, e.g.*, Tom Brant, *The Best Desktop Computers for 2019*, PCMAG (Dec. 10, 2018), https://www.pcmag.com/roundup/256884/ the-best-desktop-computers; *MacBook Pro*, APPLE, https:// www.apple.com/macbook-pro/; *Surface Devices for the Modern Workplace*, MICROSOFT, https://www.microsoft.com/en-us/ surface/business?CustomerIntent=Consumer; Jessica Dolcourt, *Samsung Galaxy S10 Plus Review*, CNET (Mar. 26, 2019), https:// www.cnet.com/reviews/samsung-galaxy-s10-plus-review/.

44. *Identity Fraud Hits All-Time High with 16.7 Million U.S. Victims in 2017, According to New Javelin Strategy & Research Study*, JAVELIN (Feb. 6, 2018), https://www.javelinstrategy.com/press-release/ identity-fraud-hits-all-time-high-167-million-us-victims-2017-according-new-javelin.

45. For instance, a family reported that a stranger hacked into and spoke to a child through their Nest camera. Narmeen Choudhury, *First on PIX11: Home Monitoring System Hacked by Stranger; LI Family Doesn't Know How Long They've Been Watched*, PIX11 (Oct. 30, 2018), https://pix11.com/2018/10/30/home-monitoring-system-hacked-by-stranger-li-family-doesnt-know-how-long-theyve-been-watched/. Another family reported that a stranger remotely activated their baby monitor and Next camera. Amy B. Wang, *'I'm in Your Baby's Room': A Hacker Took Over a Baby Monitor and Broadcast Threats, Parents Say*, WASH. POST (Dec. 20, 2018), https://www.washingtonpost.com/technology/2018/ 12/20/nest-cam-baby-monitor-hacked-kidnap-threat-came-device-parents-say/?utm_term=.23ba25e96ebb. Note that stolen credentials may have been at fault.

46. Kaushal Kafle et al., *A Study of Data Store-Based Home Automation*, CODASPY 2019 (Dec. 4, 2018), https://arxiv.org/pdf/ 1812.01597.pdf.

47. *Id.* at 4.

48. Jack Wallen, *Five Nightmarish Attacks That Show the Risks of IoT Security*, ZDNET (June 1, 2017), https://www.zdnet. com/article/5-nightmarish-attacks-that-show-the-risks-of-iot-security/ (reporting that "cybercriminals shut down the heating of two buildings in the city of Lappeenranta, Finland"

in a distributed denial-of-service attack that caused the heating controllers to continually reboot the system such that the heating never actually kicked on; this was especially significant because the temperatures in Finland dip well below freezing in November).

49. Cesar Cerrudo, *Hacking Washington DC Traffic Control Systems*, IOACTIVE (July 31, 2014), http://blog.ioactive.com/2014/07/hacking-washington-dc-traffic-control.html.

50. *Id.*

51. *Id.*

52. Kelly Jackson Higgins, *4 Hurdles to Securing the Internet of Things*, INFO. WK. (Sept. 4, 2014), http://www.darkreading.com/informationweek-home/4-hurdles-to-securing-the-internet-of-things/d/d-id/1306978.

53. *Id.*

54. Press Release, Marketer of Internet-Connected Home Security Video Cameras Settles FTC Charges It Failed to Protect Consumers' Privacy, Fed. Trade Comm'n (Sept. 4, 2013), https://www.ftc.gov/news-events/press-releases/2013/09/marketer-internet-connected-home-security-video-cameras-settles.

55. *Id.*

56. Dara Kerr, *FTC and TrendNet Settle Claim over Hacked Security Cameras*, CNET (Sept. 3, 2013), http://www.cnet.com/news/ftc-and-trendnet-settle-claim-over-hacked-security-cameras.

57. Mark Stanislav, *Top 3 Security Issues in Consumer IoT and Industrial IoT*, IOT-INC (Mar. 4, 2015), http://www.iot-inc.com/top-3-iot-security-issues-connected-products-transcript/.

58. *Id.*

59. Andrei Costin, Jonas Zaddach, Aurélien Francillon, & Davide Balzarotti, *A Large-Scale Analysis of the Security of Embedded Firmwares*, USENIX (Aug. 20, 2014), https://www.usenix.org/system/files/conference/usenixsecurity14/sec14-paper-costin.pdf.

60. Mario Ballano Barcena & Candid Wueest, *Insecurity in the Internet of Things*, SYMANTEC (Mar. 12, 2015), https://www.symantec.com/content/en/us/enterprise/iot/b-insecurity-in-the-internet-of-things_21349619.pdf.

61. *Id.*

62. SCHNEIER, *supra* note 6, at 45.

63. *See, e.g.*, Maria Korolov, *What Is a Botnet? And Why They Aren't Going Away Anytime Soon*, CSO (Feb. 27, 2019), https://www.

csoonline.com/article/3240364/what-is-a-botnet-and-why-they-arent-going-away-anytime-soon.html.

64. *Id.*

65. Wallen, *supra* note 48.

66. Lily Hay Newman, *The Botnet That Broke the Internet Isn't Going Away*, Wired (Dec. 9, 2016), https://www.wired.com/2016/12/botnet-broke-internet-isnt-going-away/.

67. *Id.*

68. *See, e.g.*, Josh Fruhlinger, *The Mirai Botnet Explained: How Teen Scammers and CCTV Cameras Almost Brought Down the Internet*, CSO (Mar. 9, 2018), https://www.csoonline.com/article/3258748/the-mirai-botnet-explained-how-teen-scammers-and-cctv-cameras-almost-brought-down-the-internet.html.

69. *See* Schneier, *supra* note 6, at 37 ("the only way for you to update the firmware in your hackable DVR is to throw it away and buy a new one").

70. Brian Krebs, *Mirai Botnet Authors Avoid Jail Time*, Krebs on Sec. (Sept. 19, 2018), https://krebsonsecurity.com/tag/mirai-botnet/.

71. *DNS Overview*, Dyn, https://dyn.com/dns/.

72. Lily Hay Newman, *What We Know about Friday's Massive East Coast Internet Outage*, Wired (Oct. 21, 2016), https://www.wired.com/2016/10/internet-outage-ddos-dns-dyn/; *see also* Josh Fruhlinger, *supra* note 68; Wallen, *supra* note 48.

73. Newman, *supra* note 72.

74. *Id.*

75. Wallen, *supra* note 48.

76. Andy Greenberg, *Hackers Remotely Kill a Jeep on the Highway—With Me in It*, Wired (July 21, 2015), https://www.wired.com/2015/07/hackers-remotely-kill-jeep-highway/.

77. *See, e.g.*, Lily Hay Newman, *Medical Devices Are the Next Security Nightmare*, Wired (Mar. 2, 2017), https://www.wired.com/2017/03/medical-devices-next-security-nightmare/; Iain Thomson, *Wi-Fi Baby Heart Monitor May Have the Worse IoT Security of 2016*, Register (Oct. 13, 2016), https://www.theregister.co.uk/2016/10/13/possibly_worst_iot_security_failure_yet/?mt=1476453928163; Selena Larson, *FDA Confirms That St. Jude's Cardiac Devices Can Be Hacked*, CNN (Jan. 9, 2017), https://money.cnn.com/2017/01/09/technology/fda-st-jude-cardiac-hack/.

78. Andy Greenberg, *Hackers Can Disable a Sniper Rifle—Or Change Its Target*, Wired (July 29, 2015), https://www.wired.com/2015/07/hackers-can-disable-sniper-rifleor-change-target/.

79. *Are 'Smart Guns' the Answer for Improved Policing?*, POLICEONE (Aug. 3, 2017), https://www.policeone.com/police-products/firearms/articles/390257006-Are-smart-guns-the-answer-for-improved-policing/.

80. *See, e.g.*, Colin Jeffrey, *Canada's Next-Generation Military Smart Gun Unveiled*, NEW ATLAS (Feb. 16, 2015), https://newatlas.com/smart-gun-evolution-military-weapon/36091/.

81. *SCADA StrangeLove*, http://www.scada.sl/ (last visited June 9, 2019).

82. Margaret Rouse, *Honeypot*, TECHTARGET, https://searchsecurity.techtarget.com/definition/honey-pot (explaining that a "honeypot" is a used as a decoy to lure cyberattacks by looking like a potential target on the Internet and to detect, deflect, or study hacking attempts).

83. *Honey, I Hacked the SCADA! Industrial CONTROLLED Systems!* RSA CONF., https://www.youtube.com/watch?v=QAl2GkhT4Jg.

84. *Id.*

85. Paul Roberts, *Hacker Charged in Breach of New York Dam*, SEC. LEDGER (Mar. 25, 2016), https://securityledger.com/2016/03/hacker-charged-in-breach-of-new-york-dam/.

86. Candid Wueest, *Targeted Attacks against the Energy Sector*, SYMANTEC (Jan. 13, 2014), https://www.symantec.com/content/en/us/enterprise/media/security_response/whitepapers/targeted_attacks_against_the_energy_sector.pdf, at 10.

87. William J. Broad, John Markoff, & David E. Sanger, *Israeli Test on Worm Called Crucial in Iran Nuclear Delay*, N.Y. TIMES (Jan. 15, 2011), https://www.nytimes.com/2011/01/16/world/middleeast/16stuxnet.html.

88. Nicole Perlroth & Clifford Krauss, *A Cyberattack in Saudi Arabia Had a Deadly Goal: Experts Fear Another Try*, N.Y. TIMES (Mar. 15, 2018), https://www.nytimes.com/2018/03/15/technology/saudi-arabia-hacks-cyberattacks.html; *see also* Anshu Mittal, Andrew Slaughter, & Paul Zonneveld, *Protecting the Connected Barrels: Cybersecurity Upstream Oil and Gas*, DELOITTE (June 26, 2017), https://www2.deloitte.com/insights/us/en/industry/oil-and-gas/cybersecurity-in-oil-and-gas-upstream-sector.html?id=us:2el:3pr:dup3960:awa:dup:MMDDYY (describing the results of a study on cyberattacks that are targeting crude oil and natural gas companies and growing in frequency, sophistication, and impact).

89. Samuel Gibbs, *Triton: Hackers Take Out Safety Systems in 'Watershed' Attack on Energy Plant*, GUARDIAN (Dec. 15, 2017), https://www.theguardian.com/technology/2017/dec/15/triton-hackers-malware-attack-safety-systems-energy-plant.

90. Robert M. Lee, Michael J. Assante, & Tim Conway, *Analysis of the Cyber Attack on the Ukrainian Power Grid*, E-ISAC & SANS ICS (Mar. 18, 2016), https://www.nerc.com/pa/CI/ESISAC/Documents/E-ISAC_SANS_Ukraine_DUC_18Mar2016.pdf.

91. Donghui Park, Julia Summers, & Michael Walstrom, *Cyberattack on Critical Infrastructure: Russia and the Ukrainian Power Grid Attacks*, UNIV. WASH. HENRY M. JACKSON SCH. OF INT'L STUD. (Oct. 11, 2017), https://jsis.washington.edu/news/cyberattack-critical-infrastructure-russia-ukrainian-power-grid-attacks/; *see Ukraine Power Cut 'Was Cyber-Attack,'* BBC (Jan. 11, 2017), https://www.bbc.com/news/technology-38573074; Alyza Sebenius, *Will Ukraine Be Hit by Yet Another Holiday Power-Grid Hack?*, ATLANTIC (Dec. 13, 2017). https://www.theatlantic.com/technology/archive/2017/12/ukraine-power-grid-hack/548285/.

92. BRUCE SCHNEIER, CLICK HERE TO KILL EVERYBODY: SECURITY AND SURVIVAL IN A HYPER-CONNECTED WORLD 2 (2018).

93. Peter Behr, *Cyberattackers Have Penetrated U.S. Infrastructure Systems—NSA Chief*, ENERGY WIRE (Nov. 21, 2014), https://www.eenews.net/energywire/stories/1060009391; Richard J. Campbell, *Cybersecurity Issues for the Bulk Power System*, CONG. RES. SERV. (June 10, 2015), https://fas.org/sgp/crs/misc/R43989.pdf; Mission Support Center: Idaho National Laboratory, *Cyber Threat and Vulnerability Analysis of the U.S. Electric Sector*, US DEP'T OF ENERGY (Aug. 2016), https://www.energy.gov/sites/prod/files/2017/01/f34/Cyber%20Threat%20and%20Vulnerability%20Analysis%20of%20the%20U.S.%20Electric%20Sector.pdf.

94. *Dragonfly: Western Energy Sector Targeted by Sophisticated Attack Group*, SYMANTEC (Oct. 20, 2017), https://www.symantec.com/blogs/threat-intelligence/dragonfly-energy-sector-cyber-attacks.

95. *Alert (TA18-074A): Russian Government Cyber Activity Targeting Energy and Other Critical Infrastructure*, DHS CISA (Mar. 15, 2018), https://www.us-cert.gov/ncas/alerts/TA18-074A; Brian Naylor, *Russia Hacked US Power Grid—So What Will the Trump Administration Do about It?*, NPR (Mar. 23, 2018), https://www.

npr.org/2018/03/23/596044821/russia-hacked-u-s-power-grid-so-what-will-the-trump-administration-do-about-it; *see* Julian Borger, *US Accuses Russia of Cyber-Attack on Energy Sector and Imposes New Sanctions*, Guardian (Mar. 15, 2018), https://www.theguardian.com/us-news/2018/mar/15/russia-sanctions-energy-sector-cyber-attack-us-election-interference.

96. *IOActive and Embedi Uncover Major Security Vulnerabilities in ICS Mobile Applications*, IOActive (Jan. 11, 2018), https://ioactive.com/article/ioactive-and-embedi-uncover-major-security-vulnerabilities-in-ics-mobile-applications/.

97. *Id.*

98. *Id.*

99. *See, e.g.*, Jeff Goldman, *20 Cyber Security Startups to Watch in 2018*, eSecurity Planet (Feb. 26, 2018), https://www.esecurityplanet.com/network-security/top-cyber-security-startups-2018.html (highlighting Armis, MagicCube, and Xage Security as companies to watch); *see also* Lindsey O'Donnell, *15 Cool IoT Security Startups That Are Keeping Connected Devices Safe*, CRN (Apr. 17, 2017), https://www.crn.com/slide-shows/internet-of-things/300084589/15-cool-iot-security-startups-that-are-keeping-connected-devices-safe.htm/1; Jeff Vance, *10 Hot IoT Security Startups to Watch*, NetworkWorld (May 2, 2019), https://www.networkworld.com/article/3391413/10-hot-iot-security-startups-to-watch.html.

100. *IoT Security*, Cisco, https://www.cisco.com/c/en/us/solutions/internet-of-things/iot-system-security.html.

101. Benedikt Abendroth, Aaron Kleiner, & Paul Nicholas, *Cybersecurity Policy for the Internet of Things*, Microsoft (2017), https://blogs.microsoft.com/wp-content/uploads/2017/05/IoT_WhitePaper_5_15_17.pdf.

102. *Cloud*, Tech Terms, https://techterms.com/definition/cloud (last visited June 9, 2019) ("The term 'cloud' comes from early network diagrams, in which the image of a cloud was used to indicate a large network, such as a WAN. The cloud eventually became associated with the entire Internet, and the two terms are now used synonymously. The cloud may also be used to describe specific online services, which are collectively labeled 'cloud computing.'").

103. *See, e.g.*, Samantha Lee, *The Cloud-Computing Market Is Set to Double to $116 Billion by 2021—These 3 Charts Show Why*

That's Probably Good News Only for Amazon, Google, Microsoft, and Alibaba, Bus. Insider (Nov. 20, 2018), https://www. businessinsider.com/goldman-sachs-cloud-computing-market-forecast-aws-microsoft-azure-google-cloud-2018-11 (estimating that, in 2019, Amazon will have 47%, Microsoft will have 22%, Alibaba will have 8%, and Google will have 7% of the public cloud market share, i.e., a combined 84%).

104. *IoT Platform*, Alibaba Cloud, https://www.alibabacloud.com/ product/iot (last visited June 9, 2019); *Internet of Things, Cloud IoT Core: Documentation: Device Security*, Google Cloud, https:// cloud.google.com/iot/docs/concepts/device-security (last visited June 9, 2019).

105. *AWS IoT Device Defender FAQs*, AWS, https://aws.amazon.com/ iot-device-defender/faq/ (last visited June 9, 2019).

106. *Azure IoT Security*, Microsoft, https://azure.microsoft.com/en-us/overview/iot/security/.

107. Galen Hunt, *Introducing Microsoft Azure Sphere: Secure and Power the Intelligent Edge*, Microsoft Azure (Apr. 16, 2018), https:// azure.microsoft.com/en-us/blog/introducing-microsoft-azure-sphere-secure-and-power-the-intelligent-edge/; *see Azure Sphere*, Microsoft Azure, https://azure.microsoft.com/en-us/ services/azure-sphere/.

108. *See, e.g.*, Kim Knickle, *Microsoft Azure Sphere Marks Turning Point for IoT in Manufacturing*, IoT Agenda, https:// internetofthingsagenda.techtarget.com/opinion/Microsoft-Azure-Sphere-marks-turning-point-for-IoT-in-manufacturing.

109. Hunt, *supra* note 107.

110. *See, e.g.*, Andrew Larkin, *Disadvantages of Cloud Computing*, Cloud Academy (June 26, 2018), https://cloudacademy.com/ blog/disadvantages-of-cloud-computing/.

111. *Id.*; Galen Hunt, George Letey, & Edmund B. Nightingale, *The Seven Properties of Highly Secure Devices*, Microsoft, https:// www.microsoft.com/en-us/research/wp-content/uploads/ 2017/03/SevenPropertiesofHighlySecureDevices.pdf (last visited June 9, 2019) (the seven properties are: hardware-based root of trust; small trusted computing base; defense in depth; compartmentalization; certificate-based authentication; renewable security; and failure reporting).

112. *Wireless Industry Announces New Cybersecurity Certification Program for Cellular-Connected IoT Devices*, CTIA (Aug. 21, 2018),

https://www.ctia.org/news/wireless-industry-announces-internet-of-things-cybersecurity-certification-program.

113. *Landmark IoT Security Summit Gathers Industry Cybersecurity Experts and Leaders to Build Cross-Sector Guidelines for Securing Connected Devices*, COUNCIL TO SECURE THE DIGITAL ECON. (Mar. 21, 2019), https://securingdigitaleconomy.org/wp-content/uploads/2019/03/Release_CSDE-IOT-Meeting.pdf.

114. *BSA Framework for Secure Software*, BSA, https://www.bsa.org/reports/bsa-framework-for-secure-software.

115. *Device Identifier Composition Engine (DICE) Architectures*, TRUSTED COMPUTING GROUP, https://trustedcomputinggroup.org/work-groups/dice-architectures/ (explaining its goal to enhance security and privacy on systems with a Trusted Platform Module (TPM) as well as provide viable security and privacy foundations for IoT systems without a TPM (due to power, resource, or other constraints)).

116. *Alibaba*, HACKERONE, https://hackerone.com/alibaba; *Vulnerability Reporting*, AWS, https://aws.amazon.com/security/vulnerability-reporting/ (last visited June 9, 2019); *Report a Security or Privacy Vulnerability*, APPLE, https://support.apple.com/en-us/HT201220 (last visited June 9, 2019); *Information*, FACEBOOK, https://www.facebook.com/whitehat/ (last visited June 9, 2019); *How Google Handles Security Vulnerabilities*, GOOGLE, https://www.google.com/about/appsecurity/ (last visited June 9, 2019); *IBM*, HACKERONE, https://hackerone.com/ibm (last visited June 9, 2019); *Product Security at Intel*, INTEL, https://www.intel.com/content/www/us/en/corporate-responsibility/product-security.html (last visited June 9, 2019); *Coordinated Vulnerability Disclosure*, MICROSOFT, https://www.microsoft.com/en-us/msrc/cvd (last visited June 9, 2019); *Security Reporting*, SAMSUNG MOBILE SEC., https://security.samsungmobile.com/securityReporting.smsb (last visited June 9, 2019). Alibaba and IBM enlist the help of HackerOne. A broader group from the Cybersecurity Tech Accord, of which Microsoft is a member, have also announced their support for coordinated vulnerability disclosure. *The Cybersecurity Tech Accord Supports the GFCE's Call for Industry-Wide Adoption of Transparent Policies for Coordinated Vulnerability Disclosure (CVD)*, TECH ACCORD (Sept. 10, 2018), https://cybertechaccord.org/supports-gfce-call-for-cvd/.

117. For instance, in the United States, the Department of Commerce National Telecommunications and Information Administration hosted a multistakeholder process with representatives from industry, government, the security researcher community, and civil society to discuss best practices for collaboration. *Multistakeholder Process: Cybersecurity Vulnerabilities*, NAT'L TELECOMM. AND INFO. ADMIN. (Dec. 15, 2016), https://www.ntia.doc.gov/other-publication/2016/multistakeholder-process-cybersecurity-vulnerabilities. In announcing a shift toward coordinated vulnerability disclosure in 2010, Microsoft also referenced the long-running debate between different parts of the security community about how best to structure disclosure. *Announcing Coordinated Vulnerability Disclosure*, MICROSOFT, https://blogs.technet.microsoft.com/msrc/2010/07/22/announcing-coordinated-vulnerability-disclosure/.

118. *Coordinated Vulnerability Disclosure*, GLOBAL F. ON CYBER EXPERTISE, https://www.thegfce.com/initiatives/r/responsible-disclosure-initiative-ethical-hacking; *What Is a Vulnerability Disclosure Policy and Why You Need One*, HACKERONE (Aug. 30, 2018), https://www.hackerone.com/blog/What-Vulnerability-Disclosure-Policy-and-Why-You-Need-One (citing the European Commission's reference to the importance of more companies adhering to a vulnerability disclosure policy as well as supportive language and efforts from other government and civil society organizations in the United States and Europe).

119. *About HackerOne*, HACKERONE, https://www.hackerone.com/about; *We Are the #1 Crowdsourced Security Platform*, BUGCROWD, https://www.bugcrowd.com/about/ (last visited June 9, 2019).

120. *Vulnerability Disclosure Policy: What Is It, Why You Need One, and How to Get Started*, HACKERONE, https://www.hackerone.com/sites/default/files/2018-11/vulnerability-disclosure-policy.pdf (last visited June 9, 2019).

121. Greenberg, *supra* note 76; Greenberg, *supra* note 78; Chapman, *supra* note 33; Paul, *supra* note 34.

122. SCHNEIER, *supra* note 92, at 2.

123. *Id*. at 2–3.

124. *Id*. at 3.

125. *Id*. at 33.

126. *Id*. at 5.

Chapter 4

* This chapter is based on years of distilled research in the field of
IoT governance. As such, earlier versions of selections from this
chapter have previously been published in reverse chronological
order as follows: SCOTT J. SHACKELFORD, MANAGING CYBER
ATTACKS IN INTERNATIONAL LAW, BUSINESS, AND RELATIONS: IN
SEARCH OF CYBER PEACE (2014); Scott J. Shackelford, *Toward
Cyberpeace: Managing Cyber Attacks through Polycentric Governance*,
62 AM. U. L. REV. 1273 (2013). Readers are encouraged to consult
these sources for additional discussion of the covered topics.
Special thanks go to Professor Fred Cate for his helpful comments
and critiques on this chapter.

1. *See* Max Roser & Esteban Ortiz-Ospina, *World Population Growth*,
OUR WORLD IN DATA (2013; last updated May 2019), https://
ourworldindata.org/world-population-growth.

2. *Id.*

3. Matt Reimann, *How the First Mass-Market Camera Led to the Right
to Privacy and 'Roe v. Wade,'* TIMELINE (Mar. 9, 2017), https://
timeline.com/how-the-first-mass-market-camera-led-to-the-
right-to-privacy-and-roe-v-wade-4fb4cd87df7a (noting that "the
'Kodak fiend' got that name, of course, from Eastman Kodak, the
company whose cameras made photography affordable to the
amateur. This phenomenon was only accelerated by the release
of their Kodak Brownie, a prism-shaped camera with a price tag
of $1—cheap enough to be marketed to the masses.").

4. *Id.*

5. Samuel D. Warren & Louis D. Brandeis, *The Right to Privacy*,
4 HARV. L. REV. 193, 195 (1890) (calling for the common law to
protect the privacy of the individual).

6. *See* Dorothy J. Glancy, *The Invention of the Right to Privacy*, 21
ARIZ. L. REV. 1, 4 (1979).

7. Warren & Brandeis, *supra* note 5, at 195 n.4. *But see* Glancy, *supra*
note 6, at 3 n.13 (stating that "Thomas Cooley appears to have
coined the phrase 'the right to be let alone' in his TREATISE ON
THE LAW OF TORTS 29 (1st ed. 1879)").

8. Ben Bratman, *Brandeis, & Warren, The Right to Privacy and the
Birth of the Right to Privacy*, 69 TENN. L. REV. 623, 623 (2002).

9. Reimann, *supra* note 3; *see* Josephine Wolff, *Losing Our
Fourth Amendment Data Protection*, N.Y. TIMES (Apr. 28,
2019), https://www.nytimes.com/2019/04/28/opinion/

fourth-amendment-privacy.html?smid=nytcore-ios-share
(discussing the erosion of privacy protections in modern US
Supreme Court rulings).

10. *See* Fred H. Cate & Beth E. Cate, *The Supreme Court and
Information Privacy*, 2 INT'L DATA PRIVACY L. 255, 255 (2012).

11. *See generally* Daniel J. Solove, *Conceptualizing Privacy*, 90 CALIF.
L. REV. 1087 (2002) (advocating a pragmatic approach to
conceptualizing privacy). This research was first published as
Scott J. Shackelford, *Fragile Merchandise: A Comparative Analysis
of the Privacy Rights of Public Figures*, 19 AM. BUS. L.J. 125, 125–27
(2012).

12. *See, e.g.,* Leonid Bershidsky, *Let Users Sell Their Data
to Facebook*, BLOOMBERG (Jan. 31, 2019), https://
www.bloomberg.com/opinion/articles/2019-01-31/
facebook-users-should-be-free-to-sell-their-personal-data.

13. Daniel J. Solove, *A Taxonomy of Privacy*, 154 U. PENN. L. REV. 477,
490 (2006).

14. *See* Lee Rainie, *Americans' Complicated Feelings about Social Media
in an Era of Privacy Concerns*, PEW RESEARCH CTR. (Mar. 27,
2018), https://www.pewresearch.org/fact-tank/2018/03/27/
americans-complicated-feelings-about-social-media-in-an-era-
of-privacy-concerns/; Samuel Gibbs, *We Know People Care about
Privacy, So Why Won't They Pay for It*, GUARDIAN (July 8, 2016),
https://www.theguardian.com/technology/2016/jul/08/we-
know-people-care-about-privacy-so-why-wont-they-pay-for-it.

15. HENRY DAVID THOREAU, WALDEN, OR LIFE IN THE WOODS (1854).

16. *See* Edward Wyatt & Tanzina Vega, *Stage Set for Showdown on
Online Privacy*, N.Y. TIMES, Nov. 10, 2010, at B1 (examining
privacy rights related to tracking of Internet usage).

17. *See Smart Speaker Recordings Reviewed by Humans*, BBC (Apr. 11,
2019), https://www.bbc.com/news/technology-47893082.

18. *See, e.g.,* Alix Langone, *Here's How Facebook or Any Other App
Could Use Your Phone's Microphone to Gather Data*, MONEY (Mar.
30, 2018), http://money.com/money/5219041/how-to-turn-off-
phone-microphone-facebook-spying/.

19. *See* Christopher Mims, *Privacy Is Dead: Here's What Comes Next*,
WALL ST. J. (May 6, 2018), https://www.wsj.com/articles/
privacy-is-dead-heres-what-comes-next-1525608001; Farhad
Manjoo, *It's Time to Panic about Privacy*, N.Y. TIMES, https://
www.nytimes.com/interactive/2019/04/10/opinion/

internet-data-privacy.html?smid=nytcore-ios-share (last visited June 12, 2019).

20. Jim Edwards, *Google's Top Futurist Says Your "Privacy May Be an Anomaly,"* Bus. Insider (Nov. 22, 2013), https://www.businessinsider.com.au/google-vinton-cerf-declares-an-end-to-privacy-2013-11.

21. Herman T. Tavani, *Philosophical Theories of Privacy: Implications for an Adequate Online Privacy Policy*, 38 Metaphilosophy 1, 6 (2007) (quoting Alan F. Westin, Privacy and Freedom (1967)).

22. Margalit Fox, *Alan F. Westin, Who Transformed Privacy Debate before the Web Era, Dies at 83*, N.Y. Times (Feb. 22, 2013), https://www.nytimes.com/2013/02/23/us/alan-f-westin-scholar-who-defined-right-to-privacy-dies-at-83.html.

23. *NSTAC Report to the President on the Internet of Things*, Nat'l Sec. Telecomm. Advisory Comm. (Nov. 19, 2014), https://www.dhs.gov/sites/default/files/publications/NSTAC%20Report%20to%20the%20President%20on%20the%20Internet%20of%20Things%20Nov%202014%20%28updat%20%20%20.pdf.

24. Brad Stone & Brian Stelter, *Facebook Withdraws Changes in Data Use*, N.Y. Times, Feb. 19, 2009, at B1.

25. *See* Kevin Granville, *Facebook and Cambridge Analytica: What You Need to Know as Fallout Widens*, N.Y. Times (Mar. 19, 2018), https://www.nytimes.com/2018/03/19/technology/facebook-cambridge-analytica-explained.html.

26. Laurel Wamsley, *Facebook Has Behaved Like 'Digital Gangsters,' UK Parliament Report Says*, NPR (Feb. 18, 2019), https://www.npr.org/2019/02/18/695729829/facebook-has-been-behaving-like-digital-gangsters-u-k-parliament-report-says.

27. *See* Louise Matsakis, *What to Look for in Your Facebook Data—And How to Find It*, Wired (Mar. 28, 2018), https://www.wired.com/story/download-facebook-data-how-to-read/.

28. Lee Rainie, *Americans' Complicated Feelings about Social Media in an Era of Privacy Concerns*, Pew Res. Ctr. (Mar. 27, 2018), http://www.pewresearch.org/fact-tank/2018/03/27/americans-complicated-feelings-about-social-media-in-an-era-of-privacy-concerns/.

29. *Id.*; Derek Hawkins, *The Cybersecurity 202: "A Wake-up Call": OPM Data Stolen Years Ago Surfacing Now in Financial Fraud Case*, Wash. Post (June 20, 2018), https://www.washingtonpost.

com/news/powerpost/paloma/the-cybersecurity-202/
2018/06/20/the-cybersecurity-202-a-wake-up-call-opm-
data-stolen-years-ago-surfacing-now-in-financial-fraud-case/
5b2924ca1b326b3967989b66/?utm_term=.70e772b70c72.

30. ROBERT KING MERTON, SOCIAL THEORY AND SOCIAL STRUCTURE
429 (1968).

31. *See* Casey Newton, *Facebook Has Been Paying Teens $20 a
Month for Total Access to Their Phone Activity*, VERGE (Jan. 29,
2019), https://www.theverge.com/2019/1/29/18202880/
facebook-research-enterprise-root-certificate-onavo-techcrunch.

32. *Id.*

33. *Id.* (noting that "The Research app requires that users install a
custom root certificate, which gives Facebook the ability to see
users' private messages, emails, web searches, and browsing
activity. It also asks users to take screenshots of their Amazon
order history and send it back to Facebook.").

34. Shobhit Seth, *How Much Can Facebook Potentially Make from
Selling Your Data?*, INVESTOPEDIA (Apr. 11, 2018), https://www.
investopedia.com/tech/how-much-can-facebook-potentially-
make-selling-your-data/.

35. Sacha Molitorisz, *It's Time for Third-Party Data Brokers to Emerge
from the Shadows*, CONVERSATION (Apr. 4, 2018), https://
theconversation.com/its-time-for-third-party-data-brokers-to-
emerge-from-the-shadows-94298.

36. *What Are Data Brokers—And What Is Your Data Worth?*, WEBFX,
https://www.webfx.com/blog/general/what-are-data-brokers-
and-what-is-your-data-worth-infographic/ (last visited Mar.
23, 2019).

37. Mytheos Holt, *How Much Is Your Data Worth?*, HILL (Dec.
11, 2018), https://thehill.com/opinion/technology/
420816-how-much-is-your-data-worth.

38. *Id.* (noting that heavy social media use has been correlated with
a higher risk of depression); Concerns Regarding Social Media
and Health Issues in Adolescents and Young Adults, Am. College
of Obstetricians & Gynecologists (Feb. 2016), https://www.acog.
org/Clinical-Guidance-and-Publications/Committee-Opinions/
Committee-on-Adolescent-Health-Care/Concerns-Regarding-
Social-Media-and-Health-Issues-in-Adolescents-and-Young-
Adults?IsMobileSet=false.

39. Holt, *supra* note 37.
40. *See, e.g.,* Dylan Walsh, *How Much Is Your Private Data Worth—And Who Should Own It?*, INSIGHTS BY STAN. BUS. (Sept. 19, 2018), https://www.gsb.stanford.edu/insights/how-much-your-private-data-worth-who-should-own-it.
41. *Id.*
42. *See, e.g.,* ROGER MCNAMEE, ZUCKED: WAKING UP TO THE FACEBOOK CATASTROPHE (2019).
43. *See* Scott J. Shackelford, *'NotPetya' Ransomware Attack Shows Corporate Social Responsibility Should Include* Cybersecurity, CONVERSATION (June 27, 2017), https://theconversation.com/notpetya-ransomware-attack-shows-corporate-social-responsibility-should-include-cybersecurity-79810.
44. *See, e.g.,* Rachel Kraus, *Facebook Rolls Out GDPR Privacy Checkups Worldwide*, MASHABLE (May 24, 2018), https://mashable.com/2018/05/24/facebook-gdpr-worldwide-compliance/#Wx1biPUwSaqV.
45. *See, e.g.,* Maya Kosoff, *Mark Zuckerberg Quietly Moves 1.5 Billion Users' Rights out of Europe's Reach*, VANITY FAIR (Apr. 19, 2018), https://www.vanityfair.com/news/2018/04/mark-zuckerberg-quietly-moves-15-billion-facebook-user-rights-out-of-europes-reach.
46. *Zuckerberg: Facebook Is in 'Arms Race' with Russia*, BBC (Apr. 11, 2018), https://www.bbc.com/news/world-us-canada-43719784.
47. *See* Press Release, Facebook Launches New Initiative to Help Scholars Assess Social Media's Impact on Elections, Facebook (Apr. 9, 2018), https://newsroom.fb.com/news/2018/04/new-elections-initiative/.
48. *See* Nilay Patel, *Facebook's $5 Billion FTC Fine Is an Embarrassing Joke*, VERGE (July 12, 2019), https://www.theverge.com/2019/7/12/20692524/facebook-five-billion-ftc-fine-embarrassing-joke.
49. Arjun Kharpal, *Social Media Users Treated as 'Experimental Rats,' EU Data Watchdog Says as He Urges More Changes from Facebook*, CNBC (Apr. 6, 2018), https://www.cnbc.com/id/105113671.
50. *Is Connectivity a Human Right?*, FACEBOOK, https://www.facebook.com/isconnectivityahumanright (last visited Mar. 26, 2019); *cf.* Maeve Shearlaw, *Facebook Lures Africa with Free Internet—But What Is the Hidden Cost?*, GUARDIAN (Aug. 1, 2016), https://www.theguardian.com/world/2016/aug/01/facebook-free-basics-internet-africa-mark-zuckerberg

(exploring the hidden costs of free Internet services). An earlier version of research first appeared as Scott J. Shackelford, *Should Cybersecurity Be a Human Right? Exploring the 'Shared Responsibility' of Cyber Peace*, 55 Stan. J. Int'l L. 155 (2019).

51. *See* Kurt Wagner & Rani Molla, *Facebook's User Growth Has Hit a Wall*, Recode (July 25, 2018), https://www.recode.net/2018/7/25/17614426/ facebook-fb-earnings-q2-2018-user-growth-troubles.

52. *See Internet Access Is a 'Human Right,'* BBC (Mar. 8, 2000), http:// news.bbc.co.uk/2/hi/technology/8548190.stm.

53. Margalit Fox, *Alan F. Westin, Who Transformed Privacy Debate before the Web Era, Dies at 83*, N.Y. Times (Feb. 22, 2013), https:// www.nytimes.com/2013/02/23/us/alan-f-westin-scholar-who- defined-right-to-privacy-dies-at-83.html.

54. *See* International Covenant on Civil and Political Rights, Dec. 19, 1966, 999 U.N.T.S. 171, 6 I.L.M. 368 (entered into force Mar. 23, 1976, and ratified by the United States June 8, 1992) [hereinafter ICCPR]; Michael J. Dennis, *Application of Human Rights Treaties Extraterritorially in Times of Armed Conflict and Military Occupation*, 99 Am. J. Int'l L. 119, 119 (2005); Nat'l Research Council, Technology, Policy, Law, and Ethics Regarding U.S. Acquisition and Use of Cyberattack Capabilities 281 (William A. Owens, Kenneth W. Dam, & Herbert S. Lin eds., 2009) [hereinafter National Academies].

55. The Right to Privacy in the Digital Age, Nov. 1, 2013, U.N. Doc. A/ C.3/68/L.45 (2013), http://daccess-dds-ny.un.org/doc/UNDOC/ GEN/N13/544/07/PDF/N1354407.pdf?OpenElement; *see* Violet Blue, *Despite US Opposition, UN Approves Rights to Privacy in the Digital Age*, ZDNet (Nov. 27, 2013), http://www.zdnet.com/ despite-us-opposition-un-approves-rights-to-privacy-in-the- digital-age-7000023708/ (reporting "it is the first such document to establish privacy rights and human rights in the digital sphere").

56. *See* Guiding Principles on Business and Human Rights: Implementing the United Nations "Protect, Respect and Remedy" Framework, U.N. Hum. Rts. 24 (2011), http://www.ohchr.org/Documents/Publications/ GuidingPrinciplesBusinessHR_EN.pdf.

57. *See, e.g.*, Press Release, UN Human Rights Council Resolution on Protection of Human Rights on the Internet a Milestone for Free Speech, Says OSCE Representative, Org. for Sec. & Co-Operation in Eur. (July 5, 2016), http://www.osce.org/fom/250656.

58. G20 LEADERS' COMMUNIQUÉ (Nov. 15–16, 2015), https://
    www.g20.org/Content/DE/_Anlagen/G7_G20/2015-g20-
    abschlusserklaerung-eng.pdf?__blob=publicationFile&v=3.

59. *See* Shackelford, *supra* note 50; *see also* Ann Väljataga, *Tracing*
    Opinio Juris *in National Cyber Security Strategy Documents*, NATO
    CCDCOE, at 4 (2018), http://ccdcoe.com/uploads/2019/
    01/Tracing-opinio-juris-in-NCSS-2.docx.pdf ("National cyber
    security strategies, on the contrary, while not being designed to
    contain legally binding (customary) norms, do communicate a
    state's general position as to the rules and principles in cyber
    state practice and scholarly opinion, viewed as grey zones.")

60. REPUBLIC OF TURK., MINISTRY OF TRANSP., MAR. AFFAIRS &
    COMM., NATIONAL CYBER SECURITY STRATEGY AND 2013–
    2014 ACTION PLAN 16 (2013), https://ccdcoe.org/library/
    publications/national-cyber-security-organisation-turkey/
    ("The principles of rule of law, fundamental human rights
    and freedoms and protection of privacy should be accepted
    as essential principles."); STRATEGY FOR PERSONAL DATA
    PROTECTION IN REPUBLIC OF MACEDONIA 2-12-16, at 4 (arguing
    that "personal data protection . . . includes human rights").

61. These nations include: Australia, Austria, Estonia, Czech
    Republic, Germany, Italy, Macedonia, Netherlands, Poland,
    Russia, Spain, Sweden, Switzerland, Turkey, the United
    Kingdom, and the United States.

62. These nations include: Armenia, Australia, Hungary, Italy,
    Romania, the United Kingdom, and the United States. This
    research was first published as Scott J. Shackelford, *Protecting*
    Intellectual Property and Privacy in the Digital Age: The Use
    of National Cybersecurity Strategies to Mitigate Cyber Risk, 19
    CHAPMAN L. REV. 445 (2016) (the appendices of this article
    contain references to the applicable national cybersecurity
    strategies referencing civil rights and civil liberties).

63. These nations include Armenia, Australia, Austria, Canada,
    Estonia, Czech Republic, Finland, Italy, Japan, Lithuania,
    Macedonia, Netherlands, Nigeria, Norway, Qatar, Slovakia, Spain,
    Switzerland, Turkey, the United Kingdom, and the United States.

64. *Reflections on the Right to Privacy*, N.Y. TIMES (June 28, 2011),
    https://www.nytimes.com/2011/06/29/opinion/l29search.html.

65. These nations include: Aghanistan, Australia, Austria, Canada,
    Chile, Croatia, Denmark, Dubai, Egypt, Finland, France,

Greece, Iceland, India, Italy, Jamaica, Japan, Kenya, Lithuania, Luxembourg, Malta, Mauritania, Mongolia, Montenegro, Netherlands, New Zealand, Nigeria, Norway, Pakistan, Poland, Portugal, Qatar, Romania, Samoa, Saudie Arabia, Slovakia, Slovenia, Spain, Trinidad and Tobago, Turkey, Uganda, the United Kingdom, the United States, and Zimbabwe.

66. These nations include: Australia, Austria, Belgium, Bosnia, Bulgaria, Canada, Chile, Croatia, Czech Republic, Egypt, Estonia, Finland, France, Gambia, Greece, Hungary, Iceland, Italy, Jamaica, Japan, Kenya, Malta, Mongolia, Montenegro, Netherlands, New Zealand, Norway, Poland, Portugal, Romania, Serbia, Slovakia, Slovenia, Spain, Sweden, Switzerland, Turkey, Ukraine, the United Kingdom, the United States, and Zimbabwe.

67. *See, e.g.*, Scott J. Shackelford, *Understanding Cybersecurity Due Diligence*, HUFF. POST (Sept. 16, 2016), https://www.huffpost.com/entry/understanding-cybersecuri_b_8140648.

68. Bhaskar Chakravorti, *Facebook's Fake Pivot to Privacy*, FORBES (Mar. 11, 2019), https://www.forbes.com/sites/bhaskarchakravorti/2019/03/11/facebooks-fake-pivot-to-privacy/#76902cbcb37a.

69. *See* Jane Wakefield, *Facebook and Google Need Ad-Free Options, Says Jaron Lanier*, BBC (Apr. 11, 2018), https://www.bbc.com/news/technology-43639712.

70. *See* Cardiff Garcia & Stacey Vanek Smith, *Dollars for Data*, NPR (Mar. 26, 2018), https://www.npr.org/sections/money/2018/03/26/597036173/dollars-for-data.

71. *See, e.g.*, Russell Brandom, *After Facebook Hearing, Senators Roll Out New Bill Restraining Online Data Use*, VERGE (Apr. 10, 2018), https://www.theverge.com/2018/4/10/17221046/facebook-data-consent-act-privacy-bill-markey-blumenthal.

72. *See* Makena Kelly, *FTC Secures Authority to Open Antitrust Probe into Facebook*, VERGE (June 3, 2019), https://www.theverge.com/2019/6/3/18650845/ftc-authority-facebook-amazon-google-antitrust-investigation-justice-department.

73. *See* Draft NIST Privacy Framework: An Enterprise Risk Management Tool (Apr. 30, 2019), https://www.nist.gov/sites/default/files/documents/2019/04/30/nist-privacy-framework-discussion-draft.pdf.

74. OECD GUIDELINES ON THE PROTECTION OF PRIVACY AND TRANSBORDER FLOWS OF PERSONAL DATA, https://www.oecd.

org/internet/ieconomy/oecdguidelinesontheprotectionofprivac
yandtransborderflowsofpersonaldata.htm (last updated 2013).

75. Shackelford, *supra* note 11.

76. *See Internet of Things (IoT) Connected Devices Installed Base
    Worldwide from 2015 to 2025 (in Billions)*, STATISTA, https://
    www.statista.com/statistics/471264/iot-number-of-connected-
    devices-worldwide/ (last visited Mar. 28, 2019). For a collection
    of other IoT stats and graphics, see Ana Bera, *80 Mind-Blowing
    IoT Statistics*, SAFE AT LAST (Feb. 25, 2019), https://safeatlast.co/
    blog/iot-statistics/.

77. *See, e.g.*, Rob LeFebvre, *Amazon Fixed an Exploit That Allowed
    Alexa to Listen All the Time*, ENGADGET (Apr. 25, 2018), https://
    www.engadget.com/2018/04/25/amazon-fixed-exploit-alexa-
    listen/.

78. Peter Newman, *Here's Why Hackers Are Unlikely to Target
    Smart Speakers like Amazon Echo or Google Home, According to a
    Cybersecurity Expert*, Bus. INSIDER (Sept. 6, 2018), https://www.
    businessinsider.com/jake-williams-cybersecurity-expert-smart-
    speaker-hacking-2018-9.

79. *Big Data: What It Is and Why It Matters*, SAS, https://www.
    sas.com/en_us/insights/big-data/what-is-big-data.html (last
    visited Mar. 30, 2019).

80. Rolf H. Weber, *Internet of Things: Privacy Issues Revisited*, 31
    COMPUTER L. & SEC. REV. 618, 618 (2015).

81. Mackenzie Adams, *Big Data and Individual Privacy in the Age
    of the Internet of Things*, 7 TECH. INNOVATION MGMT. REV. 12, 13
    (2017); Jacob Morgan, *A Simple Explanation of 'The Internet of
    Things,'* FORBES (May 13, 2014), http://www.forbes.com/sites/
    jacobmorgan/2014/05/13/simple-explanation-internet-things-
    that-anyone-can-understand/#572b4c086828.

82. *See* Branden Ly, *Never Home Alone: Data Privacy Regulations for the
    Internet of Things*, 2017 U. ILL. J.L. TECH. & POL'Y 539, 540 (2017).

83. Adams, *supra* note 81, at 14.

84. Charith Perera et al., *Big Data Privacy in the Internet of Things Era*,
    IT PRO, May/June 2015, at 32.

85. *Id.* at 33.

86. Adams, *supra* note 81, at 16.

87. *See* Lindsey Washington, *The Big Debate on Privacy in Big
    Data*, DIPLOMATIC COURIER (Apr. 30, 2018), https://www.
    diplomaticcourier.com/2018/04/30/the-big-debate-on-privacy-
    in-big-data/.

88. Perera, *supra* note 84, at 18.

89. *See id.* at 20.

90. *Healthy Pets, Healthy People*, CDC, https://www.cdc.gov/ healthypets/health-benefits/index.html (last visited Mar. 30, 2019).

91. Andrew Liszewski, *Hasbro Now Has a Toy Line for Seniors Starting with a Lifelike Robotic Cat*, GIZMODO (Nov. 18, 2015), https:// gizmodo.com/hasbro-now-has-a-toy-line-for-seniors-starting-with-a-l-1743122884.

92. *See, e.g., Top Threats and Responses for Older Adults*, UNIV. TEX. AT AUSTIN CTR. FOR IDENTITY, https://identity.utexas.edu/older-adults/top-threats-and-responses-for-older-adults. (last visited Mar. 30, 2019).

93. Marc DaCosta, *Smart-Home Robots Are Using Their Cuteness to Spy on You Better*, N.Y. MAG. (Aug. 8, 2018), http://nymag.com/ intelligencer/smarthome/smart-home-robots-are-adorable-pets-and-also-good-at-collecting-data.html.

94. *Id.* (citing Jan Wolfe, *Roomba Vacuum Maker iRobot Betting Big on the "Smart" Home*, REUTERS (July 24, 2017), https://www.reuters. com/article/us-irobot-strategy/roomba-vacuum-maker-irobot-betting-big-on-the-smart-home-idUSKBN1A91A5).

95. *See Moral Machine*, MIT, http://moralmachine.mit.edu/ (last visited June 9, 2019); *Whom Should Self-Driving Cars Protect in an Accident?*, ECONOMIST (Oct. 27, 2018), https:// www.economist.com/science-and-technology/2018/10/27/ whom-should-self-driving-cars-protect-in-an-accident.

96. *Virtue Ethics*, STANFORD ENCYCLOPEDIA OF PHILOSOPHY (last revised Dec. 8, 2016), https://plato.stanford.edu/entries/ethics-virtue/.

97. Washington, *supra* note 87.

98. *See* Daniela Popescul & Mircea Georgescu, *Internet of Things— Some Ethical Issues*, 13 USV ANNALS OF ECON. & PUB. ADMIN. 208, 208 (2013).

99. Craig Konnoth, *Health Information Equity*, 165 COL. L. SCHOLARLY COMMONS 1317, 1317 (2017).

100. Margaret Hu, *Algorithmic Jim Crow*, 86 FORDHAM L. REV. 633 (2017).

101. *See, e.g.,* Anjanette Raymond, Scott J. Shackelford, & Emma Arrington Stone Young, *Building a Better HAL 9000: Algorithms, the Market, and the Need to Prevent the Engraining of Bias*, 15 NW. J. OF TECH. & INTELL. PROP. 215, 215 (2018).

102. Mark Ryan, *Ethics of Public Use of AI and Big Data*, 2 Orbit J. 1 (2019).

103. Mikkel Flyverbom, Ronald Deibert, & Dirk Matten, *The Governance of Digital Technology, Big Data, and the Internet: New Roles and Responsibilities for Business*, 58 Bus. & Soc'y 3 (2017).

104. Hillary Brill & Scott Jones, *Little Things and Big Challenges: Information Privacy and the Internet of Things*, 66 Am. U. L. Rev. 1183 (2017).

105. *See, e.g.*, Fred H. Cate & Viktor Mayer-Schönberger, *Notice and Consent in a World of Big Data*, 3 Int'l Data Privacy L. 67, 67 (2013).

106. *See* Shankar Vedantam, *To Read All Those Web Privacy Policies, Just Take a Month Off Work*, NPR (Apr. 19, 2012), https://www.npr.org/sections/alltechconsidered/2012/04/19/150905465/to-read-all-those-web-privacy-policies-just-take-a-month-off-work?t=1560288482612.

107. Cate & Mayer-Schönberger, *supra* note 105, at 71–73.

108. *See* Abbey Stemler, Joshua E. Perry, & Todd Haugh, *The Code of the Platform*, Georgia L. Rev. (2019).

109. *See* Scott J. Shackelford et al., *Sustainable Cybersecurity: Applying Lessons from the Green Movement to Managing Cyber Attacks*, 2016 U. Ill. L. Rev. 1995, 1995 (2016).

Chapter 5

* This chapter is based on years of distilled research in the field of IoT governance. As such, earlier versions of selections from this chapter have previously been published in reverse chronological order as follows: Scott J. Shackelford, *Smart Factories, Dumb Policy? Managing Cybersecurity and Data Privacy Risks in the Industrial Internet of Things*, 21 Minn. of L., Sci., & Tech. 1 (2019); Scott J. Shackelford, *When Toasters Attack: Enhancing the 'Security of Things' through Polycentric Governance*, 2017 U. Ill. L. Rev. 415 (2017); Scott J. Shackelford, Scott Russell, & Jeffrey Haut, *Bottoms Up: A Comparison of "Voluntary" Cybersecurity Frameworks*, 16 U.C. Davis Bus. L.J. 217 (2016); Scott J. Shackelford, Scott Russell, & Andreas Kuehn, *Unpacking the International Law on Cybersecurity Due Diligence: Lessons from the Public and Private Sectors*, 17 Chi. J. Int'l L. 1 (2016); Scott J. Shackelford, *Opinion: Forget about Safe Harbor: Modernize Global Privacy Law Instead*, Christian Science Monitor (Jan. 27, 2016), http://www.csmonitor.com/World/Passcode/Passcode-Voices/2016/0127/

Opinion-Forget-about-Safe-Harbor.-Modernize-global-privacy-law-instea; Scott J. Shackelford, *Toward Cyberpeace: Managing Cyber Attacks through Polycentric Governance*, 62 AM. U. L. REV. 1273 (2013). Readers are encouraged to consult these sources for additional discussion of the covered topics, particularly SCOTT J. SHACKELFORD, MANAGING CYBER ATTACKS IN INTERNATIONAL LAW, BUSINESS, AND RELATIONS: IN SEARCH OF CYBER PEACE (2014). Special thanks go to Professor Jeff Kosseff for his helpful comments and critiques on this chapter.

1. *See* Adi Robertson, *California Just Became the First State with an Internet of Things Cybersecurity Law*, VERGE (Sept. 28, 2018), https://www.theverge.com/2018/9/28/17874768/california-iot-smart-device-cybersecurity-bill-sb-327-signed-law.

2. *See* Eli Dourado, *Is There a Cybersecurity Market Failure?* (George Mason Univ. Mercatus Ctr., Working Paper No. 12–05, 2012), http://mercatus.org/publication/there-cybersecurity-market-failure-0 (arguing that market failures are not so common in the cybersecurity realm).

3. ANDREW W. MURRAY, THE REGULATION OF CYBERSPACE: CONTROL IN THE ONLINE ENVIRONMENT 200 (2006).

4. *See, e.g.*, *The Administration Unveils Its Cybersecurity Legislative Proposal*, WHITE HOUSE (May 12, 2011), https://obamawhitehouse.archives.gov/blog/2011/05/12/administration-unveils-its-cybersecurity-legislative-proposal (arguing for the need to strike a "critical balance between maintaining the government's role and providing industry with the capacity to innovatively tackle threats to national cybersecurity").

5. LAWRENCE LESSIG, THE FUTURE OF IDEAS: THE FATE OF THE COMMONS IN A CONNECTED WORLD 71 (2001). To help translate these insights into a regulatory framework for policymakers, Professor Yochai Benkler introduced a simplified three-layer structure composed of: (1) the "physical infrastructure," including the fiber-optic cables and routers making up the physical aspect of cyberspace; (2) the "logical infrastructure," comprising necessary "software such as the TCP/IP protocol"; and (3) the "content layer," which includes data and, indirectly, users. Yochai Benkler, *From Consumers to Users: Shifting the Deeper Structure of Regulation toward Sustainable Commons and User Access*, 52 FED. COMM. L.J. 561, 562 (2000).

6. James A. Lewis, *Sovereignty and the Role of Government in Cyberspace*, 16 BROWN J. WORLD AFF. 55, 56 (2010).

7. *See, e.g.,* Scott J. Shackelford, *Opinion: After High-Profile Hacks, It's Time for a Bolder Approach to Cybersecurity*, CHRISTIAN SCI. MONITOR (Feb. 27, 2015), http://m.csmonitor.com/World/Passcode/Passcode-Voices/2015/0227/Opinion-After-high-profile-hacks-it-s-time-for-a-bolder-approach-to-cybersecurity; FIREEYE, EVOLVING ROLE OF GOVERNMENT IN CYBER SECURITY 2 (2018), https://www.fireeye.com/content/dam/fireeye-www/solutions/pdfs/wp-evolving-role-gov.pdf; FIREEYE, HOW GOVERNMENT AGENCIES ARE FACING CYBERSECURITY CHALLENGES 2 (2018), https://www.fireeye.com/content/dam/fireeye-www/solutions/pdfs/how-govt-agencies-are-facing-cyber-security-challenges.pdf; *see also* BRUCE SCHNEIER, CLICK HERE TO KILL EVERYBODY: SECURITY AND SURVIVAL IN A HYPER-CONNECTED WORLD 117 (2018) (noting that critical infrastructure protection is difficult since it is expensive, complicated, features hybrid public–private governance, and it is politically difficult to spend the funds needed).

8. Josephine Wolff & William Lehr, *When Cyber Threats Loom, What Can State and Local Governments Do?*, 19 GEO. J. INT'L L. 67, 68 (2018).

9. *See Yahoo!, Inc. v. La Ligue Contre le Racisme et L'Antisemitisme*, 169 F. Supp. 2d 1181 (N.D. Cal. 2001), *rev'd*, 379 F.3d 1120 (9th Cir. 2005), *rev'd en banc*, 433 F.3d 1199 (9th Cir. 2006). An earlier version of this research appeared as chapter 1 in SHACKELFORD, MANAGING CYBER ATTACKS, *supra* note *

10. *See* Elissa A. Okoniewski, Yahoo!, Inc. v. LICRA: *The French Challenge to Free Expression on the Internet*, 18(1) AM. U. INT'L L. REV. 295, 296–97 (2002) (recounting how Yahoo!'s sale of Nazi memorabilia in France contravened French Penal Code R. 645-1, and acted as the basis of the private suit in the *Yahoo!* case).

11. *See* JACK GOLDSMITH & TIM WU, WHO CONTROLS THE INTERNET?: ILLUSIONS OF A BORDERLESS WORLD 5 (2006).

12. *See id.* at 10.

13. *Id.*

14. *See, e.g., Cyber Attacks Force WikiLeaks to Move Web Address*, FR. 24 (Mar. 12, 2010), http://www.france24.com/en/20101203-wikileaks-website-address-server-cyber-attacks-switzerland-france-usa (reporting that WikiLeaks had published "hundreds of confidential diplomatic cables that have given unvarnished

and sometimes embarrassing insights into the foreign policy of
the United States and its allies").

15. *See Internet Freedom: Free to Choose*, Economist (Oct. 6, 2012),
http://www.economist.com/node/21564198 ("Brazilian
authorities briefly detained Google's country boss on September
26th for refusing to remove videos from its YouTube subsidiary
that appeared to breach electoral laws.").

16. Chloe Taylor, *Social Media Execs Will Face Jail in Australia If Their
Platforms Host Violent Content*, CNBC (Apr. 4, 2019), https://
www.cnbc.com/2019/04/04/social-media-execs-will-face-jail-in-
australia-if-their-platforms-host-violent-content.html.

17. *See* Tim Stack, *Internet of Things (IoT) Data Continues to Explode
Exponentially: Who Is Using That Data and How?*, Cisco (Feb. 5,
2018), https://blogs.cisco.com/datacenter/internet-of-things-iot-
data-continues-to-explode-exponentially-who-is-using-that-data-
and-how.

18. *See, e.g.,* Mohana Ravindranath, *Who's in Charge of Regulating
the Internet of Things?*, Nextgov (Sept. 1, 2016), https://
www.nextgov.com/emerging-tech/2016/09/internet-things-
regulating-charge/131208/.

19. *Id.*

20. *New IoT Security Regulations*, Schneier on Sec., https://www.
schneier.com/blog/archives/2018/11/new_iot_securit.html (last
visited Apr. 4, 2019).

21. *See, e.g.,* Daniel Carpenter et al., *Approval Regulation and
Endogenous Consumer Confidence: Theory and Analogies to Licensing,
Safety, and Financial Regulation*, 4 Reg. & Governance 383, 383
(2010).

22. *See, e.g.,* Dan Lohrmann, *Lack of Trust in IoT Security Shows More
Regulation Is Coming*, Gov't Tech. (Nov. 5, 2017), https://www.
govtech.com/blogs/lohrmann-on-cybersecurity/lack-of-trust-in-
iot-security-means-more-regulation-is-coming.html.

23. *See id.;* Charlotte A. Tschider, *Regulating the Internet of
Things: Discrimination, Privacy, and Cybersecurity in the Artificial
Intelligence Age*, 96 Denv. L. Rev. 88, 138 (2018).

24. *See* Tschider, *supra* note 23, at 121.

25. Shinichi Kamiya et al., *What Is the Impact of Successful Cyberattacks
on Target Firms?* (Nat'l Bureau of Econ. Research, Working Paper
No. 24409, 2018), https://www.nber.org/digest/jun18/w24409.
shtml.

26. Tschider, *supra* note 23, at 90.

27. Elinor Ostrom, *Polycentric Systems as One Approach for Solving Collective-Action Problems* 1 (Ind. Univ. Workshop in Pol. Theory and Pol'y Analysis, Working Paper Series No. 08-6, 2008), http://dlc.dlib.indiana.edu/dlc/bitstream/handle/10535/4417/W08-6_Ostrom_DLC.pdf?sequence=1.

28. VINCENT OSTROM, THE MEANING OF FEDERALISM 225 (1991).

29. *See generally* POLYCENTRICITY AND LOCAL PUBLIC ECONOMIES: READINGS FROM THE WORKSHOP IN POLITICAL THEORY AND POLICY ANALYSIS (Michael D. McGinnis ed., 1999) (collecting these studies).

30. *See* Elinor Ostrom, *A Polycentric Approach for Coping with Climate Change* 6 (World Bank, Pol'y Res., Working Paper No. 5095, 2009), http://documents.worldbank.org/curated/en/480171468315567893/pdf/WPS5095.pdf.

31. *See* Scott J. Shackelford, *Governing the Final Frontier: A Polycentric Approach to Managing Space Weaponization and Debris*, 51 AM. BUS. L.J. 429 (2014).

32. SCHNEIER, supra note 7, at 24.

33. *See* Robert O. Keohane & David G. Victor, *The Regime Complex for Climate Change*, 10 (Harv. Kennedy Sch., Discussion Paper 10-33, 2009) (internal quotation marks omitted), http://belfercenter.ksg.harvard.edu/files/Keohane_Victor_Final_2.pdf.

34. *See* Henning Wegener, *Cyber Peace, in* THE QUEST FOR CYBER PEACE 77, 77 (Int'l Telecomm. Union & Permanent Monitoring Panel on Info. Sec. eds., 2011), http://www.itu.int/dms_pub/itu-s/opb/gen/S-GEN-WFS.01-1-2011-PDF-E.pdf. For a more general background on the application of polycentric governance to addressing cybersecurity, see Scott J. Shackelford, Timothy L. Fort, & Jamie Prenkert, *How Businesses Can Promote Cyber Peace*, 36 U. PENN. J. INT'L L. 353 (2015); Scott J. Shackelford et al., *Using BITs to Protect Bytes: Promoting Cyber Peace and Safeguarding Trade Secrets through Bilateral Investment Treaties*, 52 AM. BUS. L.J. 1 (2015).

35. MONROE E. PRICE & STEFAN G. VERHULST, SELF-REGULATION AND THE INTERNET 21 (2005).

36. *See id.* at 21–22.

37. Ostrom, *supra* note 27, at 2–3.

38. *See, e.g.,* Taylor Owen, *The Era of Big Tech Self-Governance Has Come to an End*, GLOBE & MAIL (Apr. 11, 2018), https://www.

theglobeandmail.com/opinion/article-the-era-of-big-tech-self-
governance-has-come-to-an-end/.

39. Jon Martindale, *FTC Head Wants the Internet of Things to
Regulate Itself*, Digital Trends (Mar. 15, 2017), https://www.
digitaltrends.com/web/ftc-iot-self-regulae/.

40. A Resolution Expressing the Sense of the Senate About a
Strategy for the Internet of Things to Promote Economic
Growth and Consumer Empowerment, S. Res. 110, 114th
Cong., 1st Sess. (2015); *see* Rita Tehan, *Cybersecurity: Legislation,
Hearings, and Executive Branch Documents*, Cong. Res.
Serv. R43317, at 12–21 (Dec. 2015), https://www.fas.
org/sgp/crs/misc/R43317.pdf; John Eggerton, *Senate
Commerce Schedules IoT Hearing*, Multichannel News
(Apr. 23, 2019), https://www.multichannel.com/news/
senate-commerce-schedules-iot-hearing.

41. *See* Jerry Brito & Tate Watkins, *Loving the Cyber Bomb? The
Dangers of Threat Inflation in Cybersecurity Policy*, 3 Harv. Nat'l
Sec. J. 39, 82 (2011) (making the case against there being a
cybersecurity market failure).

42. *See* Andrew J. Grotto & Christos Makridis, *Publicly Reported
Data Breaches: A Measure of Our Ignorance?*, Lawfare
(July 11, 2018), https://www.lawfareblog.com/publicly-
reported-data-breaches-measure-our-ignorance?utm_
source=Hoover+Daily+Report&utm_campaign=be844ea02e-
HDR_COPY_01&utm_medium=email&utm_term=0_
21b1edff3c-be844ea02e-72796245.

43. *See* Elinor Ostrom, Governing the Commons: The Evolution
of Institutions for Collective Action 212 (1990); Susan
J. Buck, The Global Commons: An Introduction 32 (1998).

44. Murray, *supra* note 3, at 148.

45. *Id*. at 163. John Locke was a seventeenth-century philosopher
who is popularly known as the Father of Liberalism. *See* Michael
Welbourne, *The Community of Knowledge*, 31(125) Phil. Q. 302,
302–04 (1981).

46. Murray, *supra* note 3, at 163. Jean-Jacques Rousseau was an
eighteenth-century Genevan philosopher who argued that
individuals are best protected from one another by forming
a moral community of equals. *See* Katrin Froese, *Beyond
Liberalism: The Moral Community of Rousseau's Social Contract*, 34
Can. J. Pol. Sci. 579, 581–82 (2001).

47. Murray, *supra* note 3, at 163.

48. *See, e.g.*, Elinor Ostrom et al., *Revisiting the Commons: Local Lessons, Global Challenges*, 284 Sci. 278, 278 (1999) (questioning policymakers' use of Garrett Hardin's theory of the "tragedy of the commons," in light of the empirical data showing self-organizing groups can communally manage common-pool resources).

49. *See, e.g.*, Gregory A. Johnson, *Organizational Structure and Scalar Stress, in* Theory and Explanation in Archeology 389, 392–94 (Colin Renfrew et al. eds., 1982).

50. *See* Murray, *supra* note 3, at 164.

51. Indeed, the retail sector established an ISAC in the wake of the 2014 Target data breach. *See Retail-ISAC Launches Cyber Sharing Portal Supported by FS-ISAC*, PR Newswire (Mar. 24, 2015), http://www.prnewswire.com/news-releases/retail-isac-launches-cyber-sharing-portal-supported-by-fs-isac-300055086.html. Other sectors, such as automobile manufacturers, have followed suit.

52. *See* Murray, *supra* note 3, at 164.

53. Price & Verhulst, *supra* note 35, at 21 According to Notre Dame Professor Don Howard, different online communities "have a complicated topology and geography, with overlap, hierarchy, varying degrees of mutual isolation and mutual interaction. There are also communities of corporations or corporate persons, gangs of thieves, and . . . on scales small and large." Don Howard, *Civic Virtue and Cybersecurity* 15 (Working Paper, 2014). What is more, Professor Howard argues that these communities will each construct norms in their own ways, and at their own rates, but that this process has the potential to make positive progress toward addressing multifaceted issues such as enhancing cybersecurity. *Id.* at 22.

54. *See* Price & Verhulst, *supra* note 35, at 21–22.

55. Ostrom, *supra* note 27, at 2–3.

56. Murray, *supra* note 3, at 125.

57. *See* Paul Hiebert, *Consumer Reports in the Age of the Amazon Review*, Atlantic (Apr. 13, 2016), https://www.theatlantic.com/business/archive/2016/04/consumer-reports-in-the-age-of-the-amazon-review/477108/.

58. *Consumer Reports Launches Digital Standard to Safeguard Consumers' Security and Privacy in Complex Marketplace*, Consumer Rep. (Mar. 6, 2017), https://www.consumerreports.

org/media-room/press-releases/2017/03/consumer_reports_
launches_digital_standard_to_safeguard_consumers_security_
and_privacy_in_complex_marketplace/.

59. Jerry Beilinson, *Glow Pregnancy App Exposed Women to Privacy
    Threats, Consumer Reports Finds*, CONSUMER REP. (July 28, 2016),
    https://www.consumerreports.org/mobile-security-software/
    glow-pregnancy-app-exposed-women-to-privacy-threats/.

60. *See* Hiebert, *supra* note 57 ("More than 120 employees, with an
    annual testing budget of approximately $25 million, evaluate
    some 3,000 products a year. The results of these impartial studies
    are then gathered, examined, and published, ad-free, in *Consumer
    Reports*."); Allen St. John, *Europe's GDPR Brings Data Portability to
    U.S. Consumers*, CONSUMER REP. (May 25, 2018), https://www.
    consumerreports.org/privacy/gdpr-brings-data-portability-to-
    us-consumers/.

61. For a thorough accounting of international cybersecurity norms
    and how they overlap, see *International Cybersecurity Norms*,
    CARNEGIE ENDOWMENT, https://carnegieendowment.org/
    publications/interactive/cybernorms (last visited Sept. 11, 2018).

62. For a deep dive on this topic, see Scott J. Shackelford & Scott
    O. Bradner, *Have You Updated Your Toaster? Transatlantic
    Approaches to Governing the Internet of Everything* (Kelley School of
    Business, Research Paper No. 18-60, July 4, 2018), https://ssrn.
    com/abstract=3208018.

63. Scott R. Peppet, *Regulating the Internet of Things: First Steps toward
    Managing Discrimination, Privacy, Security, and Consent*, 93 TEX.
    L. REV. 85, 135 (2014).

64. *FTC Report on Internet of Things Urges Companies to Adopt Best
    Practices to Address Consumer Privacy and Security Risks*, FED.
    TRADE COMM'N (Jan. 27, 2015), https://www.ftc.gov/news-
    events/press-releases/2015/01/ftc-report-internet-things-urges-
    companies-adopt-best-practices [hereinafter "FTC IoT Report"].

65. *See id.*

66. *See id.*

67. Peppet, *supra* note 63, at 39.

68. *Id.*

69. Katharine Goodloe, *Covington IoT Update: US Legislative
    Roundup on IoT*, INSIDE PRIVACY (May 9, 2018), https://www.
    insideprivacy.com/internet-of-things/covington-iot-update-u-s-
    legislative-roundup-on-iot/.

70. Allison Schiff, *IoT Is a Security Mess and Regulators Are Paying Attention*, ADEXCHANGER, (Dec. 9, 2016), https://adexchanger.com/mobile/iot-security-mess-regulators-paying-attention/.

71. W. Reece Hirsch et al., *Third Circuit Sides with FTC in Data Security with Wyndham*, NAT'L L. REV. (Sept. 8, 2015), https://www.natlawreview.com/article/third-circuit-sides-ftc-data-security-dispute-wyndham.

72. Tyler Armerding, *Can the FTC Save the IoT?*, CSO ONLINE, (Feb. 9, 2017), https://www.csoonline.com/article/3166601/can-the-ftc-save-the-iot.html.

73. *See, e.g., FTC's Bureau of Consumer Protection Staff Submits Comment on Internet of Things and Consumer Product Hazards*, FED. TRADE COMM'N (June 15, 2018), https://www.ftc.gov/news-events/press-releases/2018/06/ftcs-bureau-consumer-protection-staff-submits-comment-internet.

74. FTC IoT Report, *supra* note 64.

75. *See* Andrea Arias, *The NIST Cybersecurity Framework and the FTC*, Fed. Trade Comm'n (Aug. 31, 2016), https://www.ftc.gov/news-events/blogs/business-blog/2016/08/nist-cybersecurity-framework-ftc.

76. *See FTC Enters 'Internet of Things' Arena with TRENDnet Proposed Settlement*, INFO. L. GP. (Sept. 9, 2013), https://www.infolawgroup.com/blog/2013/09/articles/ftc/trendnet-settlement.

77. *See, e.g., FCC Regulations and Guidelines for Manufacturing IoT Devices*, TEMPO AUTOMATION (Sept. 20, 2018), https://www.tempoautomation.com/blog/fcc-regulations-and-guidelines-for-manufacturing-iot-devices/.

78. Chase Martin, *Now FCC Stepping In on IoT Regulations*, AI&IoT DAILY (Jan. 22, 2017), https://www.mediapost.com/publications/article/293367/now-fcc-stepping-in-on-iot-regulations.html.

79. "47 CFR 95.421—(CB Rule 21) What Are the Penalties for Violating These Rules?" Legal Information Institute, CORNELL L. SCH., https://www.law.cornell.edu/cfr/text/47/95.421.

80. Exec. Order No. 13636, 78 Fed. Reg. 11737 at 11740–41 (Feb. 19, 2013).

81. For more on this topic, see Scott J. Shackelford et al., *Toward a Global Standard of Cybersecurity Care?: Exploring the Implications of the 2014 Cybersecurity Framework on Shaping Reasonable National*

and International Cybersecurity Practices, 50 Tex. Int'l L.J. 287, 288–90 (2015).

82. Scott J. Shackelford & Andrew Proia, *Why Ignoring the NIST Framework Could Cost You*, Huff. Post (May 2, 2014), http:// www.huffingtonpost.com/scott-j-shackelford/why-ignoring-the-nist- fra_b_5244112.html.

83. The NIST CSF Framework Core is the main component, focusing on cybersecurity-related activities and outcomes. It includes five main groups of possible actions: identify, protect, detect, respond, and recover. Each group is further divided into categories and subcategories, each of which point to specific industry standards. The Profiles are essentially a summary of a given cybersecurity program and are used to help organizations align activities with their desired security requirements. Organizations create a "Current Profile" and a "Target Profile" to identify security gaps and establish road maps to go from the former to the latter. Finally, the NIST CSF Tiers are meant for organizations to self-rank their cybersecurity risk management practices. NIST provides four tiers, ranging from Tier 1 (Partial) to Tier 4 (Adaptive). As the tiers get higher, the practices implemented increase in rigor and sophistication. The goal is for companies to determine if they should invest resources into moving up tiers, because it is not always necessary or cost-effective to do so depending on the cyber threats they face. *Uses and Benefits of the Framework*, NIST, https://www.nist.gov/cyberframework/ online-learning/uses-and-benefits-framework (last visited Apr. 10, 2019).

84. Press Release, NIST Marks Fifth Anniversary of Popular Cybersecurity Framework, NIST (Feb. 2, 2019), https://www.nist.gov/news-events/news/2019/02/ nist-marks-fifth-anniversary-popular-cybersecurity-framework.

85. PwC, Why You Should Adopt the NIST Framework 1 (May 2014), https://www.pwc.com/us/en/increasing-it- effectiveness/publications/assets/adopt-the-nist.pdf; *see* Shackelford, Russell, & Kuehn, *supra* note *, at 1.

86. *See* Exec. Order No.13,228 on Strengthening the Cybersecurity of Federal Networks and Critical Infrastructure, 82 Fed. Reg. 32,172 (May 11, 2017).

87. *See* Tim Casey et al., *The Cybersecurity Framework in Action: An Intel Use Case*, Intel (2015), https://supplier.intel.com/static/

governance/documents/The-cybersecurity-framework-in-
action-an-intel-use-case-brief.pdf; *Applying the Cybersecurity
Framework at the University of Chicago—An Education Case
Study*, UNIV. OF CHI. (2014), http://security.bsd.uchicago.edu/
wp-content/uploads/sites/2/2016/04/BSD-Framework-
Implementation-Case-Study_final_edition.pdf.

88. *NIST Releases Version 1.1 of Its Popular Cybersecurity
Framework*, NIST (Apr. 16, 2018), https://
www.nist.gov/news-events/news/2018/04/
nist-releases-version-11-its-popular-cybersecurity-framework.

89. *See id.*

90. *See, e.g.*, Paul Otto & Brian Kennedy, *NIST Releases Draft
Framework on the Internet of Things*, HOGAN LOVELLS CHRON. OF
DATA PROTECTION (Sept. 25, 2015), http://www.hldataprotection.
com/2015/09/articles/consumer-privacy/nist-releases-draft-
framework-on-the-internet-of-things/.

91. *See* Rebecca Crootof, *The Internet of Torts*, 69 DUKE L.J. 1, 1 (2019)
("Even as the potential for harm escalates, contract and tort law
work in tandem to shield IoT companies from liability.").

92. Peppet, *supra* note 63, at 7.

93. *Id.* However, based on *LabMD Inc. v. Federal Trade Commission*,
the FTC may need to become more specific in the cybersecurity
standards it requires of businesses. In essence, the Eleventh US
Circuit Court of Appeals ruled in June 2018 that, since the FTC
had not provided specific cybersecurity standards defining
reasonableness for LabMD, a now bankrupt cancer-screening
company, the FTC's order was illegal. Alison Frankel, *There's a Big
Problem for the FTC Lurking in the 11th Circuit's LabMD Data-Security
Ruling*, REUTERS (June 7, 2018), https://www.reuters.com/article/
us-otc-labmd/theres-a-big-problem-for-the-ftc-lurking-in-11th-
circuits-labmd-data-security-ruling-idUSKCN1J32S2.

94. FTC STAFF REP., INTERNET OF THINGS: PRIVACY & SECURITY IN A
CONNECTED WORLD (2015), https://www.ftc.gov/system/files/
documents/reports/federal-trade-commission-staff-report-
november-2013-workshop-entitled-internet-things-privacy/
150127iotrpt.pdf.

95. *Id.*

96. *IoT Cyber Bill Factsheet*, https://www.warner.senate.gov/public/
_cache/files/8/6/861d66b8-93bf-4c93-84d0-6bea67235047/
8061BCEEBF4300EC702B4E894247D0E0.iot-cybesecurity-
improvement-act---fact-sheet.pdf.

97. *Id.*

98. Katharine Goodloe & Micha Nandaraj Gallo, *Senate Reintroduces IoT Cybersecurity Improvement Act*, Inside Privacy (Mar. 12, 2019), https://www.insideprivacy.com/internet-of-things/senate-reintroduces-iot-cybersecurity-improvement-act/.

99. Robertson, *supra* note 1.

100. Kimberly Underwood, *The U.S. Government Urgently Needs to Address Cyber Security Challenges*, Signal (Sept. 24, 2018), https://www.afcea.org/content/us-government-urgently-needs-address-cybersecurity-challenges.

101. Catalin Cimpanu, *GAO Gives Congress Go-Ahead for a GDPR-Like Privacy Legislation*, ZDNet (Feb. 15, 2019), https://www.zdnet.com/article/gao-gives-congress-go-ahead-for-a-gdpr-like-privacy-legislation/.

102. Robertson, *supra* note 1.

103. Josh Fruhlinger, *The Mirai Botnet Explained*, CSO Online, (Mar. 9 2018), https://www.csoonline.com/article/3258748/the-mirai-botnet-explained-how-teen-scammers-and-cctv-cameras-almost-brought-down-the-internet.html.

104. Robert Graham, *California's Bad IoT Law*, Errata Sec. (Sept. 10, 2018), https://blog.erratasec.com/2018/09/californias-bad-iot-law.html ("the point is not to add 'security features' but to remove 'insecure features.' For IoT devices, that means removing listening ports and cross-site/injection issues in web management."); Arshad Noor, *California SB-327 and the Wake-Up Call for Stronger Authentication*, CPO Mag. (Dec. 4, 2018), https://www.cpomagazine.com/cyber-security/california-sb-327-and-the-wake-up-call-for-stronger-authentication/.

105. *See* Michael Kassner, *Ohio Law Creates Cybersecurity 'Safe Harbor' for Businesses*, Tech. Rep. (Jan. 3, 2019), https://www.techrepublic.com/article/ohio-law-creates-cybersecurity-safe-harbor-for-businesses/.

106. There are also potential dormant commerce clause issues to consider in such a scenario. *See* Jack L. Goldsmith & Alan O. Sykes, *The Internet and the Dormant Commerce Clause*, 110 Yale L.J. 785, 786 (2000).

107. *See* Samm Sacks & Lorand Laskai, *China's Privacy Conundrum*, Slate (Feb. 7, 2019), https://slate.com/technology/2019/02/china-consumer-data-protection-privacy-surveillance.html.

108. *See* Yu Du & Matthew Murphy, *Data Protection and Privacy Issues in China*, HG, https://www.hg.org/legal-articles/

data-protection-and-privacy-issues-in-china-5340 (last visited Apr. 11, 2019) ("Privacy rights have been available to Chinese citizens under the Constitution and other legal regulations since the 1980's. However, due to the size and strength of government, as well as a general reluctance in the past to litigate, the laws have not been tested to a great extent."). China's push to become the global leader in 5G technology is also widely seen as a move to position it to be the leading force in IoT applications and governance. *See, e.g.,* Josh Chin, *The Internet, Divided between the US and China, Has Become a Battleground,* WALL ST. J. (Feb. 9, 2019), https://www.wsj.com/articles/the-internet-divided-between-the-u-s-and-china-has-become-a-battleground-11549688420?mg=prod/com-wsj.

109. *See, e.g.,* Mark G. McCreary, *The California Consumer Privacy Act: What You Need to Know,* N.J. L.J. (Dec. 1, 2018), https://www.law.com/njlawjournal/2018/12/01/the-california-consumer-privacy-act-what-you-need-to-know/?slreturn=20190311100925.

110. *See, e.g.,* Eric Goldman, *41 California Privacy Experts Urge Major Changes to the California Consumer Privacy Act,* TECH. & MARKETING L. BLOG (Jan. 17, 2019), https://blog.ericgoldman.org/archives/2019/01/41-california-privacy-experts-urge-major-changes-to-the-california-consumer-privacy-act.htm.

111. *See* Joseph J. Lazzarotti & Jason C. Gavejian, *State Law Developments in Consumer Privacy,* NAT'L L. REV. (Mar. 15, 2019), https://www.natlawreview.com/article/state-law-developments-consumer-privacy.

112. *See The State of Data Protection Rules around the World: A Briefing for Consumer Organizations,* CONSUMERS INT'L, at 3 (2018), https://www.consumersinternational.org/media/155133/gdpr-briefing.pdf.

113. *Commission Priority, Digital Single Market, Bringing Down Barriers to Unlock Online Opportunities Digital Single Market,* EUR. COMM'N http://ec.europa.eu/priorities/digital-single-market/index_en.htm.

114. *See Framework for Improving Critical Infrastructure,* NIST, at 4 (Apr. 2015), http://www.nist.gov/cyberframework/upload/cybersecurity_framework_bsi_2015-04-08.pdf (noting that "[t]o allow for adoption, Framework version 2.0 is not planned for the near term").

115. Eur. Comm'n, *supra* note 113.
116. Eur. Comm'n, An Environment Where Digital Networks and Services Can Prosper, http://ec.europa.eu/priorities/digital-single-market/environment/index_en.htm (last visited Dec. 16, 2017).
117. *See, e.g., Top Ten Operational Impacts of the GDPR,* Int'l Assoc. Privacy Prof., https://iapp.org/resources/article/top-10-operational-impacts-of-the-gdpr/ (last visited June 5, 2018).
118. Max Read, *The E.U.'s New Privacy Laws Might Actually Create a Better Internet,* Intelligencer (May 15, 2018), http://nymag.com/intelligencer/2018/05/can-gdpr-create-a-better-internet.html.
119. Lindsey Washington, *The Big Debate on Privacy in Big Data,* Diplomatic Courier (Apr. 30, 2018), https://www.diplomaticourier.com/2018/04/30/the-big-debate-on-privacy-in-big-data/.
120. Int'l Assoc. Privacy Prof., *supra* note 117.
121. *See* Alyssa Newcomb, *Chicago Tribune, Los Angeles Times Block European Users Due to GDPR,* NBC News (May 25, 2018), https://www.nbcnews.com/tech/tech-news/chicago-tribune-los-angeles-times-block-european-users-due-gdpr-n877591.
122. Chris Albers Denhart, *New European Union Data Law GDPR Impacts Are Felt by Largest Companies: Google, Facebook,* Forbes (May 25, 2018), https://www.forbes.com/sites/chrisdenhart/2018/05/25/new-european-union-data-law-gdpr-impacts-are-felt-by-largest-companies-google-facebook/#73b2a17f4d36.
123. Scott Gordon, *Will We Get a GDPR for the IOT?,* SC Mag. (Apr. 26, 2018), https://www.scmagazineuk.com/will-we-get-a-gdpr-for-the-iot/article/758037/.
124. *Id.*
125. *See* Int'l Assoc. Privacy Prof., *supra* note 117.
126. *The Directive on Security of Network and Information Systems (NIS Directive),* Eur. Comm'n, https://ec.europa.eu/digital-single-market/en/network-and-information-security-nis-directive (last visited Jan. 7, 2018).
127. *See, e.g.,* Alfred Ng, *Tech Companies Really Don't Want a US Version of Europe's Privacy Law,* CNET (Sept. 26, 2018), https://www.cnet.com/news/tech-companies-really-dont-want-a-us-version-of-europes-privacy-law/.

128. Michihiro Nishi, *Data Protection in Japan to Align with GDPR*, SKADDEN (Sept. 24, 2018), https://www.skadden.com/insights/publications/2018/09/quarterly-insights/data-protection-in-japan-to-align-with-gdpr.

129. Noah Apthorpe, Sarah Varghese, & Nick Feamster, *Evaluating the Contextual Integrity of Privacy Regulation: Parents' IoT Toy Privacy Norms Versus COPAA*, CORNELL UNIV. (submitted Mar. 12, 2019), https://arxiv.org/abs/1903.05152.

130. *Indian Supreme Court in Landmark Ruling on Privacy*, BBC (Aug. 24, 2017), https://www.bbc.com/news/world-asia-india-41033954; *State of Privacy India*, PRIVACY INT'L (Jan. 2019), https://privacyinternational.org/state-privacy/1002/state-privacy-india.

131. Sindhuja Balaji, *India Finally Has a Data Framework—What Does It Mean for Its Billion-Dollar Tech Industry?*, FORBES (Aug. 3, 2018), https://www.forbes.com/sites/sindhujabalaji/2018/08/03/india-finally-has-a-data-privacy-framework-what-does-it-mean-for-its-billion-dollar-tech-industry/#380096b370fe.

132. *Id.*

133. UK DEP'T BUS., INNOVATION & SKILLS, CYBER ESSENTIALS SCHEME SUMMARY (June 2014), http://www.cyberstreetwise.com/cyberessentials/files/scheme-summary.pdf.

134. *Id.*

135. *Id.*

136. *See* Charles Towers-Clark, *UK to Introduce New Law for IoT Device Security*, FORBES (May 2, 2019), https://www.forbes.com/sites/charlestowersclark/2019/05/02/uk-to-introduce-new-law-for-iot-device-security/#4b0d8688579d.

137. *See Cyber Essentials*, NAT'L CYBER SEC. CTR., https://www.cyberessentials.ncsc.gov.uk/getting-certified/ (last visited June 5, 2018).

138. Press Release, EU to Become More Cyber-Proof as Council Backs Deal on Common Certification and Beefed-Up Agency, Council of the Eur. Union (Dec. 19, 2018), https://www.consilium.europa.eu/en/press/press-releases/2018/12/19/eu-to-become-more-cyber-proof-as-council-backs-deal-on-common-certification-and-beefed-up-agency/.

139. Gordon, *supra* note 121.

140. *See* Henry Belot, *Microsoft Says Encryption Laws Make Companies Wary of Storing Data in Australia*, ABC (Mar. 27, 2019), https://www.abc.net.au/news/2019-03-28/

microsoft-says-companies-are-no-longer-comfortable-storing-data/10946494.

141. Laura DeNardis & Mark Raymond, *The Internet of Things as a Global Policy Frontier*, 51 U.C. Davis L. Rev. 475 (2017), https://lawreview.law.ucdavis.edu/issues/51/2/Symposium/51-2_DeNardis_Raymond.pdf.

142. For the state of play as of early 2019, see *Trends in International Law for Cyberspace*, NATO CCDCOE (May 2019), https://ccdcoe.org/uploads/2019/05/Trends-Intlaw_a4_final.pdf.

143. *See* Scott J. Shackelford, *The Law of Cyber Peace*, 18 Chi. J. Int'l L. 1 (2017); Tallinn Manual on the International Law Application to Cyber Warfare (Michael N. Schmitt ed., 2013).

144. Tim Ryan & Leonard Navarro, *Cyber Due Diligence: Pre-Transaction Assessments Can Uncover Costly Risks*, Kroll Call (Jan. 28, 2015), https://www.kroll.com/en/insights/publications/cyber/cyber-due-diligence-pre-transaction-assessments.

145. An earlier version of this research was previously published as Shackelford, Russell, & Kuehn, *supra* note *, at 1.

146. *See* Pete Burke, *Protecting Critical Internet Infrastructure from IoT Device Risks*, GCN (Dec. 10, 2018), https://gcn.com/articles/2018/12/10/iot-critical-infrastructure.aspx.

147. G7 Declaration on Responsible States Behavior in Cyberspace (Apr. 11, 2017), https://www.mofa.go.jp/files/000246367.pdf.

148. Group of Governmental Experts on Developments in the Field of Information and Telecommunications in the Context of International Security, U.N. Doc. A/70/174 (July 22, 2015), https://carnegieendowment.org/publications/interactive/cybernorms.

149. Tallinn Manual on the International Law Application to Cyber Warfare, Rule 6 (Michael N. Schmitt ed., 2013).

150. Letter dated 9 January 2015 from the Permanent Representatives of China, Kazakhstan, Kyrgyzstan, the Russian Federation, Tajikistan, and Uzbekistan to the United Nations addressed to the Secretary General, U.N. Doc. A/69/723 (Jan. 13, 2015), https://carnegieendowment.org/publications/interactive/cybernorms.

151. G.A. Res. 217 (III) A, Universal Declaration of Human Rights, art. 12 (Dec. 10, 1948).

152. *See* Peter Schaar, *Zügellose Überwachung zurückfahren!*, Spiegel
     Online (June 25, 2013), http://www.spiegel.de/netzwelt/
     netzpolitik/peter-schaar-zu-prism-und-tempora-ueberwachung-
     zurueckfahren-a-907793.html.
153. *See, e.g.,* Ryan Gallagher, *After Snowden Leaks, Countries Want Digital
     Privacy Enshrined in Human Rights Treaty*, Slate (Sept. 26, 2013),
     https://slate.com/technology/2013/09/article-17-surveillance-
     update-countries-want-digital-privacy-in-the-iccpr.html.
154. For more on this topic, see Scott J. Shackelford, *Should
     Cybersecurity Be a Human Right? Exploring the 'Shared
     Responsibility' of Cyber Peace*, 55 Stan. J. Int'l L. 155 (2019). There
     are also other useful regional agreements to consider aside from
     GDPR, such as the APEC Cross-Border Privacy Rules (CBPR)
     system, which is composed of twenty-seven APEC nations plus
     the United States, Canada, Japan, and Mexico. These rules do
     not replace existing domestic privacy regimes, but do provide
     a minimum level of protection when national regulations are
     silent. Alex Wall, *GDPR Matchup: The APEC Privacy Framework
     and Cross-Border Privacy Rules*, Int'l Assoc. Privacy Prof. (May
     31, 2017), https://iapp.org/news/a/gdpr-matchup-the-apec-
     privacy-framework-and-cross-border-privacy-rules/#. Similarly,
     the Privacy Shield Program, which replaced the Safe Harbor
     regime that the European Court of Justice found to be illegal in
     2013, also acts as something of a de facto international standard
     for IoT firms. International Trade Administration, Privacy
     Shield Framework (2019), https://www.privacyshield.gov/
     Program-Overview.
155. Schneier, supra note 7, at 9.

Chapter 6

* This chapter is based on years of distilled research in the field
  of cybersecurity and Internet governance. As such, earlier
  versions of selections from this chapter have previously been
  published in reverse chronological order as follows: Scott
  J. Shackelford, *'NotPetya' Ransomware Attack Shows Corporate
  Social Responsibility Should Include Cybersecurity*, Conversation
  (June 27, 2017), https://theconversation.com/notpetya-
  ransomware-attack-shows-corporate-social-responsibility-
  should-include-cybersecurity-79810; Scott J. Shackelford
  et al., *Sustainable Cybersecurity: Applying Lessons from the Green*

Movement to Managing Cyber Attacks, 2016 U. ILL. L. REV. 1995;
Scott J. Shackelford, Timothy L. Fort, & Jamie D. Prenkert, *How
Businesses Can Promote Cyber Peace*, 36 U. PENN. J. INT'L L. 353
(2015); Scott J. Shackelford, *Sustainable Cybersecurity*, HUFF.
POST (Apr. 2, 2015), http://www.huffingtonpost.com/scott-j-
shackelford/sustainable-cybersecurity_b_6988050.html

1. Megan Garber, *Kennedy, Before Choosing the Moon: "I'm Not That
   Interested in Space,"* ATLANTIC (Sept. 12, 2012), https://www.
   theatlantic.com/technology/archive/2012/09/kennedy-before-
   choosing-the-moon-im-not-that-interested-in-space/262287/.
2. Alan Crameri, *Artificial Intelligence: The Fourth Industrial
   Revolution*, INFO. AGE (Oct. 3, 2018), https://www.information-
   age.com/artificial-intelligence-fourth-industrial-revolution-
   123475170/.
3. Josh Dzieza, *A History of Metaphors for the Internet*, VERGE (Aug.
   20, 2014), https://www.theverge.com/2014/8/20/6046003/
   a-history-of-metaphors-for-the-internet.
4. *Id.*
5. *Id.*
6. Dzieza, *supra* note 3.
7. Nathan Jurgenson, *Digital Dualism and the Fallacy of
   Web Objectivity*, CYBORGOLOGY (Sept. 13, 2011), https://
   thesocietypages.org/cyborgology/2011/09/13/digital-dualism-
   and-the-fallacy-of-web-objectivity/.
8. *Id.*
9. Dzieza, *supra* note 3.
10. *See also* UNDERSTANDING CYBER CONFLICT: 14 ANALOGIES (George
    Perkovich & Ariel E. Levite eds., 2017) (exploring a range of
    analogies from privateering to nuclear weapons to explain and
    better manage cyber conflict).
11. *See* Rose Eveleth, *There Are 37.2 Trillion Cells in Your
    Body*, SMITHSONIAN MAG. (Oct. 24, 2013), https://www.
    smithsonianmag.com/smart-news/there-are-372-trillion-cells-in-
    your-body-4941473/.
12. *See NIH Human Microbiome Project Defines Normal Bacterial Makeup
    of the Body*, NAT'L INST. HEALTH (June 13, 2012), https://www.
    nih.gov/news-events/news-releases/nih-human-microbiome-
    project-defines-normal-bacterial-makeup-body.
13. *See* Press Release, Number of Connected IoT Devices Will
    Surge to 125 Billion by 2030, IHS Markit Says, IHS Markit (Oct.

24, 2017), https://technology.ihs.com/596542/number-of-connected-iot-devices-will-surge-to-125-billion-by-2030-ihs-markit-says.

14. *See, e.g.*, Michael McElfresh, *Power Grid Cyber Attacks Keep the Pentagon Up at Night*, Sci. Am. (June 8, 2015), https://www.scientificamerican.com/article/power-grid-cyber-attacks-keep-the-pentagon-up-at-night/.

15. *Id.*

16. *See* Brent Rowe, Michael Halpern, & Tony Lentz, *Is a Public Health Framework the Cure* for Cyber Security?, 25 CrossTalk 30, 31–32 (2012).

17. *Id.* at 35.

18. *Id.* at 36.

19. *Is Public Health the Model for Securing the Internet of Things?*, Sec. Ledger (Aug. 28, 2015), https://securityledger.com/2015/08/is-public-health-the-model-for-securing-the-internet-of-things/.

20. *Id.; see also* Michael Imeson, *Manufacturers Face Tighter Rules on Devices*, Fin. Times (Oct. 17, 2018), https://www.ft.com/content/d21079b0-8a79-11e8-affd-da9960227309 ("Security by design is fundamental if we are to progress with the internet of things," says Margot James, UK minister for digital and the creative industries. "If consumers don't have confidence in the safety of the products they buy, it will stymie growth in this sector.").

21. *Organization*, Nat'l Inst. Health, https://www.nih.gov/about-nih/who-we-are/organization (last visited Apr. 29, 2019).

22. *See* Robert O. Keohane & David G. Victor, *The Regime Complex for Climate Change* 2, 4 (Harv. Project on Int'l Climate Agreements, Discussion Paper No. 33, 2010).

23. Joseph S. Nye Jr., *Cyber Power*, Harv. Belfer Ctr. 15 (2010), http://belfercenter.ksg.harvard.edu/files/cyber-power.pdf (making the case that cyberspace may be considered a type of common pool resource, and as such "self-organization is possible under certain conditions").

24. Mike Barlow, Governing the IoT: Balancing Risk and Regulation 2 (2016).

25. *Id.*

26. Dimiter V. Dimitrov, *Medical Internet of Things and Big Data in Healthcare*, 22 Healthcare Informatics Res. 156 (2016), https://www.ncbi.nlm.nih.gov/pmc/articles/PMC4981575/pdf/hir-22-156.pdf.

27. Scott J. Shackelford et al., *Securing the Internet of Healthcare*, 19 MINN. J.L., SCI., & TECH. 405, 406 (2018).

28. Charlie Osborne, *Locky Ransomware Used to Target Hospitals Evolves*, ZDNET (Nov. 7, 2017), http://www.zdnet.com/article/locky-ransomware-used-to-target-hospitals-evolves/.

29. *See Firmware Update to Address Cybersecurity Vulnerabilities Identified in Abbott's (Formerly St. Jude Medical's) Implantable Cardiac Pacemakers: FDA Safety Communication*, FED. DRUG ADMIN. (Aug. 29, 2017), https://www.fda.gov/MedicalDevices/Safety/AlertsandNotices/ucm573669.htm.

30. For a deep dive on this topic, see Shackelford et al., *supra* note 27.

31. SEC. LEDGER, *supra* note 19.

32. *Id.*

33. *Overview*, GAIA THEORY, http://www.gaiatheory.org/overview/ (last visited Apr. 30, 2019).

34. *Id.*

35. *See NIST Cybersecurity for IoT Program*, https://www.nist.gov/programs-projects/nist-cybersecurity-iot-program (last visited Apr. 30, 2019).

36. *Demystifying IoT Cybersecurity*, IoT CYBERSECURITY ALLIANCE 3 (2017), https://www.iotca.org/wp-content/themes/iot/pdf/IoT-Cybersecurity-Alliance-Demystifying-IoT-Cybersecurity.pdf.

37. *See NIST Plans to Draft IoT Cybersecurity Guidance That Will Impact the Private Sector*, WILEY (Oct. 23, 2017), https://www.wileyconnect.com/home/2017/10/23/nist-plans-to-draft-iot-cybersecurity-guidance-that-will-impact-the-private-sector.

38. Laurence Pitt, *The Path to Securing IoT Ecosystems Starts at the Network*, SEC. WK. (July 19, 2018), https://www.securityweek.com/path-securing-iot-ecosystems-starts-network.

39. Jeremy Robert et al., *Open IoT Ecosystem for Enhanced Interoperability in Smart Cities—Example of Metropole De Lyon*, 17 SENSORS 2849 (2017), https://www.ncbi.nlm.nih.gov/pmc/articles/PMC5751623/.

40. *See Creating a Truly Open IOT Device Management Ecosystem*, ACCELERITE (Mar. 22, 2018), https://accelerite.com/blogs/creating-a-truly-open-iot-device-management-ecosystem/.

41. *See, e.g.*, Gaia Scagnetti, *The Here and Now of Dystopian Scenarios*, MEDIUM (June 13, 2017), https://medium.com/the-state-of-responsible-internet-of-things-iot/dystopian-scenarios-and-the-internet-of-things-3836daba8e34.

42. Bruce Schneier, We Have Root: Even More Advice from Schneier on Security 67 (2019).

43. Larry B. Crowder et al., *Resolving Mismatches in U.S. Ocean Governance*, 313 Sci. 617, 617 (2006) (noting that "[i]n the United States, at least 20 federal agencies implement over 140 federal ocean-related statutes," and arguing for ecosystem-based management).

44. Paul A. Berkman & Oran R. Young, *Governance and Environmental Change in the Arctic Ocean*, 324 Sci. 339, 340 (2009).

45. *See* Charlotte Hess, *The Virtual CPR: The Internet as a Local and Global Common Pool Resource* (1995), http://dlc.dlib.indiana.edu/dlc/bitstream/handle/10535/234/iascp-95-II.pdf?sequence=1.

46. This research first appeared as Shackelford, *'NotPetya' Ransomware Attack, supra* note *.

47. Andy Greenberg, *The Untold Story of NotPetya, the Most Devastating Cyberattack in History*, Wired (Aug. 22, 2018), https://www.wired.com/story/notpetya-cyberattack-ukraine-russia-code-crashed-the-world/.

48. *Id.*

49. *Id.*

50. *How Boards of Directors Really Feel about Cyber Security Reports*, Bay Dynamics, https://baydynamics.com/resources/how-boards-of-directors-really-feel-about-cyber-security-reports/ (last visited May 5, 2019).

51. *See* Sven Herpig & Ari Schwartz, *The Future of Vulnerabilities Equities Processes around the World*, Lawfare (Jan. 4, 2019), https://www.lawfareblog.com/future-vulnerabilities-equities-processes-around-world.

52. *See* Nicole Perlroth & Scott Shane, *In Baltimore and Beyond, a Stolen NSA Tool Wreaks Havoc*, N.Y. Times (May 25, 2019), https://www.nytimes.com/2019/05/25/us/nsa-hacking-tool-baltimore.html?smid=nytcore-ios-share.

53. *See* Archie B. Carroll, *The Pyramid of Corporate Social Responsibility: Toward the Moral Management of Organizational Stakeholders*, 34 Bus. Horizons 39, 40 (1991).

54. *See, e.g.*, Markus Christen et al., *A Review of Value-Conflicts in Cybersecurity*, 1 ORBIT J. (2017), https://orbit-rri.org/ojs/index.php/orbit/article/view/28.

55. Timothy L. Fort, Business, Integrity, and Peace: Beyond Geopolitical and Disciplinary Boundaries 79 (2011).

56. *Id*. at 92 (noting that "the aggregate approach fosters freedom, but does not attend to the gaps where those outside the market can effectively negotiate contracts . . . [whereas] [t]he concession approach aligns the corporation with the nation-state with an implicit obligation to be loyal to the country of its origins").

57. *Id*. at 86.

58. Rand Beers, *Cybersecurity: A Shared Responsibility*, Dep't Homeland Sec. (Oct. 18, 2013), https://www.dhs.gov/blog/2013/10/18/cybersecurity-shared-responsibility.

59. *See* Jake Olcott, *Building Customer Trust—Cybersecurity in CSR Programmes*, Gigabit (Dec. 21. 2018), https://www.gigabitmagazine.com/big-data/building-customer-trust-cybersecurity-csr-programmes.

60. *See* Marcel Salathé, *Herd Immunity and Measles: Why We Should Aim for 100% Vaccination Coverage*, Conversation (Feb. 2, 2015), https://theconversation.com/herd-immunity-and-measles-why-we-should-aim-for-100-vaccination-coverage-36868.

61. Scott J. Shackelford, Timothy L. Fort, & Jamie D. Prenkert, *How Businesses Can Promote Cyber Peace*, 36 U. Penn. J. Int'l L. 353, 379 (2015).

62. *Id*. at 380.

63. For more on this topic, see Janine S. Hiller & Scott J. Shackelford, *The Firm and Common Pool Resource Theory: Understanding the Rise of Benefit Corporations*, 55 Am. Bus. L.J. 1, 5 (2018).

64. *See* Megan Stifel, *Securing the Modern Economy: Transforming Cybersecurity through Sustainability*, Pub. Knowledge (Apr. 2018), https://www.publicknowledge.org/assets/uploads/documents/Securing_the_Modern_Economy--Transforming_Cybersecurity_Through_Sustainability_FINAL_4.18.18_PK.pdf.

65. *Id*. at 11; Karen Walsh, *Physical and Digital Environmentalism: Lessons for Sustainable Cyber*, Peerlyst (Apr. 25, 2019), https://www.peerlyst.com/posts/physical-and-digital-environmentalism-lessons-for-sustainable-cyber-karen-walsh.

66. *See, e.g.*, Andrew S. Goudie, The Human Impact on the Natural Environment: Past, Present, and Future 326–29 (2013).

67. Michael Rotman, *Cuyahoga River Fire*, CLEVELAND HIST. http://
clevelandhistorical.org/items/show/63 (last visited Nov.
19, 2013).

68. *Chemical Spill Turns Rhine Red*, BBC: ON THIS DAY, http://news.
bbc.co.uk/onthisday/hi/dates/stories/november/1/newsid_
4679000/4679789.stm (last visited May 13, 2019).

69. *See* Justin McCurry, *Japanese Schoolchildren Fed Toxic Dolphin
Meat*, GUARDIAN (Sept. 5, 2007), https://www.theguardian.com/
world/2007/sep/05/japan.justinmccurry.

70. *See* Weihong Qian & Yafen Zhu, *Climate Change in China from 1880
to 1998 and Its Impact on the Environmental Condition*, 50 CLIMATE
CHANGE 419, 419–20 (2001); Jonathan Watts, *China Makes Gain in
Battle against Desertification but Has Long Fight Ahead*, GUARDIAN
(Jan. 4, 2011), http://www.theguardian.com/world/2011/jan/
04/china-desertification.

71. *See, e.g., DDT: A Brief History and Status*, ENVTL. PROTECTION
AGENCY, https://www.epa.gov/ingredients-used-pesticide-
products/ddt-brief-history-and-status.

72. *See* Adriene Hill, *Wet Towels in Hotel Rooms Is a Corporate Goal*,
MARKETPLACE (Sept. 18, 2013), http://www.marketplace.org/
topics/sustainability/wet-towels-hotel-rooms-corporate-goal.

73. *Id.*

74. *Id.*

75. *See* Michael Hickins, *Turning Cybersecurity into a Competitive
Advantage*, WALL ST. J. (Feb. 20, 2013), http://blogs.wsj.com/
cio/2013/02/20/the-morning-download-turning-cybersecurity-
into-a-competitive-advantage/; THE LAW REQUIRES IT, BUT
CUSTOMERS DEMAND IT: CYBER SECURITY AND PRIVACY ARE GOOD
BUSINESS, FINANCIER WORLDWIDE (Apr. 2016), https://www.
financierworldwide.com/the-law-requires-it-but-customers-
demand-it-cyber-security-and-privacy-are-good-business. For a
discussion of cybersecurity best practices being deployed by the
private sector to enhance cybersecurity, see Shackelford, Fort, &
Prenkert, *supra* note 61.

76. *See* DANIEL C. ESTY & ANDREW WINSTON, GREEN TO GOLD: HOW
SMART COMPANIES USE ENVIRONMENTAL STRATEGY TO INNOVATE,
CREATE VALUE, AND BUILD A COMPETITIVE ADVANTAGE 2 (2009).

77. *See* SHACKELFORD, MANAGING CYBER ATTACKS, *supra* note *, at
225–28.

78. Hill, *supra* note 72.

79. *See* Tom Relihan, *These Are the Cyberthreats Lurking in Your Supply Chain*, MIT Sloan (Feb. 19, 2019), https://mitsloan.mit.edu/ideas-made-to-matter/these-are-cyberthreats-lurking-your-supply-chain; David Inserra & Steven P. Bucci, *Cyber Supply Chain Security: A Crucial Step Toward U.S. Security, Prosperity, and Freedom in Cyberspace*, Heritage Found. (Mar. 6, 2014), http://www.heritage.org/research/reports/2014/03/cyber-supply-chain-security-a-crucial-step-toward-us-security-prosperity-and-freedom-in-cyberspace.

80. *See About GRI*, Global Reporting Initiative, https://www.globalreporting.org/Information/about-gri/Pages/default.aspx (last visited May 5, 2019).

81. *See Sustainability Disclosure Database*, GRI, http://database.globalreporting.org/ (last visited May 5, 2019).

82. *Id.*

83. *See, e.g.*, Matt Egan, *Survey: Investors Crave More Cyber Security Transparency*, Fox Bus. (Mar. 4, 2013), https://www.foxbusiness.com/markets/survey-investors-crave-more-cyber-security-transparency.

84. *Id.*

85. Div. of Corp. Fin., US Sec. & Exch. Comm'n, CF Disclosure Guidance: Topic No. 2 Cybersecurity (Oct. 13, 2011), https://www.sec.gov/divisions/corpfin/guidance/cfguidance-topic2.htm; Joel Bronstein, *The Balance between Informing Investors and Protecting Companies: A Look at the Division of Corporation Finance's Recent Guidelines on Cybersecurity Disclosure Requirements*, 13 N.C. J.L. & Tech. On. 257, 271 (2012) (citing *TSC Indus., Inc. v. Northway, Inc.*, 426 U.S. 438, 449 (1976), which defined "material" as "a substantial likelihood that the disclosure of the omitted fact would have been viewed by the reasonable investor as having significantly altered the 'total mix' of information made available").

86. *See, e.g., SEC Staff Provides Guidance on Disclosure Obligations Relating to Cybersecurity Risks and Cyber Incidents*, WSGR Alert (Oct. 18, 2011), http://www.wsgr.com/WSGR/Display.aspx?SectionName=publications/PDFSearch/wsgralert-cybersecurity-risks.htm [hereinafter WSGR Alert]; Chris Strohm, *SEC Chairman Reviewing Company Cybersecurity Disclosures*, Bloomberg (May 13, 2013), http://www.bloomberg.com/news/2013-05-13/

sec-chairman-reviewing-company-cybersecurity-disclosures.html (reporting that the SEC is exploring strengthening cyber attack disclosure requirements).

87. Rob Scott, *SEC Demands Better Disclosure for Cybersecurity Incidents and Threats*, HELPNET SEC. (Apr. 30, 2019), https:// www.helpnetsecurity.com/2019/04/30/sec-demands-better-disclosure-for-cybersecurity-incidents-and-threats/.

88. *Id.*

89. Alexander Koskey & Matthew White, *SEC Issues Risk Alert on Regulation S-P*, JD SUPRA (May 3, 2019), https://www.jdsupra.com/legalnews/sec-issues-risk-alert-on-regulation-s-p-61498/.

90. *See Green Building Leadership Is LEED*, US GREEN BUILDING COUNCIL, https://new.usgbc.org/leed (last visited May 13, 2019).

91. *Id.*

92. *Id.*

93. *See, e.g., Perspectives on the Framework*, NIST, https://www.nist.gov/cyberframework/perspectives (last visited May 5, 2019).

94. *See* Christopher P. Skroupa, *An Approach 'Essential to Creating Robust, Sustainable Cyber Security,'* FORBES (Feb. 27, 2018), https://www.forbes.com/sites/christopherskroupa/2018/02/27/an-approach-essential-to-creating-robust-sustainable-cyber-security/#51f16cc33793.

Chapter 7

* This chapter and the conclusion are based on years of distilled research in the field of cybersecurity and privacy. As such, earlier versions of selections from this chapter have previously been published in reverse chronological order as follows: Scott J. Shackelford, *Smart Factories, Dumb Policy? Managing Cybersecurity and Data Privacy Risks in the Industrial Internet of Things*, 21 MINN. OF L., SCI., & TECH. 1 (2019); Scott J. Shackelford, *Securing the Internet of Healthcare*, 19 MINN. OF L., SCI., & TECH. 405 (2018); Scott J. Shackelford & Steve Myers, *Block-by-Block: Leveraging the Power of Blockchain Technology to Build Trust and Promote Cyber Peace*, 19 YALE J. OF L. & TECH. 334 (2017); Scott J. Shackelford, *The Law of Cyber Peace*, 18 CHI. J. INT'L L. 1 (2017); Scott J. Shackelford, *Opinion: How to Make Democracy Harder to Hack*, CHRISTIAN SCI. MONITOR (July 29, 2016), http://www.csmonitor.com/World/Passcode/Passcode-Voices/2016/

0729/Opinion-How-to-make-democracy-harder-to-hack; Scott J. Shackelford et al., *Using BITs to Protect Bytes: Promoting Cyber Peace and Safeguarding Trade Secrets through Bilateral Investment Treaties*, 52 AM. BUS. L.J. 1 (2015); Scott J. Shackelford, *Toward Cyberpeace: Managing Cyber Attacks through Polycentric Governance*, 62 AM. U. L. REV. 1273 (2013). Interested readers are encouraged to consult these sources for additional discussion of the covered topics, particularly SCOTT J. SHACKELFORD, MANAGING CYBER ATTACKS IN INTERNATIONAL LAW, BUSINESS, AND RELATIONS: IN SEARCH OF CYBER PEACE (2014).

1. GEORGE SAVILE MARQUIS OF HALIFAX, THE COMPLETE WORKS OF GEORGE SAVILE, FIRST MARQUESS OF HALIFAX 249 (1912).
2. *See Significant Cyber Incidents*, CSIS, https://www.csis.org/programs/cybersecurity-and-governance/technology-policy-program/other-projects-cybersecurity (last visited May 6, 2019).
3. *5 Cybersecurity Trends to Expect in 2019*, AT&T BUS., https://www.business.att.com/learn/tech-advice/5-cybersecurity-trends-to-expect-in-2019.html (last visited May 6, 2019).
4. *See, e.g.*, Tara Swaminatha, *Corporate Boards Will Face the Spotlight in Cybersecurity Incidents*, CSO (Mar. 8, 2018), https://www.csoonline.com/article/3261405/corporate-boards-will-face-the-spotlight-in-cybersecurity-incidents.html.
5. *See* AT&T BUS., *supra* note 3.
6. *Id.*
7. For a deep dive on this topic, see SHACKELFORD, MANAGING CYBER ATTACKS, *supra* note *.
8. Henning Wegener, *Cyber Peace, in* THE QUEST FOR CYBER PEACE 77, 78 (Hamadoun I. Toure & Perm. Monitoring Panel on Info. Sec. eds., 2011), http://www.itu.int/dms_pub/itu-s/opb/gen/S-GEN-WFS.01-1-2011-PDF-E.pdf.
9. *Digital Peace*, MICROSOFT, https://digitalpeace.microsoft.com/ (last visited Nov. 5, 2018).
10. Johan Galtung, *Violence, Peace, and Peace Research*, 6 J. PEACE RES. 167, 168 (1969).
11. *See, e.g.*, Martin Luther King Jr., *Nonviolence and Racial Justice*, CHRISTIAN CENTURY 118, 119 (1957) (arguing "true peace is not merely the absence of some negative force—tension, confusion, or war; it is the presence of some positive force—justice, good will, and brotherhood").

12. *See* Johan Galtung, *Peace, Positive and Negative, in* THE
    ENCYCLOPEDIA OF PEACE PSYCHOLOGY 1, 1 (Daniel J. Christie
    ed., 2011).

13. ROBERT SCHÜTZE, EUROPEAN CONSTITUTIONAL LAW 177 (2012)
    (citing to OXFORD ENGLISH DICTIONARY).

14. David E. Sanger, *U.S. Declines to Sign Declaration Discouraging Use
    of Cyberattacks*, N.Y. TIMES (Nov. 12, 2018), https://www.nytimes.
    com/2018/11/12/us/politics/us-cyberattacks-declaration.html;
    *Indiana University among First to Endorse Paris Call for Trust and
    Security in Cyberspace*, IU NEWSROOM (Nov. 12, 2018), https://
    news.iu.edu/stories/2018/11/iu/releases/12-paris-call-for-trust-
    and-security-in-cyberspace.html.

15. Milton Mueller, *The Paris IGF: Convergence on Norms, or Grand
    Illusion?*, INTERNET GOVERNANCE PROJECT (Nov. 9, 2018), https://
    www.internetgovernance.org/2018/11/09/the-paris-igf-
    convergence-on-norms-or-grand-illusion/ (arguing that "there
    will be no effective operationalization of norms until there is
    agreement on the status of cyberspace as a global commons, a
    non-sovereign space").

16. Romain Dillet, *With the Paris Call, Macron Wants to Limit
    Cyberattacks*, TECH CRUNCH (Nov. 12, 2018), https://techcrunch.
    com/2018/11/12/with-the-paris-call-macron-wants-to-limit-
    cyberattacks/.

17. Press Release, Cybersecurity: Paris Call of 12 November 2018 for
    Trust and Security in Cyberspace, France Diplomatie, https://
    www.diplomatie.gouv.fr/en/french-foreign-policy/digital-
    diplomacy/france-and-cyber-security/article/cybersecurity-
    paris-call-of-12-november-2018-for-trust-and-security-in.

18. *See* Garrett Hinck, *Private-Sector Initiatives for Cyber Norms: A
    Summary*, LAWFARE (June 25, 2018), https://www.lawfareblog.
    com/private-sector-initiatives-cyber-norms-summary.

19. Obama White House, *The Comprehensive National Cybersecurity
    Initiative*, WHITE HOUSE, https://obamawhitehouse.archives.
    gov/issues/foreign-policy/cybersecurity/national-initiative (last
    visited May 13, 2019).

20. The notion of including humans in conceptions of cyberspace
    and cybersecurity is nothing new. *See* James A. Winnefeld Jr.,
    Christopher Kirchhoff, & David M. Upton, *Cybersecurity's Human
    Factor: Lessons from the Pentagon*, HARV. BUS. REV. (Sept. 2015),
    https://hbr.org/2015/09/cybersecuritys-human-factor-lessons-
    from-the-pentagon, along with the work on human factors.

21. WHITE HOUSE, NATIONAL CYBER STRATEGY OF THE UNITED STATES OF AMERICA (Sept. 2018), https://www.whitehouse.gov/wp-content/uploads/2018/09/National-Cyber-Strategy.pdf.

22. *See About Us: Non-Governmental Organizations,* ONLINE TRUST ALLIANCE, https://otalliance.org/about-us/non-governmental-organizations-ngos (last visited Nov. 9, 2017).

23. *See Cybersecurity and Internet Governance,* OSTROM WORKSHOP, https://ostromworkshop.indiana.edu/research/internet-cybersecurity/index.html (last visited Nov. 9, 2017); CYBER FUTURE FOUND., http://cyberfuturefoundation.org/ (last visited Nov. 9, 2017).

24. ICT4PEACE, https://ict4peace.org/what-we-do/ (last visited Nov. 1, 2018).

25. *See Cyber Peace Working Group,* OSTROM WORKSHOP, https://ostromworkshop.indiana.edu/research/internet-cybersecurity/index.html (last visited May 11, 2019); *Cybersecurity Working Group,* CORNELL UNIV., https://einaudi.cornell.edu/working-group/cybersecurity (last visited May 11, 2019).

26. Scott J. Shackelford, *Is It Time for a Cyber Peace Corps?,* CONVERSATION (Oct. 25, 2017), https://theconversation.com/is-it-time-for-a-cyber-peace-corps-85721.

27. *See* Matt Lewis, *Obama Loves Martin Luther King's Great Quote—But He Uses It Incorrectly,* DAILY BEAST (Jan. 16, 2017), https://www.thedailybeast.com/obama-loves-martin-luther-kings-great-quotebut-he-uses-it-incorrectly.

28. *See* Ana Bera, *80 Mind-Blowing IoT Statistics (Infographic),* SAFEATLAST (Feb. 25, 2019), https://safeatlast.co/blog/iot-statistics/.

29. *Id.*; Ekaterina Novoseltseva, *IoT Projects That Will Change the World,* APIUMHUB (Nov. 2, 2017), https://apiumhub.com/tech-blog-barcelona/iot-projects-will-change-world/?utm_source=datafloq&utm_medium=ref&utm_campaign=datafloq.

30. *See* Bera, *supra* note 28.

31. SMART DUBAI, https://www.smartdubai.ae/about-us (last visited May 11, 2019).

32. SMART NATION, https://www.smartnation.sg/what-is-smart-nation/initiatives (last visited May 11, 2019).

33. *See* Amanda Coletta, *Quayside, Toronto's Google-Linked Smart City, Draws Opposition Over Privacy, Costs,* WASH. POST (May 7, 2019), https://www.washingtonpost.com/world/the_americas/quayside-torontos-google-linked-smart-city-draws-

opposition-over-privacy-costs/2019/05/05/e0785500-6d12-11e9-
bbe7-1c798fb80536_story.html?utm_term=.28cd715a7165; Nick
Schifrin, *Chinese Tech Makes Cities 'Smart,' But Critics Say It Spreads
Authoritarianism*, PBS Newshour (Oct. 1, 2019), https://www.
pbs.org/newshour/show/is-this-chinese-technology-a-trojan-
horse-for-spreading-authoritarianism.

34. Michele Bertoncello & Dominik Wee, *Ten Ways Autonomous
Driving Could Redefine the Automotive World*, McKinsey &
Co. (June 2015), https://www.mckinsey.com/industries/
automotive-and-assembly/our-insights/ten-ways-autonomous-
driving-could-redefine-the-automotive-world.

35. *See* James Cook, *A Complete History of Internet-Connected Fridges*,
Bus. Insider (Jan. 5, 2016), https://www.businessinsider.
com/the-complete-history-of-internet-fridges-and-connected-
refrigerators-2016-1.

36. David Pegg, *Facebook Labelled "Digital Gangsters" by Report on
Fake News*, Guardian (Feb. 17, 2019), https://www.theguardian.
com/technology/2019/feb/18/facebook-fake-news-
investigation-report-regulation-privacy-law-dcms.

37. *See* Julia Angwin, *How the Government Could Fix Facebook*,
Atlantic (Apr. 5, 2018), https://www.theatlantic.com/
technology/archive/2018/04/four-ways-to-fix-facebook/
557255/. *See generally* Jeff Kosseff, The Twenty-Six Words That
Created the Internet (2019).

38. *Internet of Things Quotes*, https://internetofthings.net/internet-
things-quotes/ (last visited May 6, 2019).

39. *See* Maciej Kranz, *What We Can Learn from China about IoT*,
Forbes (May 5, 2018), https://www.forbes.com/sites/
forbestechcouncil/2018/03/05/what-we-can-learn-from-china-
about-iot/#2b1ac5f937af.

40. *See* Kelvin Chan & Karel Janicek, *Cyber Officials Call for
Coordinated 5G Security Approach*, AP (May 3, 2019), https://
www.apnews.com/132800027bf24f95aa9f0c950f96343d.

41. *See* Bernard Marr, *Chinese Social Credit Score: Utopian Big Data
Bliss or Black Mirror on Steroids?*, Forbes (Jan. 21, 2019), https://
www.forbes.com/sites/bernardmarr/2019/01/21/chinese-
social-credit-score-utopian-big-data-bliss-or-black-mirror-on-
steroids/#48df224748b8; *The Chinese Surveillance State*, N.Y.
Times (May 6, 2019), https://www.nytimes.com/2019/05/06/
podcasts/the-daily/china-surveillance-uighurs.html; Chris

Buckley & Paul Mozur, *How China Uses High-Tech Surveillance to Subdue Minorities*, N.Y. TIMES (May 22, 2019), https://www.nytimes.com/2019/05/22/world/asia/china-surveillance-xinjiang.html?smid=nytcore-ios-share.

42. Marr, *supra* note 41.
43. *Id*.
44. *See* Samira Shackle, *China Is Actively Exporting Its Model of the Internet*, NEW HUMANIST (Mar. 26, 2019), https://newhumanist.org.uk/articles/5441/china-is-actively-exporting-its-model-of-the-internet.
45. *See* Scott J. Shackelford & Amanda N. Craig, *Beyond the New 'Digital Divide': Analyzing the Evolving Role of Governments in Internet Governance and Enhancing Cybersecurity*, 50 STAN. J. INT'L L.119 (2014).
46. *What Is Edge Computing?*, HEWLETT PACKARD, https://www.hpe.com/emea_europe/en/what-is/edge-computing.html (last visited June 10, 2019).
47. Jeffrey Lee, *How Mesh Networking Will Make IoT Real*, HACKERNOON (May 8, 2018), https://hackernoon.com/how-mesh-networking-will-make-iot-real-b5b88baab63b.
48. *See* Jack Stewart, *Self-Driving Cars Use Crazy Amounts of Power, And It's Becoming a Problem*, WIRED (Feb. 6, 2018), https://www.wired.com/story/self-driving-cars-power-consumption-nvidia-chip/.
49. *See* Peter Levine, *The End of Cloud Computing*, https://a16z.com/2016/12/16/the-end-of-cloud-computing/ (last visited May 6, 2019).
50. Barry Manz, *Why Mesh Networks Matter at the Edge*, ENTERPRISE IoT INSIGHTS (May 30, 2018), https://enterpriseiotinsights.com/20180529/channels/fundamentals/why-mesh-networks-matter-at-the-edge-Tag35-Tag99.
51. Trent Gillies, *Why Most of Three Square Market's Employees Jumped at the Chance to Wear a Microchip*, CNBC (Aug. 13, 2017), https://www.cnbc.com/2017/08/11/three-square-market-ceo-explains-its-employee-microchip-implant.html.
52. Lucy Rowlands, *Brain–Computer Interface Gives People with Paralysis Full Control of a Tablet Computer*, PHYSICS TODAY (Dec. 11, 2018), https://physicsworld.com/a/brain-computer-interface-gives-people-with-paralysis-full-control-of-a-tablet-computer/.

53. *See* Wenyao Xu Feng Lin & Zhangpeng Jin, *The Fugure of Passwords? Your Brain*, Fast Co. (Oct. 26, 2018), https://www.fastcompany.com/90257174/the-future-of-passwords-your-brain.

54. Duncan Graham-Rowe, *Wheelchair Makes the Most of Brain Control*, MIT Tech. Rev. (Sept. 13, 2010), https://www.technologyreview.com/s/420756/wheelchair-makes-the-most-of-brain-control/.

55. *See The New Politics of the Internet: Everything Is Connected*, Economist (Jan. 5, 2013), http://www.economist.com/news/briefing/21569041-can-internet-activism-turn-real-political-movement-everything-connected [hereinafter *New Politics*] (discussing the ideas of Professor Kevin Werbach, who has suggested that the Internet "lowers the barriers to organisation," potentially to the point that mailing lists could replace painstaking institution building); *Digital Do-Gooders: Why Do We Help Strangers Online?*, BBC (Sept. 25, 2013), http://www.bbc.co.uk/news/magazine-24207047 (reporting that "educated people around the world have about a trillion hours of free time each year that could be contributed to collaborative projects, a phenomenon . . . [Clay Shirky] calls 'cognitive surplus' ").

56. Paul Stokes, *IoT Applications in Agriculture: The Potential of Smart Farming on the Current Stage*, Medium (Oct. 2, 2018), https://medium.com/datadriveninvestor/iot-applications-in-agriculture-the-potential-of-smart-farming-on-the-current-stage-275066f946d8; Tom Raftery, *What Will the Internet of Things Look Like in 2027? 7 Predictions*, D!gitalist Mag. (Mar. 29, 2017), https://www.digitalistmag.com/iot/2017/03/29/what-will-internet-of-things-look-like-in-2027-7-predictions-04998096.

57. Bruce Schneier, Click Here to Kill Everybody: Security and Survival in a Hyper-Connected World 84 (2018).

58. *See 4 Ways Cybersecurity Automation Should Be Used*, Palo Alto Networks Cyberpedia, https://www.paloaltonetworks.com/cyberpedia/4-ways-cybersecurity-automation-should-be-used (last visited May 6, 2019).

59. *See* Luke Irwin, *How Long Does It Take to Detect a Cyber Attack?*, IT Governance (Mar. 14, 2019), https://www.itgovernanceusa.com/blog/how-long-does-it-take-to-detect-a-cyber-attack.

60. *See* Naveen Joshi, *Can AI Become Our New Cybersecurity Sheriff?*, Forbes (Feb. 4, 2019), https://www.forbes.com/sites/cognitiveworld/2019/02/04/can-ai-become-our-new-cybersecurity-sheriff/#2d71f3e636a8.

61. *Report Details AI and ML Cybersecurity Arms Race*, DARK READING (Feb. 20, 2019), https://www.darkreading.com/analytics/report-details-ai-and-ml-cybersecurity-arms-race/d/d-id/1333926.

62. Sourabh Bumb et al., *Bringing the Power of AI to the Internet of Things*, WIRED (2018), https://www.wired.com/brandlab/2018/05/bringing-power-ai-internet-things/.

63. *Id.*

64. Ben Dickson, *Machine Learning Will Be Key to Securing IoT in Smart Homes*, IOT SEC. FOUND. (Jul. 7, 2016), https://www.iotsecurityfoundation.org/machine-learning-will-be-key-to-securing-iot-in-smart-homes/.

65. Blockchain technology is based on cryptographic principles that are designed to promote data integrity. For more on this topic, see Shackelford & Myers, *Block-by-Block, supra* note *, at 334; Shackelford et al., *Securing the Internet of Healthcare, supra* note *, at 405.

66. Kevin Jackson, *What Is Blockchain?*, SCI. NODE (Nov. 14, 2018), https://sciencenode.org/feature/What%20is%20blockchain.php.

67. *The Trust Machine*, ECONOMIST (Oct. 31, 2015), https://www.economist.com/leaders/2015/10/31/the-trust-machine.

68. *See* Kyle Torpey, *Prediction: $10 Billion Will Be Invested in Blockchain Projects in 2016*, COIN J. (Jan. 22, 2016), http://coinjournal.net/prediction-10-billion-will-be-invested-in-blockchain-startups-in-2016/.

69. *See* PRIMAVERA DE FILIPPI & AARON WRIGHT, BLOCKCHAIN AND THE LAW: THE RULE OF CODE 156 (2018).

70. *Id.* at 158 ("One's mind need not wander far to imagine what would happen if a malicious actor hacked a centralized service provider managing fleets of self-driving cars or gained control of millions of connected devices used to manage human health or even an entire city.").

71. Stevan Mcgrath, *Resolving IoT Security Issues with Blockchain Technology*, HACKERNOON (Jan. 21, 2019), https://hackernoon.com/resolving-iot-security-issues-with-blockchain-technology-3ffb36357094.

72. FILIPPI & WRIGHT, *supra* note 69, at 156. One example of this approach is a so-called Block Chain Gateway, which informs users of all the devices (and their privacy policies) connected to a given platform by using smart contracts. *See* Shi-Cho Cha et al., *Privacy-Aware and Blockchain Connected Gateways*

for Users to Access Legacy IoT Devices, IEEE (2017), https://
ieeexplore-ieee-org.proxyiub.uits.iu.edu/stamp/stamp.
jsp?tp=&arnumber=8229327.

73. *See* Jason Koebler, *Society Is Too Complicated to Have a President,
Complex Mathematics Suggest*, MOTHERBOARD (Nov. 7, 2016),
https://www.vice.com/en_us/article/wnxbm5/society-is-
too-complicated-to-have-a-president-complex-mathematics-
suggest.

74. *Id.*

75. *See* Nellie Bowles, *Thermostats, Locks, and Lights: Digital Tools
of Domestic Abuse*, N.Y. TIMES (June 23, 2018), https://www.
nytimes.com/2018/06/23/technology/smart-home-devices-
domestic-abuse.html.

76. Bruce Schneier, *Real-World Security and the Internet of Things*,
SCHNEIER ON SEC. (July 28, 2016), https://www.schneier.com/
blog/archives/2016/07/real-world_secu.html.

77. Remarks of Commissioner Rebecca Kelly Slaughter, *Rising
the Standard: Bridging Security and Transparency to the Internet
of Things?*, NEW AMERICA (July 26, 2018), https://www.ftc.
gov/system/files/documents/public_statements/1395854/
slaughter_-_raising_the_standard_-_bringing_security_and_
transparency_to_the_internet_of_things_7-26.pdf.

78. *Plan to Secure Internet of Things with New Law*, BBC (May 1, 2019),
https://www.bbc.com/news/technology-48106582 (law would
require "unique passwords by default," clearly state "for how
long security updates would be made available," and "offer a
public point of contact to whom any cybersecurity vulnerabilities
may be disclosed").

79. SCHNEIER, *supra* note 57, at 185.

80. *See, e.g.,* Scott J. Shackelford & Scott O. Bradner, *Have You Updated
Your Toaster? Transatlantic Approaches to Governing the Internet of
Everything* (Kelley School of Business, Research Paper No. 18-60,
July 4, 2018), available at https://ssrn.com/abstract=3208018.

81. *See* Bruno S. Frey & Felix Oberholzer-Gee, *The Cost of Price
Incentives: An Empirical Analysis of Motivation Crowding-Out*, 87
AM. ECON. REV. 746 (1997); Elinor Ostrom, *Beyond Markets and
States: Polycentric Governance of Complex Economic Systems*, 100
AM. ECON. REV. 641, 656 (2010) (citing Andrew F. Reeson & John
G. Tisdell, *Institutions, Motivations, and Public Goods: An Experimental
Test of Motivational Crowding*, 68 J. ECON. BEHAVIOR & ORG.

273 (2008) (finding "externally imposed regulation that would theoretically lead to higher joint returns 'crowded out' voluntary behavior to cooperate").

82. *See, e.g.,* Ostrom, *supra* note 81, at 656.

83. SCHNEIER, *supra* note 57, at 102.

84. Interview with Elinor Ostrom, Distinguished Professor, Indiana University—Bloomington, in Bloomington, Ind. (Oct. 13, 2010).

85. NIST is helping with this process, such as by focusing on a guide for secure communications by IoT manufacturers. *See Securing Small-Business and Home Internet of Things (IoT) Devices*, NIST SPECIAL PUBLICATION 1800-15 (Apr. 2019), https://www.nccoe. nist.gov/sites/default/files/library/sp1800/iot-ddos-nist-sp1800-15-preliminary-draft.pdf.

86. SCHNEIER, *supra* note 57, at 131.

87. *See, e.g.,* HOUSE REPUBLICAN CYBERSECURITY TASK FORCE, 112TH CONG., RECOMMENDATIONS OF THE HOUSE REPUBLICAN CYBERSECURITY TASK FORCE 5, 8, 14 (2011).

88. *See The Business of Insuring Intangible Risks Is Still in Its Infancy*, ECONOMIST (Aug. 23, 2018), https://www. economist.com/finance-and-economics/2018/08/23/ the-business-of-insuring-intangible-risks-is-still-in-its-infancy.

89. *See* Adam Satariano & Nicole Perlroth, *Big Companies Thought Insurance Covered a Cyberattack: They May Be Wrong*, N.Y. TIMES (Apr. 15, 2019), https://www.nytimes.com/2019/04/15/ technology/cyberinsurance-notpetya-attack.html#click=https:// t.co/ymBtwrNIHF.

90. For a rundown on these cybersecurity best practices, see US FED. TRADE COMM'N, PROTECTING PERSONAL INFORMATION: A GUIDE FOR BUSINESS, https://www.ftc.gov/tips-advice/business-center/guidance/protecting-personal-information-guide-business (last visited Sept. 25, 2018).

91. SCHNEIER, *supra* note 57, at 108–9 (calling for a top 10 list of IoT standards, including: (1) transparency, (2) making it possible to patch software, (3) test software before it is released, (4) "enable secure default operation, (5) "fail predictably," (6) "use standard protocols and implementations," (7) "avoid known vulnerabilities, (8) "preserve offline functionality," (9) "encrypt and authenticate data," and (10) "support responsible security research").

92. *Id.* at 113.

93. *Id.* at 155.

94. *See* Scott J. Shackelford, *The U.S. Needs an NTSB for Cyberattacks*, Wall St. J. (June 4, 2019), https://www.wsj.com/articles/the-u-s-needs-an-ntsb-for-cyberattacks-11559700060.

95. *See* Janaki Chadha, *Three Ideas for Solving the Cybersecurity Skills Gap*, Wall St. J. (Sept. 18, 2018), https://www.wsj.com/amp/articles/three-ideas-for-solving-the-cybersecurity-skills-gap-1537322520; Scott J. Shackelford, *What Cybersecurity Investigators Can Learn from Airplane Crashes*, Conversation (Feb. 21, 2018), https://theconversation.com/what-cybersecurity-investigators-can-learn-from-airplane-crashes-91177; Shackelford, *Is It Time for a Cyber Peace Corps?*, *supra* note 26.

96. *See* Michael Kassner, *Ohio Law Creates Cybersecurity "Safe Harbor" for Businesses*, Tech. Rep. (Jan. 3, 2019), https://www.techrepublic.com/article/ohio-law-creates-cybersecurity-safe-harbor-for-businesses/.

97. Schneier, *supra* note 57, at 84.

98. *See* Scott J. Shackelford et al., *Rethinking Active Defense: A Comparative Analysis of Proactive Cybersecurity Policymaking*, 41 U. Penn. J. Int'l L. 1 (2019); Anastasios Arampatzis, *The Gap between US Federal and State Policies for IoT Security*, Tripwire (Oct. 10, 2018), https://www.tripwire.com/state-of-security/government/federal-state-policies-iot-security/; Phil Goldstein, *What Massachusetts Can Do to Combat IoT Security Threats*, St. Tech. (Oct. 16, 2018), https://statetechmagazine.com/article/2018/10/what-massachusetts-can-do-combat-iot-security-threats.

99. *See* Scott J. Shackelford, Scott Russell, & Jeffrey Haut, *Bottoms Up: A Comparison of "Voluntary" Cybersecurity Frameworks*, 16 U.C. Davis Bus. L.J. 217 (2016).

100. Schneier, *supra* note 57, at 145.

101. *Id.* at 146–49 (calling for the creation of a National Cyber Office, drawing from historical precedents of other technologies like aircraft leading to new governmental entities).

102. *Id.* at 120, 125 (calling for ex ante and ex post rules, as well as those focusing on disclosure).

103. *Id.* at 152–54 (noting the speed, scope, and efficacy challenges of cyber regulations, citing the failures of the CAN-SPAM Act to "stop spam").

104. *Id.* at 129.

105. *See, e.g.*, Natasha Cohen, *The Need for a Federalist Approach to Cybersecurity*, New America (Mar. 29, 2019), https://www.

newamerica.org/cybersecurity-initiative/c2b/c2b-log/need-federalist-approach-cybersecurity/.

106. *G7 Leaders Approve Historic Cybersecurity Agreement*, Bos. Globe F. (June 6, 2016), https://bostonglobalforum.org/2016/06/g7-leaders-produce-historic-cybersecurity-agreement/.

107. Peter Apps, *IMF Cyber Attacks Boosts Calls for Global Action*, Reuters (June 13, 2011), https://www.reuters.com/article/us-imf-cyberattack-idUSTRE75A20720110613.

108. *See History of Organic Farming in the United States*, SARE, https://www.sare.org/Learning-Center/Bulletins/Transitioning-to-Organic-Production/Text-Version/History-of-Organic-Farming-in-the-United-States (last visited May 11, 2019).

109. *Id.*

110. *See* George H. Waltz Jr., *Making the Death Seat Safer*, 157(1) Pop. Sci. 82 (July 1950).

111. Schneier, *supra* note 57, at 74.

112. *See* Security Planner, https://securityplanner.org/#/ (last visited May 11, 2019).

113. *See Cybersecurity and Internet Governance*, Ostrom Workshop, https://ostromworkshop.indiana.edu/research/internet-cybersecurity/index.html (last visited Nov. 9, 2017); Cyber Future Found., http://cyberfuturefoundation.org/ (last visited Nov. 9, 2017).

114. ICT4Peace, https://ict4peace.org/what-we-do/ (last visited Nov. 1, 2018).

115. Schneier, *supra* note 57, at 100.

116. *See* James Kaplan, Wolf Richter, & David Ware, *Cybersecurity: Linchpin of the Digital Enterprise*, McKinsey & Co. (July 2019), at 5.

117. *See* Kelly Sheridan, *Cyber-Security Skills Shortage Leaves Companies Vulnerable*, Info. Wk. (Aug. 1, 2016), https://www.informationweek.com/strategic-cio/security-and-risk-strategy/cybersecurity-skills-shortage-leaves-companies-vulnerable/d/d-id/1326463; Schneier, *supra* note 57, at 141.

118. *See* Xuanyan Ouyang, *Wanted: Students to Enter Cybersecurity Field*, UPI (Aug. 19, 2016), https://www.upi.com/Business_News/2016/08/19/Wanted-Students-to-enter-cybersecurity-field/1501471626441/.

119. *See* Sheridan, *supra* note 117.

120. *See* Rebecca Grant, *The U.S. Is Running Out of Nurses*, Atlantic (Feb. 3, 2016), https://www.theatlantic.com/health/archive/2016/02/nursing-shortage/459741/.

121. *See Information Security Analysts*, Bureau of Labor Stat., https://www.bls.gov/ooh/computer-and-information-technology/information-security-analysts.htm (last visited Sept. 14, 2017).

122. *See CyberCorps® Scholarship for Service (SFS)*, Nat'l Sci. Found., https://www.nsf.gov/funding/pgm_summ.jsp?pims_id=504991 (last visited Sept. 14, 2017).

123. *See* BLS, *supra* note 121.

124. *See* Sheridan, *supra* note 117.

125. *See, e.g.*, Jeff Kauflin, *The Fast-Growing Job with a Huge Skills Gap: Cyber Security*, Forbes (Mar. 16, 2017), https://www.forbes.com/sites/jeffkauflin/2017/03/16/the-fast-growing-job-with-a-huge-skills-gap-cyber-security/#463f44425163.

126. *See* Sheridan, *supra* note 117; Zach Noble, *Closing Cybersecurity's Race Gap*, FCW (Oct. 9, 2015), https://fcw.com/articles/2015/10/09/minority-cyber-zach-noble.aspx.

127. This message is at the heart of Indiana University's M.S. in Cybersecurity Risk Management, which includes core coursework from three of IU's globally ranked schools—the Kelley School of Business, School of Informatics and Computing, and the Maurer School of Law—along with an applied capstone project allowing students to apply what they have learned by working with real-world clients through the IU Cybersecurity Clinic. *See Cybersecurity Programs*, Ind. Univ., https://cybersecurityprograms.indiana.edu/ (last visited Sept. 14, 2018).

128. *See Identity Theft First Aid*, Cal. Off. Privacy Protection, https://oag.ca.gov/idtheft/first-aid (last visited May 14, 2019); *Protect Yourself from Identity Theft*, IRS (Jan. 2012), https://www.irs.gov/pub/irs-utl/oc_protect_yourself_from_identity_theft_final.pdf.

129. Ken Hess, *10 Security Best Practice Guidelines for Consumers*, ZDNet (Mar. 5, 2013), http://www.zdnet.com/10-security-best-practice-guidelines-for-consumers-7000012171/; *Microsoft Protect*, Microsoft, http://www.microsoft.com/protect/fraud/phishing/feefraud.aspx (last visited Feb. 1, 2014).

130. William Gibson, Neuromancer 52 (1984).

131. Bruce Schneier, *Click Here to Kill Everyone*, N.Y. MAG. (Jan. 27, 2017), http://nymag.com/intelligencer/2017/01/the-internet-of-things-dangerous-future-bruce-schneier.html.

132. *See* Adam Thierer, *Putting Privacy Concerns about the Internet of Things in Perspective*, INT'L ASSOC. PRIVACY PROF. (Feb. 3, 2014), https://iapp.org/news/a/putting-privacy-concerns-about-the-internet-of-things-in-perspective.

133. *See* Paul M. Schwartz & Edward J. Janger, *Notification of Data Security Breaches*, 105 MICH. L. REV. 913, 922 (2007).

134. Franklin D. Roosevelt, Address at Oglethorpe University in Atlanta, Georgia (May 22, 1932), http://www.presidency.ucsb.edu/ws/?pid=88410.

135. RACHEL CARSON, SILENT SPRING 3 (1962).

136. *Id*.

INDEX

Tables are indicated by *t* following the page number

For the benefit of digital users, indexed terms that span two pages (e.g., 52–53) may, on occasion, appear on only one of those pages.